Für Ihr Engagement und Ihre Unterstützung im Rahmen des VN - Sonderlehrganges

➤➤ Personal für VN-Stäbe ◀◀

---

vom 5. bis 23. Juli 1993

---

an der

HEERESUNTEROFFIZIERSCHULE III

danke ich Ihnen herzlich

Ihr

Generalinspekteur der Bundeswehr

Bonn, im Juli 1993

Armour Tactics in the Second World War

Rudolf Steiger

The author, historian and former Swiss Armoured Corps officer, uses unique documents in this book in which he describes tank tactics during the first two years of the Second World War, a period which saw the employment of armour in the Polish, Western and Russian campaigns. After a short history of the tank as a weapon of war, the author studies several tactical aspects such as 'Armour on the Offensive', 'The Encirclement of the Enemy', 'Armour and Infantry', and 'Tank against Tank'. He pays particular attention to the first year of 'Operation Barbarossa', using the files of the 2nd Panzer Army whose commander, Guderian, could be described as the 'father' of the German armoured force.

Rudolf Steiger, Militärische Führungsschule Eidgenössische Technische Hochschule Zürich

STUDIES IN MILITARY HISTORY
Militärgeschichtliches Forschungsamt

General Editors: Günter Roth and Wilhelm Deist

In preparation
Horst Boog (ed.), *The Conduct of the Air War in the Second World War: An International Comparison*
Klaus Reinhardt, *Before Moscow: The Turning Point?*

Armour Tactics in the Second World War

Panzer Army Campaigns of 1939–41 in German War Diaries

Rudolf Steiger

Translated by
Martin Fry

BERG

New York / Oxford
Distributed exclusively in the US and Canada by
St Martin's Press, New York

English edition
first published in 1991 by
Berg Publishers Limited
Editorial offices:
165 Taber Avenue, Providence, RI 02906, USA
150 Cowley Road, Oxford, OX4 1JJ, UK

English edition © Militärgeschichtliches Forschungsamt, 1991
Originally published as *Panzertaktik im Spiegel deutscher*
                            Kriegstagebücher 1939 bis 1941
Translated from the German by permission of the publishers
© Rombach & Co. GmbH Freiburg

Library of Congress Cataloging-in-Publication Data
Steiger, Rudolf, 1946–
    Armour tactics in the Second World War : Panzer army
      campaigns of 1939–1941 in German war diaries / Rudolf Steiger :
      translated from the German.
      p.   cm.—(Studies in military history : vol. 1)
      Includes bibliographical references.
      ISBN 0–85496–694–3
      1. World War. 1939–1945—Tank warfare.   2. World War. 1939–1945–
    –Germany.   I. Title.   II. Series.
    D793.S73   1991
    940.54′1—dc20   90–39939
                                                                               CIP

British Library Cataloguing in Publication Data
Steiger, Rudolf
    Armour tactics in the Second World War : Panzer army campaigns of
    1939–41 in German war diaries. – (Studies in military history v.1)
    1. World War 2. Army operations by Germany. Heer. Armoured combat
    vehicles. Tanks
    I. Title   II. Series
    940.541343

ISBN 0–85496–694 3

Printed and bound in Great Britain by
Billing and Sons Ltd, Worcester

Contents

Contents

General Foreword

The following book opens the new series entitled 'Studies in Military History', in which the Militärgeschichtliches Forschungsamt (MGFA) will present translated works that have made a considerable contribution to historical research, not only in view of their theme, methodology and formulation, but also in respect of their findings. A prime example of this approach can be seen in the ten-volume series 'Germany and the Second World War', the first volume of which, *The Build-Up of German Aggression*, was published in 1990 by Oxford University Press. Apart from monographic books, the MGFA is keen to give readers of English access to collections of essays and lectures in order to make known the scientific findings of research projects and, above all, specialised conferences organised by the MGFA.

Professor Rudolf Steiger's work on World War Two armour tactics was the subject of enormous interest when it first appeared. Within a short time four editions were necessary and the German version has been out of print for some time. I hope the following translation will satisfy the great demand for the book and at the same time continue the trend towards an international discussion of central issues in military history.

Dr. Günter Roth
Brig.-Gen., Amtschef (Head),
Militärgeschichtliches Forschungsamt

Author's Preface to the English Edition

I am pleased that this dissertation has been published four times in German between 1973 and 1977. Its publication in English, however, almost twenty years after it first appeared, is both a singular honour and a great challenge.

It represents a challenge for me above all because questions and uncertainties have arisen in the meantime, such as: should a book written in the early 1970s not be revised or at least enlarged to include the specialist literature which has appeared since then? Are the results of research carried out twenty years ago still valid and defensible without limitation and revision?

My opinion is that these legitimate questions can be answered as follows. The special feature of this book is the verbatim presentation of (mostly) previously unpublished war diary entries concerning aspects of armour tactics, divided into themes, and not the mere representation of secondary literature. Because the main aim of this research was to portray German armour's successes, difficulties and limitations in the clear and unerring light of its war diaries, this book cannot and indeed should not be simply revised or rewritten. I am especially grateful to the Militärgeschichtliches Forschungsamt and Berg Publishers for their agreement on this point, and I thank Martin Fry in particular for his competent translation.

Why was it possible for the German armoured force to defeat both Poland in 1939 and France in 1940 in lightning campaigns? And why did what was meant to be a lightning campaign against Russia, in the summer of 1941, turn into a protracted war of attrition? Did the German armoured force, accustomed to victory, fail because of adverse terrain or climate, because of overstretched supply lines, or because of their underestimation of the Red Army?

The answers to these and other questions can be found in this book, answers captured for posterity, during lightning campaigns both won and lost, in the daily entries in German armour war diaries.

Rudolf Steiger
Zürich, 1990

Preface to the German Edition

The starting point for this book was the question of the relationship between imagination (theory) and reality (practice) in German tank tactics between 1939 and 1941. In the light of war diaries kept by German armoured units, I wish to point out the tactical conditions for the seemingly incredible successes achieved by the German armoured force in the Polish and Western campaigns. From these diaries, however, we can also see the difficulties and limits of the use of tanks, limits which became clear as early as the first year of the Russian campaign. In this connection we should be most interested in those events which are either hardly mentioned by historians or even marked as 'impossible', but which are, nevertheless, captured for posterity in war documents.

It is not until the thrust of armoured forces becomes delayed, in the short term, the medium term or even, as often happened, is jeopardized due to natural or artificial obstacles, that tank tactics reveal their true fascination. For this reason, German commitment of armour in France and Russia was considered in greater detail than in Poland, where the superiority of the Wehrmacht was so obvious that only limited conclusions can be gained from these operations by military historians. This book does not seek to provide a chronological account of the war in the years 1939 to 1941, but rather to look at as many aspects of tank tactics as possible. It is therefore divided only into themes.

There is a wealth of information for military historians concerning the war years 1939 to 1941. This is both valuable and necessary as the background to this book. However, my main sources are exclusively German panzer unit war diaries, in other words previously unpublished military documents. Why were war diaries kept at all? How accurate are they? In a memorandum of German Army High Command we read that: 'War diaries are documentary evidence of the actions of a command HQ or of a unit during mobilisation, on border patrol, in wartime and on special duties . . . A daily report on each day is to be given. How the events are described is left open, but the description itself must be precise and exhaustive.'[1]

No doubt Army High Command had the intention of obtaining the most accurate possible portrayal of actual events with the aid of war diaries. In addition to this, the battle reports and detailed situation maps, contained in the diaries were used to evaluate the latest war experiences.[2]

If we look at them carefully enough, we see that written sources cannot be objective. They are always coloured by the author's emotions, his mood at the time, and by his philosophy of life, to a greater or lesser extent. Thus war diaries carry the mark of their authors; their value as historical evidence varies according to the personality of the war diarist, his training and how good his relationship with his commanding officer was.[3]

Thousands of war diaries were processed for this book. The level of consensus was often such that there can be no doubt about the value, as historical evidence, of war diaries kept by candidates for the General Staff or by trained General Staff Officers.[4]

Because the war diaries of the panzer units employed in the Polish campaign were full of gaps or even missing, I had to limit my research to the years 1940/41. The files of Panzer Groups von Kleist and Guderian were used for the Blitzkrieg in France; those of 2nd and 3rd Panzer Armies for the first year of the Russian campaign. It should be obvious that the documents of 2nd Panzer Army were paid special attention, since its Commander-in-Chief was no less than the creator of the German tank force, General Guderian himself.

I would like to thank Professors R. von Albertini and W. Schaufelberger for supervising this book and for their

1. Oberkommando des Heeres, Ausb. Abt. (II), Gen.St.d.H. Nr. 900/39 of 27 November 1939.
2. Alongside each war diary several supplementary volumes were kept. Cf. below pp. 152ff.
3. The following terms are used in this book: Commander (Kommandeur) = leader of a unit (C.O.), Tank Commander (Kommandant).
4. Cf. P.E. Schramm, Kriegstagebuch des OKW vol. IV, 2nd. half-vol. Frankfurt am Main, 1961, pp. 1760–9.

suggestions, which were especially useful. My thanks also go to the Federal Archive / Military Archive (Bundesarchiv / Militärarchiv) in Freiburg i. Br., where I was allowed unrestricted access to war diaries. Also thanks to the staff of the Armed Forces Historical Research Office (Militärgeschichtliches Forschungsamt), above all to Dr U. von Gersdorff and Lieutenant Colonel (GS) Dr G. Brausch for their many hints. Last of all, thanks to my parents, without whom this book would not have been completed.

1
General Survey

1.1 Tanks as Auxiliary Weapons

The notion of sallying forth against the enemy with 'iron wagons' is an old and understandable one. Speed and protection had always been decisive factors on the battlefield. As early as 1482, in a letter to a friend, Leonardo da Vinci wrote: 'I am making secure, covered carts which will be impregnable, and, when they appear in the midst of the battle, even the largest enemy armies will be forced to retreat.'[1]

The era of the modern tank began with the invention of the combustion engine and the caterpillar track. Firepower, manoeuvrability and armour were combined in one weapon. On 15 September 1916, forty-nine tanks of the British 4th Army achieved local victories during the Battle of the Somme and, a year later, on 20 September 1917, nine British tank battalions overran German positions on a wide front. The battle of Cambrai is rightly called the genesis of armour.[2]

It is true that the commitment of armour displaced cavalry on the battlefield and forced the infantry to take cover in trenches, an unworthy role for the 'queen of the battlefield', but despite this the tanks remained a backup weapon in support of the infantry until the end of the First World War.

After the First World War, the Allies suddenly seemed to recognise the implications of tanks. In any case they were afraid

---

1. A. Halle and C. Demand, *Panzer, Illustrierte Geschichte der Kampfwagen*, Berne, Munich, Vienna, 1971, p. 19. In their book the authors chart the history of the tank from the chariot to today's panzers.
2. Cf. J.F.C. Fuller, *Die entartete Kunst Krieg zu führen 1789–1961*, Cologne, 1964, pp. 193ff. Cf. W.K. Nehring, *Die Geschichte der deutschen Panzerwaffe 1916–1945*, Frankfurt am Main and Berlin, 1969, p. 19.

1

that the Germans would develop their own armour.[3] It was all the more amazing, then, if not to say incomprehensible, that the British War Ministry decided, in the winter of 1918, to discontinue the designing of tanks and to cancel planned projects.[4] The French also refused to draw conclusions from the experience obtained with the new weapon. General Estienne and Colonel de Gaulle found their demands for independence for the motorised arm falling on deaf ears. Neither in Britain, France nor Russia was the tank force seen as a tool of operative command. The tank's place was at the side of the infantry.

Therefore, in a combat situation, tank units were to fight only in conjunction with the foot soldiers. Naturally, organisational and technical improvements were made,[5] but the fact was overlooked not only that tanks were a new kind of weapon, but that a new kind of warfare was also needed. With this went a new concept of command and control, which required entirely different means of support and implementation.[6] 'Armies learn only from defeat. That explains why an army which had been victorious in one war so often loses the next.'[7]

After the German tank operations in Poland and France in 1939 and 1940, this statement by Liddell Hart was acknowledged to be true. But by then it was too late!

1.2 The German Tank Divisions

After the 'tankless period'[8] from 1919 to 1934, the real struggle began in the Army of the German Reich over operational doctrine of armour. Guderian and his staff encountered great resist-

---

3. Article 171 of the Treaty of Versailles of 28 June 1919: 'It is also forbidden to produce in or to export to Germany tanks, armoured vehicles or anything similar which can serve a warlike purpose.'

4. Cf. Halle and Demand, *Illustrierte Geschichte*, pp. 78–9.

5. From 1933 onwards the French began to build new types of tanks to form pure panzer brigades, but the basic strategy remained the same – tanks remained auxiliary weapons.

6. Cf. H. Senff, *Die Entwicklung der Panzerwaffe im deutschen Heer zwischen den beiden Weltkriegen*, Frankfurt am Main, 1969, p. 85.

7. Quoted from Liddell Hart, in D. Orgill, *The Tank. Studies in the Development and Use of a Weapon*, London, 1970, p. 85.

8. An exhaustive study of the development of the German armoured force is given by Nehring, *Panzerwaffe*.

ance to their new ideas.[9] Should the tanks be under the control of the infantry or should they be used on open terrain in the operational sense, for deep penetration, turning movements and envelopments?[10]

On 16 March 1935, the Reich Government restored Germany's military sovereignty, and that August saw a four-week manoeuvre at Munsterlager training area with an 'Exercise Tank Division' taking part. The Commander-in-Chief of the Army, General Freiherr von Fritsch, seemed very impressed with the performance of the new unit,[11] and on 27 September 1935, the former 'Inspektion der Kraftfahrtruppen' ('Motorised Units Inspectorate') was renamed the 'Kommando der Panzertruppe' ('Armoured Command').

On 15 October 1935, the first three tank divisions were activated. This was the first break with the conventional principles of warfare. In 1937, further tank regiments were activated,[12] four infantry regiments were fully motorised, and the formation of light divisions was at the planning stage.[13]

In the autumn of the same year, on the final day of a large Wehrmacht exercise, Major-General Guderian commanded an armoured attack, with air support, in which no less than 800 tanks took part.[14] Tank war began to take shape – a war in which it was no longer armour and infantry but rather large mechanised units alone which achieved results of hitherto unknown dimensions. Those who had followed the development of the German armoured force were not surprised at the successes during the blitz campaigns against Poland and France.

9. Nehring attributes the creation of the Panzer Unit to the former Motorised Service led by Generals Erich von Tschischwitz, Alfred von Vollard Bockelberg, Oswald Lutz and Colonel Heinz Guderian.

10. The sceptical attitude taken by General Ludwig Beck to Guderian's plans is given in more detail by Senff, *Entwicklung der Panzerwaffe*, pp. 28ff.

11. Cf. Nehring, *Panzerwaffe*, p. 89.

12. Cf. H. Guderian, *Erinnerungen eines Soldaten*, Heidelberg, 1951, p. 29. 1st Panzer Div., C.O., Lieut.-General von Weichs; 2nd Panzer Div., C.O., Col. Heinz Guderian; 3rd Panzer Div., C.O., Maj.-General Ernst Fessmann. On 1 November 1935 Lieut.-Gen. Lutz was promoted to be the first general of the Panzer Unit and named as the first 'Commanding General'.

13. Using the example of the French 'division légère mécanique', the first four light divisions were activated. After the Polish campaign they were changed into armoured divisions. Cf. 2. Le. Div. Abt. Ia, Nr. 389/39 geheim of 5 October 1939: 'The light divisions were too weak to attack, too strong for reconnaissance'.

14. Cf. Nehring, *Panzerwaffe*, p. 93.

The plan to commit operational tank forces was no secret. *Heigl's Taschenbuch der Tanks*, as early as 1938, says the following about tank warfare:

> The special qualities [of the armoured force] rule out the idea of tying them to cavalry or foot soldiers. The countries which still do this are, consciously or unconsciously, throwing away any progress already gained by limiting the speed and manoeuvrability of the new weapon to the tactical and strategic pace of the existing armies. When allowed to move freely and swiftly, a panzer unit is the great deciding factor in the hand of the strategist and commander, with an effect like lightning, quick and irresistible.[15]

1.3 The Experiences of Two Campaigns

1.3.1 The Polish Campaign

On 1 September 1939, Poland was attacked by the German Wehrmacht. Four weeks later the war was at an end. An opponent had been completely routed, although his armed force was numerically almost equal. What had happened?

Poland had relied for her security upon a linear form of defence. She had returned to the combat principles of the First World War in the hope of defending everything and losing nothing. The 500 or so tanks, which also dated from the First World War, were assigned to companies and regiments. The air force, part of the army, was also out of date and only partly operational. On the other hand, the Polish Army had eleven cavalry brigades[16] – the situation was desperate even before the war began!

It was no difficult baptism of fire for the German armoured force. Exactly according to plan,[17] the leading tanks, ahead of the infantry, penetrated the Polish defence 'veil' without worrying about open flanks.[18] Other tank companies attacked the

---

15. G.P. Zezschwitz (ed.), *Heigl's Taschenbuch der Tanks. Part III. Der Panzerkampf*, new edition, Munich, 1971, p. 1.

16. Cf. XIX. A.K. mot., Abt. Ia, Anlagen zum KTB, Einsatz Ost 1–25 September 1939, Gefundene Feindunterlagen, Teil 1, dated 1–6 September 1939.

17. The operation plan was formulated by the Army High Command (OKH) without any real interference from Hitler.

18. Cf. below pp. 31ff.

enemy wings from Slovakia and in the Polish corridor, broke through them in one thrust, without stopping, and again pushed deep into Polish territory, approaching each other from the north and south. In a gigantic pincer movement the whole Polish Army was bottled up. The campaign in Poland was the birth of modern mobile warfare.

To be sure, the performance of the German armoured companies made a deep impression everywhere. There was no doubt that armour, together with the air force, had been decisive in ending the campaign so quickly and with such light casualties. It is important to remember, however, against what type of opponent these successes had been achieved.

The enemy, mostly units of the Suwalki Cavalry Brigade, which was to be found in front of and behind the corps' sector in the last few days, has . . . fled.[19]

There are herds of fine horses running around the area. They belonged to the Pomorska Cavalry Brigade.[20]

The (Polish) squadrons ride up with sabres drawn. It is like the beginning of the First World War. Unfortunately the Polish cavalrymen don't want to believe, or aren't allowed to, that German panzers are made of steel and not wood and cardboard.

Machine-gun fire is devastating in its effect on the enemy cavalry lines. But they still don't give up, they ride back, regroup and attack again.[21]

In view of such fighting, it should be no surprise to learn that German casualties in the armoured force were light relative to the results: 'Our own losses during five days of combat are very light compared to the positive and speedy victory. Dead, about 1%, wounded, about 2%'.[22] During a visit to XIX. Motorised Army Corps, Hitler expressed his appreciation of the armoured force's performance as follows: 'My trust in the armoured force

19. XIX. A. K., mot. Abt. Ia, KTB Nr. 1, Lagebeurteilung of 14 September 1939.
20. 3rd Pz. Div. Bericht des Lieut.-Gen. Frhr. Geyr von Schweppenburg, p. 15.
21. *Geschichte der 3. Pz. Div. Berlin-Brandenburg, 1939–1945*, published by Traditionsverband der Division, Berlin, 1967, p. 17.
22. XIX. A.K., mot. Abt. Ia, KTB Nr. 1, of 5 September 1939.

was always boundless'.[23] Indeed, after seeing how well it had fared, there was every reason for this trust – but the conditions under which this experience was obtained were much too simple:

> Tank losses due to enemy action amount to between 6–8 vehicles out of an approximate total of 350, the vast majority of which can boast many hits.[24]

> Tank Regiment 5, for example, has only one fallen officer (due to barrel-burst) and one fallen man.[25]

Without doubt, the Polish campaign was a revolutionary event in military terms. Guderian's views on the use of armoured units had proved to be completely correct. Only if they were kept separate from the infantry could they launch advances which were decisive for both the battle and the war. However, the Poles had made the baptism of fire a little too easy for the German armoured force. The belief that there were no obstacles tough enough for armoured forces was as premature as it was misguided![26]

1.3.2   The Western Campaign

> *Jamais une grande puissance militaire n'a été écrasée aussi vite et aussi inexorablement.*[27]
> (*Never had a great military power been crushed as quickly and as completely.*)

Certain legends die hard, especially when they hide one's own mistakes. After the success of the German armoured force in Poland, the French High Command should also have realised

---

23. Ibid, of 6 September 1939.
24. Ibid, of 5 September 1939.
25. Ibid, of 5 September 1939. During the Eastern campaign, against an equal opponent, the casualty figures looked totally different. Cf. Halder, KTB, vol. 3, Verlustmeldung of 14 December 1941!
Casualties from 22 June–10 December 1941: Wounded 18,220 officers and 561,575 N.C.O.s and men; Losses: 6,827 officers and 155,972 N.C.O.s and men; Missing, 562 officers and 31,955 N.C.O.s and men. Total casualties, 775,087 men = 24.22% of the Eastern Army.
26. Cf. 'Einzelschilderungen aus dem Feldzug in Polen', in *Militärwissenschaftliche Rundschau*, Bd. 1, 1940, p. 31.
27. L. Saurel, *La Tragédie de juin 1940*, Paris, 1966, p. 5.

that tanks could not just be used for supporting infantry. The Allied armoured forces were both numerically and technically superior to the Germans.[28]

However, this superiority could not be brought into play since: 'The commitment of the enemy's tanks was noticeably fragmented.'[29]

Perhaps the most important factor in the blitz campaign in the West must be seen in the notion of position warfare which prevailed in the French command: 'The enemy's reliance upon methodical strategy, an exaggerated need for safety and the outdated use of his armour played a great part in our early success and, to some extent, spoiled us.'[30]

On 10 May 1940,[31] almost all the German armoured units made a thrust north of the Maginot Line through the Ardennes, thought to be tank-proof terrain.[32] Via Amiens and Abbéville, they reached the Channel coast in ten days, thus cutting the Allied Army in two. Due to an incomprehensible order by Hitler, that the panzer corps should stop before they reached Dunkirk, the majority of the British Expeditionary Corps was able to escape by sea almost at the last second, something which had hardly seemed possible:

Do not attack Dunkirk, leave it to the Luftwaffe.[33]

Dunkirk is to be attacked by the Luftwaffe alone.[34]

Now that the British had left, the Allied Northern Army Group had been put out of the battle, and Panzer Groups Guderian and

---

28. There were about 2,600 German panzers as against 4,800 Allied tanks. The 'char B' was superior to all German tanks in weaponry and armour; the 'Somua' was about the same as the Panzer IV.
29. Panzergruppe Guderian, Abt. Ia, Nr. 502/40 geheim, of 22 August 1940. Out of around 3,000 French tanks, only 1,160 were in armoured units, the other approx. 1,800 tanks were divided into 'splinter units'. Cf. H. Hoth, 'Das Schicksal der französischen Panzerwaffe im ersten Teil des Westfeldzuges 1940' in *Wehrkunde*, Bd. 7, 1958, pp. 367–8.
30. Panzergruppe von Kleist, Abt. Ia. Nr. 3,422/40 geheim, of 9 August 1940.
31. Hitler had wanted to attack France on 12 November 1939. The date of the attack was postponed no less than 29 times until 10 May 1940.
32. The operational idea for the Western campaign came from the Chief of the General Staff of Army Group A, Lieut.-Gen. von Manstein.
33. Panzergruppe von Kleist, Abt. Ia, KTB of 26 May 1940.
34. Ibid, of 28 May 1940. Cf. General von Arnim, *Lebenserinnerungen*, Part IV,

von Kleist were sent southwards from Reims in order to cut the French army in two. On 17 June this massive tank wedge reached the Swiss border. France's fate seemed to be sealed when, on 18 June, the French government asked for a ceasefire, which came into effect a week later.

On 19 July, Hitler said in a Reichstag speech: 'German armour has taken its place in world history with this war.'[35] One thing is certain – the success of the blitz campaign in France would not have been possible without the German armoured force. However, the blindness of the French High Command was also a major factor!

It was characteristic of the operations in the summer of 1940 that the German Wehrmacht fought against an army which was still basking in the aura of 'victoire et gloire' of 1918. France had more and better tanks than the German aggressor in 1940. What the military leadership lacked was the knowledge of how to employ modern armour.

If the French had not blindly trusted the protection of the Maginot Line, and had the tanks not been spread along the whole front, but rather kept in reserve for massive counterblows against enemy penetration, then perhaps the blitz campaign in Poland might have been the only one.[36]

In a daily report by 1st Panzer Division we read: 'The hurried retreat and the total impossibility of pinning us down at the defences which they had specially for this purpose has left a deep impression. It can clearly be seen that the troops flooding back in retreat had wanted to fight behind good defences.'[37] The statement of a French prisoner sounds very similar: 'We have been betrayed! . . . The army had always been assured that the defences we had to hold were strong and secure. Now it has been shown that these were penetrated in a few days.'[38] After a campaign of only six weeks against the most powerful military force on the continent of Europe, the Wehrmacht High Command could report on 26 June 1940: 'The Army has, at this time,

p. 4. Cf. H.A. Jacobsen, *Dünkirchen. Ein Beitrag zur Geschichte des Westfeldzuges 1940*, Neckargemünd, 1958.
35. H.W. Borchert, *Panzerkampf im Westen*, Berlin, 1940, p. 3.
36. Cf. Nehring, *Panzerwaffe*, p. 174.
37. 1. Pz. Div., Abt. Ia, Tagesmeldung of 17 May 1940.
38. XIX. Pz. Korps, Abt. Ic, Gefangenenmeldung, date scorched.

completed the tasks assigned to it after the overwhelming victory in the West.'[39]

During the following weeks, questionnaires were sent out by the Army Commander-in-Chief to all units, from division upwards, so as to learn from recent events and to collate combat reports: 'Have our principles of command, commitment and battle been proved correct regarding the armoured forces?'[40] At Army High Command the dangers inherent in the experience gained in the Western campaign seemed to have been realised; in any case there was a clear warning: 'We must be careful that individual combat experience based on events during the Western campaign are not falsely generalised. The unit is to be trained to fight against an equal opponent.'[41]

During the Western campaign, German commanders had learned to commit tank units en masse and to let them move freely. But they had been spared most of the many difficulties of armour strategy because the enemy had conducted a 'war of missed chances'.[42]

Combat experience cannot be made up for by exercises, however realistic, and this must be taken into account in any judgment of armed forces. On the other hand, experience should not be overestimated. It is true that it can prevent old mistakes being made again. But it can become unpredictable when we think we can recognise future events as a result of our own small amount of experience.

1.4 Operation Barbarossa

1.4.1 *The Aura of Invincibility*

Even after successful combat experience, both command and unit should be made aware of possible crises again and again, because only those who expect crises have a chance of overcoming them.[43] According to Guderian, however, the German Wehrmacht's

39. OKH, Gen.St.d.H., Op. Abt., (Ia) Nr. 375/40 Geh.Kdos of 26 June 1940.
40. OKH, Gen.St.d.H., Org. Abt., (1. St.) (I) Nr. 2,980/40 geheim, Anl. 1, 2.
41. OB d.H., Ausb. Abt.(Ia) Nr. 3,000/40 geheim of 7 October 1940.
42. Cf. A. Goutard, *1940. La guerre des occasions perdues*, Paris, 1956. Cf. W.L. Shirer, *The collapse of the Third Republic*, London, 1970.
43. Cf. K. Zeitzler, 'Krisenlagen', in *Wehrkunde*, Bd. 1961, pp. 2–8.

success, especially the victory so quickly won in the West, had impressed the High Command to such an extent that they had deleted the word 'impossible' from their vocabulary.[44]

General Blumentritt, Chief of Staff of 4th Army during the Russian campaign, said regarding Operation Barbarossa: 'We should not forget the reputation and the aura of invincibility which precedes our Wehrmacht everywhere.'[45] The same trend can be seen in the words of one Air Chief Marshal (Luftwaffengeneral): 'We had already become veterans, who knew what to do and who had everything we required for a quick victory in mobile warfare.'[46] Russian military historians also emphasise the Germans' superior experience in carrying out extensive operations: 'Another very great factor was that the German army had amassed great experience in executing large-scale military operations, using the most modern technology, in two years of war in Europe.'[47]

Without doubt the German Wehrmacht had experience of mobile warfare such as no other army possessed in the spring of 1941. What was missing, however, was the critical appraisal of this experience. For example, there was the question of whether, and to what degree, the experience obtained in the West was valid in the case of a war against Russia. 'Nothing can impede the triumphant advance of the young German armoured force, neither road-blocks nor marshland nor even rivers.'[48] It is necessary to have a healthy trust in one's own weaponry, but to believe that one is invincible is most dangerous. Those who see a connection between the lack of critique of the successes achieved, the aura of invincibility and the mistakes in planning made by the Wehrmacht during Operation Barbarossa are surely not wrong to do so.

44. Cf. Guderian, *Erinnerungen*, p. 128.
45. AOK 4, Abt. Ia, Nr. 211/41 Geh.Kdos.Chefs., of 8 May 1941.
46. A. Kesselring, *Soldat bis zum letzten Tag*, Bonn, 1953, p. 114.
47. J.J. Minz et al., *Der Große Vaterländische Krieg der Sowjetunion*, Berlin, 1947, p. 39. Cf. A.M. Samsonov, *Die große Schlacht vor Moskau 1941–1942*, Berlin, 1959, pp. 23–4. Cf. P.A. Shilin, *Die wichtigsten Operationen des Großen Vaterländischen Krieges 1941–1945*, Berlin, 1958, p. 25.
48. H. Guderian, *Mit den Panzern in Ost und West. Erlebnisberichte von Mitkämpfern aus den Feldzügen in Polen und Frankreich 1939/40*, Berlin, Prague, Vienna, 1942, p. 89, picture key.

1.4.2 The Underestimation of the Red Army

On 23 November 1939, Hitler had said to his generals: 'The fact is that the Russian army is not worth much at the moment. It will stay that way for the next year or two.'[49] What remained for the next two years was this fatal underestimation and not the poor state of the Red Army.[50]

After the achievements of the French campaign, Hitler lost all sense of what was possible in military operations. On 18 December 1940, he issued order No. 21, codenamed 'Barbarossa': 'The German Wehrmacht must be prepared . . . to subdue Soviet Russia in a speedy campaign.'[51] Clearly the talk on the German side was only of short campaigns now, regardless of the enemy or of his terrain!

While it is true that Army High Command, a month later, referred to the great number of Russian soldiers, their simplicity, toughness and courage, as well as to the wide expanses of Russia, its judgment was only slightly different to that of Hitler: 'The [Russian] army is not yet a complete instrument of combat. It will be beaten every time by a modern enemy whose commanders put speedy and large-scale operations into effect.'[52]

In a map exercise conducted by 2nd Panzer Army, there was a note that the Russian command relied upon schematism, and that the population would not take part in any active resistance.[53] In 1941, the German Wehrmacht would have to learn the hard way that Russia had been underestimated, not only militarily but also both economically and politically.[54] On the 51st day of

49. P. de Mendelssohn, *Die Nürnberger Dokumente*, Hamburg, 1947, pp. 295–6.

50. A. Hillgruber considers the underestimation of the opponent's strength and the overestimation of one's own to be the most portentous component of the continuing errors made by the Germans. Cf. H. Hillgruber, 'Unternehmen Barbarossa' in A. Hillgruber (ed.), *Probleme des Zweiten Weltkrieges*, Cologne and Berlin, 1967, p. 106. Cf. E. Moritz, 'Die Einschätzung der Roten Armee durch den faschistischen Generalstab vom 1935–1941' in *Zeitschrift für Militärgeschichte*, Bd. 2, 1969, pp. 154–70.

51. OKW, W.FSt., Abt. L(I), Nr. 33,408/40 Geh.Kdos.Chefs., F.H.Qu. of 18 December 1940.

52. OKH, Abt. Fremde Heere Ost, Merkblatt über die Eigenarten der russischen Kriegführung, undated.

53. Cf. Pz. AOK 2, Abt. Ia, Nr. 25/41 Geh.Kdos.Chefs., of 14 March 1941.

54. Cf. O. Groehler, 'Zur Einschätzung der Roten Armee durch die faschistische Wehrmacht' in *Zeitschrift für Militärgeschichte*, Bd. 6, 1968, pp. 724–38. Cf. E.

the Russian campaign (a blitz campaign was already a thing of the past) the Army Chief of General Staff wrote in his diary: 'It is becoming more and more obvious that the Russian colossus . . . has been underestimated. We calculated around 200 enemy divisions at the beginning of the war. Now we know of at least 360 . . . And, when we destroy a dozen of them, the Russians put another dozen in their place.'[55]

In November 1941, as the German reserves began to dry up and the supply organisation was threatening to fall apart,[56] the commander of 2nd Panzer Army reported to Central Army Group: 'The enemy is bringing up new reinforcements, mostly made up of Siberian divisions who are fresh, well-trained and eager to fight.'[57]

Not only were the manpower reserves of the Red Army underestimated, but above all the Russian armoured force itself.[58] It can be said that the German armoured force had superior battle tactics, since the Russians employed their tanks in a similar way to the Poles and the French, in other words, as support for the infantry. However, for the Germans to ignore their matériel inferiority in the belief that they were tactically superior was dangerous. An inferiority based on tactics can be made good in a comparatively short time, whereas a matériel gap can only be closed after a long time, or sometimes not at all, during a war.[59]

1.4.3   Assessing Terrain and Climate

Too little importance is often attached to the fact that the influence of terrain and climate has been increased due to motorisation and mechanisation: 'In 24 hours the panzer division can

---

Hesse, *Der sowjetrussische Partisanenkrieg 1941–1944 im Spiegel deutscher Kampfanweisungen und Befehle*, Göttingen, 1969.

55. Halder, KTB, Bd. 3 of 11 August 1941. Cf. Pz. AOK 2, Abt. Ic, extracts from OKH, O.Qu.IV, Abt. Fremde Heere Ost, Nr. 1,620/41 Geh.Kdos.Chefs. of 31 August 1941. On their entry into the war the Red Army had about 12 million men fit for combat, and between 15 July and 10 August about 100 new divisions were raised.

56. Cf. below pp. 95ff.

57. Pz. AOK 2, Abt. Ia, KTB Nr. 1 of 20 November 1941, 5.

58. Cf. below pp. 78ff.

59. While the Russians, some months later, began to concentrate their tanks in larger units, it was not possible for the German war industry to constantly build more and better panzers.

travel 150–200 kilometres using fully-tracked vehicles and 250–300 kilometres using other vehicles.'[60] This is what the technical manual says, but it had very little to do with reality. It only makes sense to discuss the distance achieved by mechanised units while on the road if the terrain and climatic conditions are also considered. Terrain has a much greater influence on strategic plans and employment in action than strict regulations.

Terrain can provide tanks with stand-by areas and camouflage, or it can leave them fully open to the enemy air force. Woods, rivers, boggy country or other obstacles can pull armoured forces apart or force them to travel dangerously close together.[61]

I will deal in more detail with the 'mud and winter war' in Russia later.[62] Suffice it to say at this point that both difficult terrain and climate can make commitment of armour risky or even impossible.[63] Even if the German military command had counted on a blitz campaign against Russia, it was unforgivable that they had omitted to draw up winter tactics carefully enough, and at the right time, at least as a precautionary measure.[64] Thus, in 1941, Wehrmacht units had to suffer the bitter blow of their armoured columns becoming bogged down, first in the sand, then in the mud and finally in the snow and ice.[65] In the report by 4th Panzer Division we read that:

Panzer divisions are units which rely on reasonable weather. In the case of more than 15 degrees of frost, or rain which turns roads into quagmires, breakdowns occur which bear no relation to whatever minor successes are achieved. If the unit is forced to retreat under such conditions, there are losses in matériel which can be catastrophic.[66]

60. OKH, Richtlinien für Führung und Einsatz der Pz. Div., dated 3 December 1940, p. 30.
61. Cf. below pp. 87, 100ff.
62. Cf. below pp. 95ff.
63. Cf. Pz. AOK 2, Abt. Ia, Anlage 16 zum KTB Nr. 1 of 18 November 1941, p. 2.
64. Cf. M. Fretter-Pico, 'Herbst- und Winterkrieg im Osten', in *Europäische Sicherheit. Rundschau der Wehrwissenschaften*, issue of 2 March 1951, p. 25.
65. Cf. H. Guderian, *Panzer-Marsch. Aus dem Nachlaß des Schöpfers der deutschen Panzerwaffe*, ed. by O. Munzel, Munich, 1956, p. 64.
66. 4. Pz. Div. Abt. Ia, Anlage KTB, Nr. 71/42 geheim Beantwortung Fragebogen OKH, Erfahrungen Ostfeldzug, of 12 March 1942, p. 2.

On 18 November 1941, 2nd Panzer Army reported: 'During the Russian campaign we faced problems of terrain and climate hitherto unknown to us.'[67] It is understandable that many problems of armoured warfare were unknown before the Russian campaign. However, it is difficult to understand how little the spartan Russian road network, the great distances, the autumn mud period and the question of supply support were taken into account.

1.4.4 A Long 'Blitz Campaign'

On 22 June 1941, at 0300 hours, Operation Barbarossa, the German Wehrmacht's attack on Russia, began. The operational plan was to annihilate the main part of the Russian army in western Russia in a blitz campaign with an extensive advance of tank wedges, and to prevent the enemy from drawing back into the vast Russian hinterland.[68]

On 3 July the Army Chief of General Staff noted in his diary: 'I am not saying too much when I maintain that the campaign against Russia was won within 14 days.'[69] Indeed, the reports of the first days and weeks made one believe that the impossible had become reality – the Red Army had been smashed and Russia conquered in one blitz campaign. By the middle of July, 2nd and 3rd Panzer Armies of Central Army Group were in the region of Smolensk. Encirclement battles of hitherto unknown dimensions mostly ended with the complete destruction of Russian formations.[70] A gap of 650 kilometres separated the armoured forces from the Polish demarcation line, but there were still 350 kilometres between them and Moscow.

In reality, the Red Army was weakened for a long time,[71] but in no way was it beaten. The Russians drew steadily back eastwards, but certainly not on crutches, as German war propaganda had it.[72] Thanks to the element of surprise the

---

67. Pz. AOK 2, Abt. Ia Anlage 16 zum KTB Nr. 1, of 18 November 1941, p. 2.
68. Cf. L. Besymenski, *Sonderakte 'Barbarossa'*, Stuttgart, 1968.
69. Halder, KTB, Bd. 3, of 3 August 1941.
70. Cf. below pp. 35ff.
71. Cf. *Pravda* of 23 February 1957, article by Marshal of the Soviet Union R.J. Malinovski on the July days of 1941, 'We fell back because we simply could not stop the enemy'. Cf. Shilin, *Die wichtigsten Operationen*, p. 93.
72. Cf. 'Der Durchbruch durch die Stalinlinie', in *Deutsche Wehrmacht* of 25 July 1941, p. 537.

German armoured forces had had early successes, which seemed to point to a blitz campaign.[73] However, the Red Army was able to learn from its defeats without falling apart. Its reserves of manpower were almost limitless, as was the space at its disposal!

In spite of countless small victories, 4th Panzer Division reported after five weeks of the campaign: 'The Russian command appears to work to a plan – as always cleverly retreating.'[74]

And while the Red Army slowly recovered, began to organise its troops and even launch local counter-offensives,[75] the effects of the constant German operations made themselves felt. Tank breakdowns, tank knockouts and shortage of fuel had gone beyond what was tolerable. The number of combat-ready tanks fell daily.

It is not enough for armoured forces simply to be victorious. They must also be able to keep on fighting. And that became their main problem.[76] Until the start of the mud period and the cold snap which followed, the Wehrmacht had achieved countless tactical victories and a huge territorial gain. But a definite victory had not been reached by the end of 1941. The aim of defeating Russia in a blitz campaign had not been achieved.

In the following chapters we will consider individual aspects of tank tactics as they are reflected in German war diaries.

73. Cf. below pp. 19ff.
74. 4. Pz. Div. Abt. Ia, Anlagen der Gef.Berichte zum KTB, of 27 July 1941.
75. Cf. Pz. AOK 2, Abt. Ic, KTB Nr. 1, of 8 July 1941. 'Enemy on offensive in front of 17th and 18th Pz. Div.'
76. Cf. 4th Pz. Div. Abt. Ia, Anlagen zum KTB, Nr. 71/42 geheim Beantwortung Fragebogen OKH, Erfahrungen Ostfeldzug, of 12 March 1941. For the Russian campaign the German armoured force had 3,580 tanks, thus only 1,000 more than for the campaign against France, which is 10 times smaller geographically. Cf. OKH, Bericht des Generalinspekteurs der Pz. Trp. Nr. 3,940/44 Geh. Kdos. H. Qu. of 7 November 1944.

2

Armour on the Offensive

The following tactical principles were valid for the German
armoured force as early as 1938:

> Panzer units are the most potent offensive weapons on land. Their
> commitment is the climax of a battle and must force the enemy into a
> position where he can either offer further resistance or can no longer
> even prevent an invasion by non-armoured units.[1]

> The tank attack is the basic mode of combat of the armoured
> forces . . . Even on the defensive the tank attack, at the right time
> and in the right place, is always more effective than a static front, and
> is therefore desirable.[2]

2.1 Hammer Blows on Weak Front Sectors

> *The best strategy is always to be very strong, first in general, and
> then at the decisive point . . . Incredible though it sounds, it is a
> fact that armies have been divided and separated countless times,
> without the commander having any clear reason for it, simply
> because he vaguely felt that this was the way things ought to be
> done.*[3]

Whereas this vague common instinct had not yet been
suppressed in Poland and France, one could read in the German
Handbook of Modern Military Science as early as two years
before the Polish campaign 'that panzer offensives will normally
only be successful when the necessary mass effect has been
achieved by concentration of forces in the correct area. The tank

---

1. *Heigl's Taschenbuch der Tanks*, p. 262.
2. Ibid, p. 263.
3. Carl von Clausewitz, *On War*, Princeton, N.J., 1976, p. 204.

brigade is the smallest combat unit which should be entrusted with an independent mission.'[4]

The Polish campaign showed that armour commitment is successful when the tanks are under one command:

> Commitment in small units is pointless, since the antitank weapons then have the advantage and can pick off individual tanks. They should be commited in battalion strength whenever possible.[5]

> The use of platoons and even individual tanks led to failures and unnecessary losses.[6]

In armour operation in particular, it could be constantly seen that it is vital to concentrate all one's forces on one point. Any division of power led to avoidable losses.[7] 'If you can use a few panzer companies, then you can use the whole brigade.'[8] In order to be able to speak of hammer-blows on weak sectors of the front, not only are a larger number of tanks needed, but also very narrow sectors of attack, in order to allow the large force to become effective:

> Thus the offensive width, when the division is attacking out of a position with the infantry in front of them, will be about half the width of the infantry division, and with the panzer brigade in front of them the width will be about 800 to 1000 metres.[9]

> In this case the attack sector must be kept very narrow in order to concentrate the forces for the breakthrough. If necessary each corps must confine itself to one route.[10]

4. H. Franke, *Handbuch der neuzeitlichen Wehrwissenschaften*, vol. 2, Berlin and Leipzig, 1937, p. 389. Cf. Ibid, p. 388.
5. XV. A.K. mot. Abt. Ia, KTB, Erfahrungen aus der Schlacht an der Lysa-Gora, of 13 September 1939.
6. 2. le. Div. Abt. Ia, Nr. 389/39 geheim of 5 October 1939. Cf. H. Hoth, 'Der Kampf von Panzerdivisionen in Kampfgruppen in Beispielen der Kriegsgeschichte' in *Wehrkunde*, vol. 11, 1959, p. 584, 'The less tanks there are available, the more urgent the need for them to be organised under one command'.
7. Cf. OKH, Richtlinien für Führung und Einsatz der Panzerdivision, of 3 December 1940, p. 3.
8. Pz. Gr. Guderian, Abt. Ia, Nr. 557/40 geheim of 17 October 1940 (Änderungsvorschläge zu den Richtlinien für die Führung der Pz. Div. geh. D66+, by General Schmidt).
9. OKH, Richtlinien für Führung und Einsatz der Panzerdivision, of 3 December 1940, p. 21.
10. Pz. Gr. Guderian, Abt. Ia, Nr. 133/40 Geh.Kdos.Chefs., of 2 October 1940, p. 2.

With so many tanks in one place at the spearhead of the attack, such situations as these came about: 'At 0630 sharp . . . the Panzer Brigade goes on the offensive. Tank alongside tank, wave upon wave rolls away. The attack continues. The French jump up in horror and run for their lives or surrender. Thus the attack becomes like a manoeuvre.'[11]

The situation became catastrophic for the defenders when not just individual panzer divisions but Mobile Units of between four and twelve divisions attacked within a relatively narrow sector:

> Once formed the Mobile Unit is a tight one. It must not be torn apart until the mission has ended.[12]

> In its short life-time Panzer Group von Kleist has had the privilege of playing a decisive role in the victory over France, having been in constant action since the beginning of the Western offensive.
> For the first time in military history a 'pedigree' motorised Army Group was set up.[13] The course of the campaign completely fulfilled the expectations made of it.[14]

Linear defence strategies were not a viable concept against hammer-blows from large armoured forces. However, powerful mechanised counterattacks were more likely to succeed. 'On the 18.8. the Russians succeeded for the first time since the 27.7. in concentrating several divisions in one powerful thrust instead of advances by individual battalions.'[15]

After the Western campaign, it was noted in the files of Panzer Group von Kleist that the strategy had paid off. The decisive role had been played by: 'The concentration of as many tanks as possible in the point of main effort – no dissipation or

---

11. 1. Pz. Div. Abt. Ia, Gef. Bericht des Inf. Regt. 1, of 10 June 1940.

12. Pz. Gr. von Kleist, Abt. Ia, Chef des Gen.St., Richtlinien für die Führung Schneller Gruppen, Entwurf dated 20 Oktober 1940, p. 5. Cf. Ibid, p. 6. Mobile Units should ideally be under the Army High Command and an Army Group. Under an Infantry Arm there was always the danger of the employment being too limited.

13. Panzer Group von Kleist contained: 5 Pz. Divisions; 3 Motorised Infantry Divisions; 1,250 tanks; 362 armoured scout cars; 41,140 motor vehicles; 134,370 men.

14. Pz. Gr. von Kleist, Abt. Ia, KTB, undatiertes Schlußwort nach Ende des Westfeldzuges.

15. 9. Armee, Abt. Ia, OB, Nr. 3,696/41, Geh.Kdos.Chefs., of 20 August 1941.

employment of tanks which is too weak.'[16] And after the first year of the Russian campaign one could even read in the combat report of one Panzer Division: 'It is seen as vitally necessary that the employment of tanks under company strength is forbidden.'[17]

2.2 The Use of Surprise

> *This desire [i.e. surprise] is more or less basic to all operations, for without it superiority at the decisive point is inconceivable.*[18]

It can be crucial to completely surprise the enemy especially when the moment of surprise is exploited by armoured units: 'The speed of the Panzer and Motorised Divisions is vital for the surprise of the enemy. Speed must not be given away by having too much time for reconnaissance, consideration, giving and passing on of orders.'[19]

On 10 May 1940 the theoretical rules about the effect of surprise attacks proved to be correct:

> 1st and 2nd Panzer Divisions took prisoner over 100 (Belgian) Ardennes Riflemen, who were totally surprised by the attack.[20]

> Advance of divisions during the night ran smoothly . . . no resistance . . . Captured Luxembourg customs guards admitted complete surprise.[21]

The reports of captured Frenchmen and Englishmen told over and over again of their complete shock at the sudden advance of German armoured units:

> Nowhere is the advance of panzer divisions met by organised resistance . . . A good example of this is the fact that a British battery was surprised during an exercise.[22]

---

16. Pz. Gr. von Kleist, Abt. Ia, Nr. 3,422/40 geheim of 9 August 1940. Stellungnahme zu den Erfahrungsberichten des XIX. Pz. K.
17. 12. Pz. Div. Abt. Ia, Erfahrungsbericht of 24.1.42.
18. C. von Clausewitz, *On War*, p. 198.
19. Pz. Gr. von Kleist, Abt. Ia, Nr. 369/40 Geh.Kdos. of 6 April 1940.
20. XIX. Pz. Korps Abt. Ia, Abendmeldung of 10 May 1940.
21. Ibid, Morgenmeldung of 10 May 1940.
22. XIX. Pz. Korps Abt. Ic, KTB, Tagesmeldung, date burned.

Opponents, who had been fighting in Belgium and had been beaten, had wanted to regroup and defend, but they were surprised by the thrust of the panzer divisions.[23]

The following example shows that not just border patrols were surprised by the German attack:

> Lieut. Tittelbach, a fine example of an advance officer, found on 22.5., while making a reconnaissance of the next corps command post, a village south of Samer occupied by the French. They were attending Communion at the time. Thanks to his decisive action he captured, after a short show of resistance, 1 colonel, 2 majors, about 20 lieutenants and around 300 other Frenchmen.[24]

In the light of such actions it would be too easy to ascribe success merely to the exploitation of surprise . . .

The question is asked time and again: how could the largest offensive in history, Operation Barbarossa, despite the underestimation of the enemy and the lack of preparation in the opening phase, run almost to plan and without problems? One answer must be absolute surprise, which was correctly exploited by the German armoured forces and brought the Red Army dangerously close to collapse during the summer of 1941. The following reports reached the HQ of 3rd Panzer Division on the morning of the attack, 22 June 1941:

> 0325 hours, Combat Group Kleeman reports that enemy resistance is non-existent.[25]

> 0330 hours, Combat Group Androsch reports that there is no enemy reaction in their sector.[26]

> 0350 hours, Infantry Regt. 3 has already crossed (the Bug) as well as the first tanks of the Panzer Regiment.[27]

The High Command of 9th Army also reported the complete enemy surprise[28] and German Army High Command announced

---

23. Ibid.
24. Ibid, Abt. Ia, Bericht der Korps-Nachrichten-Abt. 80 über den Einsatz gegen Belgien und Frankreich, of 18 July 1940.
25. 3. Pz. Div. Abt. Ia, Anl. zum KTB Nr. 3, of 22 June 1941.
26. Ibid.
27. Ibid.
28. AOK 9, Abt. Ia, Anl. Nr. 3,320/41 geheim of 22 June 1941. Cf. Pz. AOK 3,

on 23 June: 'Enemy retreating almost everywhere, totally surprised by the attack, after weak, almost aimless resistance.'[29]

Why the countless warnings which had been sent from the Russian border areas to Moscow since the summer of 1940 had remained mostly unheeded cannot be adequately explained at this point. However, seldom has there been such clear agreement between German war diaries and the descriptions of Soviet military historians as in the portrayal of the Red Army surprised by the Wehrmacht.[30]

While the tanks of the German divisions had already crossed the Bug, Soviet Army Group 'Western Front' had not yet even been put on alarm status.[31] Soviet General Staff could not make contact with the commander-in-chief of this Army Group, since General Pavlov had gone to visit his troops, and no-one on the General Staff knew where the C-in-C was.[32]

Thus the Russian divisions started to defend singly, in an unplanned fashion or not at all, since there were neither telegraph nor radio links between the front command posts and most of the armies and independent corps.[33] According to Ic reports by the German divisions, many Russian border unit commanders were wrongly or incompletely informed.[34] Some of them waited in vain for orders from their headquarters, without at least keeping their groups on alert, 'although from the other side [of the Bug] the sound of motors and the clattering of the tank tracks could already be heard.'[35]

Abt. Ia, Feindnachrichtenblatt 6, Anl. zu Gruppenbefehl Nr. 2, of 22 June 1941.

29. OKH, Gen.St.d.H., O.Qu.IV, Abt. Fremde Heere Ost (II) Nr. 2,555/41 geheim of 23 June 1941.

30. Cf. J.G. Andronikov and W. Mostovenko, *Die Roten Panzer. Geschichte der sowjetischen Panzertruppen 1920–1960*, ed. by P.M. von Senger und Etterlin, Munich, 1963, p. 33. Cf. B.S. Telpuchovski, *Die sowjetische Geschichte des Grossen Vaterländischen Krieges 1941–1945*, edited and with a commentary by A. Hillgruber and H.A. Jacobsen, Frankfurt am Main, 1965, p. 53.

31. Cf. Shilin, *Die wichtigsten Operationen*, p. 25. Cf. G.K. Zhukov, *Erinnerungen und Gedanken*, Stuttgart, 1969, p. 234. Directive No. 2 by the People's Commissar for Defence did not reach all Army Commands until 0715 hours on the morning of the attack. However, according to Marshal Zhukov, the directive was 'obviously unrealistic . . . and could therefore not be carried out'.

32. Cf. Zhukov, *Erinnerungen*, p. 237.

33. Cf. Samsonov, *Die Große Schlacht*, p. 35. Cf. Shilin, *Die wichtigsten Operationen*, p. 49. Cf. Zhukov, *Erinnerungen*, p. 237.

34. Cf. Pz. AOK 2, Abt. Ic, Meldungen der unterstellten Verbände im KTB Nr. 1, of 22 June–18 July 1941.

35. Zhukov, *Erinnerungen*, p. 247. Cf. 18. Pz. Div. Abt. Ia, Nr. 55/40 geheim of

Because the Red Army had been surprised, the German spearhead panzers encountered the following ideal situation:

1. Poorly-prepared defences;
2. Many bridges neither destroyed nor defended;[36]
3. Anti-tank weapons not used in a concentrated way;
4. No anti-tank bases;
5. No counter-attacks by large armoured units.

Thus it can be no surprise that, by the evening of the first day of the campaign, certain Wehrmacht tank divisions were already fighting sixty kilometres deep into enemy territory.[37]

Due to the use of armoured divisions, the German commanders succeeded in catching up the slowly-retreating armies of Russian Army Group 'Western Front'.[38] The element of surprise was exploited until the enemy was encircled.[39]

2.3   The Tank Attack at Night

> *Basically, a night attack is only an intensified raid. At first glance it looks highly effective: supposedly the defender is taken unawares, while the attacker, of course, is well prepared for what is about to happen. What an uneven contest! One imagines complete confusion on one side and on the other an attacker concerned merely to profit by it. This image explains the many schemes put forward by those who have neither to lead them nor accept responsibility for them. In practice they are very rare.*[40]

---

20 November 1940. According to the combat experiences of this Pz. Div. the approach of a panzer unit is audible by day, with wind at about 1,500 metres; without wind, about 800 metres; by night, with wind, about 4,000 metres; without wind, about 2,000 metres.

36. Cf. 3. Pz. Div. Abt. Ia, KTB Nr. 3, of 24 June 1941. This Pz. Div. reports that on 24 June 1941 all bridges in their sector were usable and hardly if at all defended.

37. Cf. *Geschichte der 3. Pz. Div.*, p. 116. This division had covered around 300 kilometres up to the middle of the fourth day.

38. These were the 3rd, 4th and 10th Army. The Commander-in-Chief of Army Group 'Western Front' was replaced by Marshal Timoshenko on 2 July 1941. Cf. above, note 75, p. 15.

39. Cf. below. pp. 34, 35ff.

40. C. von Clausewitz, *On War*, p. 273.

Tank attacks at night make high demands on both the units and the commanders.[41] As we read in the report of one panzer regiment:

> Combat in darkness is not a desirable thing for armour.[42]

> Due to the onset of dusk the march became extremely difficult, especially for the tanks in the company, because they could only see a limited distance.[43]

Despite these difficulties we know that many panzer attacks at night were highly successful, for example:

1. The division's breakthrough on the Maginot Line;
2. The night attack on Arras via Cambrai on the night of 19/20 May 1940;
3. The night advance on Cherbourg.

If the division came upon the enemy on these night advances, he would be overrun, accompanied by as much firing as possible.[44]

During the Western campaign the armoured forces were able to move along good and extremely good roads, and thus it was feasible to mount attacks in darkness. During the Russian campaign, however, the conditions for night attacks became more and more difficult depending on climate and terrain:

> Night marches, attack alerts and attacks depend upon suitable roads. If these are missing, then there will be regular breakdowns. The result of this is late arrival of the unit and overtiredness. Night movements by a mobile group on difficult roads are also too costly in terms of matériel. They should therefore be the exception.[45]

From time to time houses and haystacks were shot on fire in order to increase the probability of hits:

41. Cf. OKH, Gen.St.d.H. Ausb, Ia, Nr. 1,920/40 geheim, of 18 September 1940, p. 2.
42. XIX. Pz. Korps Abt. Ia, Erfahrungsbericht des Pz. Regt. 5, of 1 October 1939. Cf. Ibid, des 3. Pz. Div., of 4 October 1939, p. 2. Cf. Ibid, des Pz. Regt. 6, of 2 October 1939.
43. 7. Pz. Div. Abt. Ia, Meldung der Pz. Abt. 101, of 23 August 1941.
44. 7. Pz. Div. Abt. Ia, Nr. 440/40 geheim, of 14 July 1940, p. 13.
45. 4. Pz. Div. Abt. Ia, Anl. zum KTB, Nr. 71/42 geheim Beantwortung Fragebogen OKH betr. Erfahrung Ostfeldzug, of 12 March 1942, p. 3.

Rothenburg, commander of Panzer Regt. 6 . . . one of the most experienced tank officers in the army, took quick action. He shot the farm building in front of him on fire, thus giving himself battlefield illumination for hours, and shot the very bravely-fought Polish infantry attacks apart with case-shot.[46]

On a dark night, light up the enemy by shooting the houses and haystacks into flames.[47]

In spite of more difficult command, rough country and high losses, night attacks became more and more important during the Russian campaign.[48] At night they were at least safe from the enemy air force, which is no minor advantage for armour in particular.[49] Panzer attacks in darkness very often served to totally smash an already shaken enemy. Therefore it was not so much a case of mounting a secretly prepared operation as of pushing home certain victory:

Attacks in fog and at night became necessary, especially when an already beaten enemy had to be annihilated and forced to break up.[50]

Victory must be exploited with all means and without pause, even at night. The beaten enemy is not to be allowed to rest.[51]

According to the combat report of 4th Panzer Division, they were often attacked at night by the Russians, above all by means of infiltration. These enemy night attacks were, however, mostly badly led and could be thrown back each time by counterattacks using often smaller forces.[52] 'The Russians themselves are very sensitive to attack at night (bad command). Our night attacks were almost always successful. Exception – minefields. They cannot be removed at night.'[53]

---

46. 3. Pz. Div. Bericht von Gen.-Lt. Frhr. Geyr von Schweppenburg, p. 10.
47. See note 45.
48. Cf. Pz. AOK 2, Abt. Ia, KTB Nr. 1, of 19 November 1941, p. 4. Cf. Ibid, Abt. Ia, KTB Nr. 1, of 20 November 1941, p. 1.
49. Cf. below, pp. 64ff.
50. H.Dv. 470/7, Ausbildungsvorschrift für die Panzertruppe, of 1 May 1941, p. 66.
51. Pz. Gr. Guderian, Abt. Ia, Anl. Nr. 557/40 geheim of 17 October 1940, p. 6.
52. Cf. 4. Pz. Div. Abt. Ia, Anl. zum KTB, Nr. 71/42 geheim Beantwortung Fragebogen OKH betr. Erfahrung Ostfeldzug, of 12 March 1942, p. 7.
53. Ibid.

Without doubt the psychological effect on the defenders played a great role in all panzer attacks at night. A German tank commander wrote on this subject: 'A nervous strain which can turn into panic when he (the defender) hears the slow sound of tanks rolling towards him, but does not see them until it is too late.'[54] Fear must have very often exceeded the actual danger in such night attacks, since one must not forget that: 'At night the tank merely makes a good target and sees little.'[55]

2.4 The Demoralisation of the Enemy

For instance, one cannot explain the effects of a victory without taking psychological reactions into account.[56]

The panzer battles of the years 1939–41 show most clearly that the effect upon morale can reach complete demoralisation. In a report from the Polish campaign we read the following about the commander of a panzer company: 'He simply drove into the wild confusion of men and machines, got out, negotiated with his machine pistol in his hand . . . With his 7 tanks and 18 crew, he took about 1,400 men prisoner.'[57] A piece of propaganda published by the German Wehrmacht High Command said: 'The cry, "German tanks are coming" was enough to make enemy battalions and regiments break up.'[58]

Well, this propaganda was not so very far from the truth, as experiences from the Western campaign show:

Numerically-superior German tanks had such a demoralising effect on enemy tank crews that they often jumped out or showed the white flag.[59]

A second 18-ton tank next to us showed no signs of damage, but had

---

54. Hofmann, 'Die Nacht, der Gehilfe des Panzermannes?' in *Die Panzertruppe*, vol. 7, 1939, p. 238.
55. 24. Pz. Div. Abt. Ia, Anl. 2 zum KTB, Nr. 365/42 geheim of 11 November 1942.
56. C. von Clausewitz, *On War*, p. 184.
57. K. Bernhard, *Panzer packen Polen*, Berlin, 1940, p. 61. Cf. XIX. Pz. Korps Abt. Ia, Ic-Meldung der 20. Inf.Div.mot. of 2 September 1939.
58. OKW, *Sieg über Frankreich. Berichte und Bilder*, Berlin, 1940, p. 154.
59. Pz. Gr. Guderian, Abt. Ia, Nr. 502/40 geheim of 22 August 1940.

been left in full working order by the crew, which seemed to have been completely depressed by the firing.[60]

On the evening of 18 May 1940 . . . Lance-Corporal Hardt ran up to a fully-operative French 3.7 ton tank with a handgrenade ready to throw. Surprised by Hardt's fearless advance, the crew of the tank surrendered. Hardt thereupon forced the driver of the tank to drive it to the company command post himself.[61]

The surprising appearance of the enemy who was certainly not expected at that time, especially the shocking and demoralising effect of the German tanks, as well as the impact of the air attacks, broke any resistance, according to the prisoners.[62]

Enemy falling back in total disorganisation from the French north front. Fleeing enemy troops have been attacked in front of the XVI. Army Corps in a spirited action and have been captured in their thousands.[63]

The situation at 2nd Pz. Div. is similar to that of 1st Pz. Div. It has reached its objective without really engaging the enemy. 2 generals and 40 officers were taken prisoner.[64]

Only a completely demoralised enemy could, for example, let 7th Panzer Division take such numbers of prisoners and captured matériel. The success record of 7th Pz. Div.:

10–29 May 1940	14,368 prisoners;
	237 tanks destroyed or captured;
	88 fields guns destroyed or captured.
5–12 June 1940	53,100 prisoners;
	117 tanks destroyed or captured;
	176 field guns destroyed or captured.[65]

For this reason Guderian did not think it wise to put too much emphasis on events which occurred during the battle in France: 'The behaviour and morale of the French during the Western campaign must not lead to our meeting any other enemy, in this

60. 8. Flak-Regt. 38, Gef. Bericht dated 17 May 1940 (burned).
61. 10. Pz. Div. Abt. Ia, Meldung von Sperrverband Oberst Müller, of 19 May 1940.
62. XIX. Pz. Korps Abt. Ic, Tagesmeldung dated 14 May 1940.
63. Pz. Gr. von Kleist, Abt. Ia, aus Gruppenbefehl Nr. 31 of 16 June 1940.
64. XIX. Pz. Korps Abt. Ic, Tagesmeldung dated 19 May 1940.
65. 7. Pz. Div. Abt. Ia, Gefangene und Beute der 7. Pz. Div., of 19 June 1940.

or any other war, with insufficient weaponry and a schematic, primitive set of tactics.'[66]

We can see from many war diaries that the British often had a markedly better fighting spirit than the French:

> While the French infantry, with the exception of the colonial divisions, seldom withstood the morale effects of a panzer attack to the final penetration, the British infantryman defended himself most doggedly, even when being rolled over by tanks in his slit trench.[67]

> British fighting while French and Belgians hardly put up any resistance.[68]

> Enemy fighting grimly and bitterly everywhere, mostly British.[69]

> The enemy is fighting doggedly and desperately in Boulogne . . . The defenders are mostly led by the British.[70]

As an example from the Russian campaign shows, the enemy was not always scared of attacking panzers: 'The enemy riflemen sat in their slit trenches until they were either run down or killed by a hand grenade or a bayonet.'[71]

If the German armoured force had the advantage of surprise and a new kind of weapon on their side, it was still true that completely demoralised opponents played a great part in the sometimes unbelievable victories. Indeed, the German tank units were a good way of wearing down the morale of enemy troops. As one training manual says:

> Live targets and non-armour-piercing weapons are to be neutralised by machine gun and grenades and, in close combat, by rolling over them with the tank.[72]

> Enemy still present is to be run over.[73]

---

66. Pz. Gr. Guderian, Abt. Ia, Nr. 502/40 geheim of 22 August 1940.
67. 7. Pz. Div. Abt. Ia, Nr. 440/40 geheim of 14 July 1940.
68. 2. Pz. Div. Abt. Ic, Meldung an XIX. Pz. Korps, date burned (probably 23 May 1940).
69. Ibid.
70. 2. Pz. Div. Abt. Ic, Tagesmeldung dated 24 May 1940.
71. LVII. Pz. Korps Abt. Ia, Gef. Bericht der 20. Pz. Div., of 5 September 1941, p. 2.
72. H.Dv. 470/7, Ausbildungsvorschrift für die Panzertruppe, of 1 May 1941, p. 31.
73. Ibid, p. 32.

Bravery and courage were not sufficient to fight against the German armoured force. This bitter experience cost the Polish cavalry dearly. However, on the other hand, a great number of soldiers and equal weaponry to the enemy's were not alone sufficient for the fight against the German armoured force either. This bitter experience cost France dearly!

2.5 Panzer Commanders Lead from the Front

> *In other words a distinguished commander without boldness is unthinkable.*[74]

When commanding armoured units in particular, the situations change so rapidly, and the opportunities to make use of good luck pass so quickly that commanders should not confine themselves to posts far behind the lines.

> One thing is sure – he who seeks formulas for commanding the Mobile Units, the pedantic type, should take off the black battledress (of the armoured force). He has no idea of its spirit.[75]

> For the Mobile Unit this motto is truer than ever, 'Better a usable order at the right time than a perfect one too late'.[76]

Simply because the surprise raid is far more characteristic of what the armoured force stands for than carefully prepared and planned attacks, armoured units can only be successfully led from the front. Entries in war diaries confirm this idea of 'leading from the front' almost without exception:

> The place of a panzer unit commander is at the front. Only he who drives ahead of his unit can lead it.[77]

> The commander must be far forward in order to influence the way the battle is run.[78]

74. C. von Clausewitz, *On War*, p. 192.

75. 3. Pz. Div. Abt. Ia, Bericht von Gen.-Lt. Frhr. Geyr von Schweppenburg, p. 28.

76. Pz. Gr. von Kleist, Abt. Ia, Chef d. Gen. St., Richtlinien für die Führung Schneller Gruppen, p. 11, outline of 20 October 1940.

77. 7. Pz. Div. Abt. Ia, Nr. 393/39 geheim, of 19 October 1939, p. 2.

78. 12. Pz. Div. Abt. Ia, Erfahrungsbericht of 24 January 1942.

Those who think these command rules merely apply at company or battalion level are mistaken:

It has been proved most effective, in all battles, when the divisional commander and his immediate staff have had their post very far forward. Only then was it possible to exploit all the chances open to them and to parry each of the enemy's countermoves.[79]

This is especially true for the divisional commander, who normally stays with his aides and the radio set at the head of the advance party.[80]

Here the advance party, led by the regimental commander with his adjutant, met up with the head of Panzer Regiment 25.[81]

Mobile Units can only be led when the commanders are far forward where the action is at its height. This goes for all commanders whatever their rank![82]

Every tankman knows that very difficult situations can arise, not only in combat, but also during any movement of large armoured units. And in such situations, which cannot be foreseen, it is vitally important that the commanding officer take control of the confusion and not just any section commander. General Guderian gives us a striking example of this: 'When General Guderian heard on the 16 May that columns of the 1st, 2nd, and 6th Panzer Divs. had collided in Montcornet, he drove there quickly and gave the divisions new march routes . . . and personally supervised the disentangling of the confused columns.'[83] Leadership from the front means more than a mere slogan, much more. Instead of unrealistic orders you then have a practical demonstration of how to fight, how to live, and, finally perhaps, how to die. 'During the attacks parts of the tank regiment came under heavy anti-tank gun fire and into the direct fire of two 7.5 cm batteries at 500 metres. There are

---

79. 7. Pz. Div. Abt. Ia, Nr. 440/40 geheim, of 14 July 1940, p. 14.
80. OKH, Richtlinien für die Führung und Einsatz der Panzerdivision, of 3 December 1940, p. 5.
81. 7. Pz. Div. Abt. Ia, Morgenmeldung des Sch. Rgt. 6, of 8 October 1941, p. 2.
82. 10. Pz. Div. Abt. Ia, Nr. 141/39 geheim, of 31 October 1939, p. 4.
83. XIX. Pz. Korps Abt. Ia, Tagesablauf des Kommandierenden Generals, of 16 May 1940.

casualties. Among others, the divisional commander's tank is hit, and he is slightly wounded.'[84]

In only five weeks of combat, from 22 June to 26 July 1941, the total casualties of 20th Pz. Div. were as follows:

Officers :   147 = 35% of marching-out strength;
N.C.O.'s :   367 = 19% of marching-out strength;
Men   : 1,571 = 11% of marching-out strength.[85]

In the war diary of 10th Pz. Div. the very high losses among officers are confirmed. From 22 June to 5 December 1941 were killed or wounded:

Officers :   351 = 63% of marching-out strength;
N.C.O.'s : 1,120 = 47% of marching-out strength;
Men   : 5,112 = 42% of marching-out strength;

Because armoured units can only be pulled into battle from the front and not pushed from behind, the losses among commanders of any rank were as unusual as the success of the young armoured force.

84. 7. Pz. Div. Abt. Ia, Kurzbericht of 14 May 1940.

85. 20. Pz. Div. Abt. Ia, Zustandsmeldung an LVII. Pz. Korps of 27 July 1941. Cf. H. von Manteuffel, *Die 7. Panzerdivision im Zweiten Weltkrieg. Einsatz und Kampf der 'Gespenster-Division' 1939–1945*, Uerdingen am Rhein, 1965, p. 273. From 22 June 1941–23 February 1942 34 officers of the Panzer Regiment were killed.

86. 10. Pz. Div. Abt. Ia, Bericht über den Einsatz im Ostfeldzug dated 22 June –5 December 1941, p. 16.

3
The Encirclement of the Enemy

The main feature of an offensive battle is the outflanking or by-passing of the defender – that is, taking the initiative.[1]

3.1 Deep Thrust with Unprotected Flanks

Before deep thrusts can be achieved, the enemy border defences must be breached.

> Attacking with the forward tanks firing, the rest of the regiment close behind, we succeeded in breaking through the deep defensive zone . . . We drove at a break-neck pace, some of us still firing, straight through the middle of the French troops.[2]

> In 8 days the unit rushed through Luxembourg, penetrated two Belgian defences by assault . . . Enemy resistance, hilly country and road-blocks did not hold us up.[3]

> Nevertheless, on this day the unit got through the Ardennes and the Meuse and thus overcame the main terrain obstacles.[4]

As soon as border defences and obstacles have been overcome, the armoured units have the perfect opportunity to exploit the initial shock and disorganisation of the enemy by using the greatest possible speed, in order to surprise him again and deny him the opportunity to rest.

For an enemy surprised by German panzer forces and divided by tank wedges there was almost no chance to regroup. More often there was complete confusion, which in many cases turned into disarray and flight:

1. C. von Clausewitz, *On War*, p. 635.
2. 7. Pz. Div. Abt. Ia, Kurzbericht of 16 May 1940.
3. Pz. Gr. von Kleist, Abt. Ia, aus dem Tagesbefehl des Kommandierenden Generals, of 17 May 1940.
4. Ibid, KTB of 16 May 1940.

> Due to a quick attack by the panzer divisions the enemy's retreat became a stampede.[5]

> And, as in the victory on the Meuse, there was a chase and we were rolling into fleeing elements.[6]

> The oncoming streams of prisoners and the amount of field guns, crawler-tractors, motor vehicles and ammunition make it obvious that the enemy's retreat has become a rout.[7]

> In so doing we overran a French mechanised division.[8]

> Ahead of the Corps, standing on the Oise, a vanquished army is flooding back southwards.[9]

Under such circumstances German armour could thrust deep into the enemy's hinterland with open flanks without fear of massive counterattacks – who could have stopped them? As early as March 1940, General von Kleist had given his Panzer Group the order that: 'The important thing is to penetrate deeply and quickly without considering what is happening to the left or right, and to continually surprise the defender'.[10]

It was mostly as a result of the enemy's linear defensive strategy that German armour during the Polish and Western campaigns could push deep into enemy territory, often with open flanks. Thus the following tactical doctrine was found to be true: 'The division should not be afraid to make deep thrusts into the enemy without worrying about unprotected flanks.'[11] Because the panzer units were given far-reaching goals from the beginning, they achieved almost unbelievable distances on the road, more reminiscent of exercises than of wartime.

> In barely 8 weeks we covered around 3,000 kilometres in combat and chase. For example, the 10th Panzer Division's daily distance on 21 June 1940 alone was 370 kilometres, that of its tank brigade almost 200 kilometres.[12]

5. Pz. Gr. von Kleist, Abt. Ia, Tagesbefehl des Kommandierenden Generals, of 11 June 1940.
6. Ibid.
7. XIX. Pz. Corps, Abt. Ic, Abendmeldung of 18 May 1940.
8. 7. Pz. Div. Abt. Ia, Nr. 440/40 geheim of 14 July 1940.
9. XIX. Pz Corps Abt. Ic, Tagesmeldung, date burned.
10. Pz. Gr. von Kleist, Abt. Ia, Nr. 217/40 Geh.Kdos.Chefs., of 12 March 1940, p. 2.
11. XXXIX. Pz. Corps Abt. Ia, Nr. 291/40 geheim, of 9 October 1940, p. 12.
12. Pz. Gr. von Kleist, Abt. Ia, KTB, of 11 July 1940.

The daily distance required for a panzer division has been greatly surpassed on some days. Also, especially in battle, much higher average speeds were reached by the tank regiment than the regulations require. The greatest distance achieved by the division on the march in one day was 340 kilometres with almost no tank breakdowns.[13]

Experiences such as this had their dangers for the planning of Operation Barbarossa, as it was thought that tank units really could achieve daily marches of between 200 and 350 kilometres.[14] However, in the first year of the Russian campaign, it was proved conclusively that these figures were only valid on French roads against a psychologically worn-out opponent: 'The secret of victory lies in the exploitation of success.'[15]

Putting this maxim into practice, the German armoured forces had broken through enemy fronts in Poland and France without fear of threat to their flanks and had caused the enemy to break up after a short time. In his Order of the Day on 26 May 1940, General Guderian praised the men of his Panzer Corps thus:

> We have seventeen days of fighting in Belgium and France behind us. About 600 kilometres separate us from the border of the German Reich. We have reached the Channel coast and the Atlantic Ocean . . . I ordered you not to sleep for 48 hours. You held out for 18 days. I forced you to face danger from both the flanks and the rear. You did not falter. Germany is proud of her armoured divisions, and I am proud to command you.[16]

3.2 Tanks in the Rear of the Enemy

'Our Group . . . played a decisive role in the great victory with our breakthrough of the Meuse defences . . . and due to our quick thrust to the Channel coast and to St Omer into the rear of the enemy.'[17]

Deep thrusts with unprotected flanks played a decisive part in

13. 7. Pz. Div. Abt. Ia, Nr. 440/40 geheim, of 14 July 1940, p. 13.
14. Cf. above, Chapter 1, note 60.
15. Cf. XXXIX. Pz. Corps Abt. Ia, Nr. 291/40 geheim, of 9 October 1940, p. 3.
16. 18.Pz. Div. Abt. Ia, Nr. 95/40 geheim, of 1 December 1940, p. 5.
17. XIX. Pz. Korps Abt. Ia, Korpstagesbefehl von General Guderian, of 26 May 1940. Cf. OKH, Gen.St.d.H./Op Abt. (IIa) Fernschreiben Nr. 3,211/40 geheim of 21 May 1940. Cf. AOK 4, Abt. Ia, Armeetagesbefehl of 23 May 1940.

the victories because they made operations in the rear of the enemy possible. The Commander-in-Chief of Army Group C wrote to General Guderian on 4 July 1940: 'Bold and resolute action to the rear of the enemy ahead of 1st and 7th Armies and further energetic support from Panzer Group largely contributed to our great victory.'[18]

The thrust by highly-mobile armoured forces, which compel the enemy to enter battle 'back to front', was, according to General Halder, the most important distinguishing feature of the Polish campaign.[19] And indeed, the 'motorised Cannae battles' of the Mobile Units, the encirclement of the enemy became the essence of mobile warfare. Admittedly, however, the Cannae scene gained a new dimension with the use of the Luftwaffe, and was widened still further by the use of paratroops.

To be fair, it must be repeated again that, in both blitz campaigns of 1939 and 1940, the defeated enemy made a great contribution to the German Wehrmacht's victory. In both Poland and France the defences were prepared in a linear fashion. As soon as the German panzer wedges had broken through these, they had only to turn round in order to attack the 'soft' rear of the enemy.

In December 1940, after the events of the blitzkrieg had been collated, German Army High Command put out new guidelines for the operation of panzer divisions. In these we read: 'Annihilation by speedy encirclement. Avoid frontal battles. Enemy must be attacked in the rear after a short time.'[20]

3.3 Envelopment and Encirclement

Enveloping operations can start from an assembly position[21] or a manoeuvre.[22] The Polish campaign was the prime example of

18. H.Gr. C, OB an den OB der Pz. Gr. Guderian, 4 July 1940. Cf. Pz. Gr. Guderian, Abt. Ia, Tagesbefehl Guderians, of 30 June 1940.
19. Cf. P. Bor, *Gespräche mit Halder*, Wiesbaden, 1950, pp. 144–5.
20. OKH, Richtlinien für die Führung und Einsatz der Panzerdivision, of 3 December 1940, p. 12.
21. Cf. Polish campaign in autumn 1939; Launch of the Western Offensive in May 1940; Starting position of Army Group Centre at the beginning of the Russian campaign in June 1941.
22. Cf. Battle near Smolensk in July 1941; battle near Kiev in September 1941; battle near Kharkov in May 1942.

an operation in which a quick victory was achieved by means of an envelopment from both sides and the subsequent encirclement.[23] Each encircling operation presumes that the commander intends to engage the enemy with reversed front. It is therefore vital to have the initiative when planning to encircle the opponent. Only then can the commander choose the time, place and object of the battle.

In most cases, being surrounded represents a crisis for those involved, which very often leads to total annihilation or to surrender.[24]

In the war diary of Panzer Group von Kleist, on 22 May 1940, we read the following entry: 'The Group must first of all fight its way up to the coast to Calais and Boulogne, in order to have the freedom at the rear to attack successfully the encircled main part of the enemy to the east.'[25] And, indeed, in May 1940, the French armies in the north-east were annihilated or taken prisoner within nine days in a gigantic encircling operation. As an Order of the Day issued by the Commander-in-Chief of German Army Group C said: 'By unceasingly pushing forward and fighting doggedly, you, and especially the armour, have managed to encircle the desperately battling enemy. Apart from heavy enemy losses, we estimate that about 500,000 men were captured, among them the Commanders-in-Chief of the 8th, 6th and 3rd French Armies and many other generals.'[26]

3.4 The Phenomenon of the Moving Pocket

After the blitz campaigns in Poland and France, Hitler believed that he could also beat the Red Army by means of large-scale enveloping operations. He was of the opinion that the border battles would be over after about four weeks, and that there would be no serious resistance after that.[27] A fatal mistake

---

23. Cf. E. Röhricht, *Probleme der Kesselschlacht*, Karlsruhe, 1958, p. 11ff. Cf. N. von Vormann, *Der Feldzug 1939 in Polen*, Weißenburg, 1958, p. 77. Cf. Guderian, *Erinnerungen*, pp. 64ff.

24. Cf. 20. Pz. Div. Abt. Ia, Meldung an LVII. Pz. Korps, of 26 August 1941, p. 3, 'Prisoner statements confirm enemy's complete collapse'. Cf. 7. Pz. Div. Abt. Ia, Morgenmeldung des Art. Regt. 78, of 9 October 1941.

25. Pz. Gr. von Kleist, Abt. Ia, KTB, of 22 May 1940.

26. H.Gr. C, Abt. Ia, Tagesbefehl von Generaloberst von Leeb, date burned.

27. Cf. OKW/WFSt./ L, IV, Chefsachen 'Barbarossa', of 30 April 1941, p. 105.

indeed, considering that in 1936 Russian commanders had spoken about letting an attacker tire himself out while pushing deep into Russian territory and then weakening him with determined counterattacks.[28]

Three years before the Russian campaign, a German military journal had drawn the readers' attention to the 'in-depth tactics' used by the Red Army,[29] but this had obviously been ignored by the experts.

The Red Army's formation on the eve of the war conformed with these 'in-depth tactics'. Out of the 149 divisions in the four western border districts, only 48 were included in the first defensive echelon. 101 divisions lay between 80 and 300 kilometres from the border. Therefore the German armoured forces, after a few days, found themselves facing a new situation. Despite great early successes, it was only ever possible to encircle parts of the enemy's forces. There was no longer a 'rear' behind a Maginot-type defensive line!

Of course, at the beginning of the Russian campaign, the excellently led armoured divisions were fully able to break through enemy fronts, make inroads and therefore create the conditions for battles of encirclement. During the first great enveloping operations near Bialystock and Minsk, they succeeded in encircling and smashing four Russian armies up to 8 July 1941. In less than three weeks twenty-two infantry divisions, seven tank divisions and nine enemy brigades had been wiped out.[30] A huge tactical victory had been achieved, but it was noted with concern that tying panzer forces down for long periods in battles of encirclement had an unexpectedly negative effect on the continuity of operations. To be sure, it was no problem to put a ring of panzer forces around a surprised opponent.[31] However, this was not the end of the story, since infantry were required to 'clean out' the area of encirclement, to take over the capture of the enemy troops. The panzer forces'

---

28. Cf. Russische Felddienstordnung, 1936, Ziffer 10, in *Militärwissenschaftliche Rundschau*, Heft 5, 1938, p. 677.

29. Cf. *Militärwissenschaftliche Rundschau*, Heft 4, 1938, pp. 557–74, and Heft 5, 1938, pp. 671–84.

30. Cf. Pz. AOK 2, Abt. Ic, KTB Nr. 1, Tagesbefehl des OB der H.Gr. Mitte, of 8 July 1941.

31. Cf. XXXXVII. Pz. Korps Abt. Ia, Anl. Nr. 609, of 31 August 1941. Cf. Ibid, Anl. Nr. 623, of 2 September 1941.

task was to keep the enemy from breaking out, and to destroy his heavy weapons by means of concentric thrusts into the encircled area: 'Concentric attack by 17th and most of 18th Panzer Division with dive-bombers against the 108th Red Tank Division in the Karbovka area of encirclement.'[32]

In the combat report by 18th Panzer Division two days later there was the laconic comment: 'The 108th Red Tank Division can be regarded as annihilated.'[33]

The further into Russia the pocket battles occurred, the more time was required for them, since the German infantry could only advance as fast as the Russians retreated. While it is true that German tank divisions succeeded in overtaking, enveloping and enclosing enemy forces, they then had to wait for their own infantry in order to turn imminent success into victory.[34]

Thus the battle for Smolensk lasted almost a month, although the 2nd Panzer Army had encircled the enemy within a few days.[35] Moreover, simply because it was the much slower infantry which determined the pace of the German advance, rather than the panzer armies, the phenomenon of the moving pocket came into being: '4th and 9th Army report daily which other east front sectors of the encircled area they can take over, little by little, from the panzer groups.'[36]

Armoured forces were often idle for days merely because they had to wait until the pocket they had formed had been cleared. Therefore the demand in the report by 4th Panzer Division seems justified: 'After the enemy has been encircled, the Panzer Division should be taken out as soon as possible and reassembled ready for other tasks.'[37] One can hear in these words the fear that armoured forces would be used as support for the infantry and not as a decisive weapon. And this fear was justified.

---

32. 18. Pz. Div. Abt. Ia, Gef. Ber. of 1 September 1941. Cf. XXXXVII. Pz. Korps Abt. Ia, Anl. Nr. 204, of 10 October 1941. Cf. Ibid, Anl. Nr. 242, of 12 October 1941.
33. 18. Pz. Div. Abt. Ia, Gef. Ber. of 3 September 1941.
34. In enclosing operations the armoured forces formed the outer ring, the infantry the inner ring. Cf. Halder, KTB vol. III, of 25 June 1941.
35. The encircling operation by 2nd Panzer Army lasted from 13 to 16 July, whereas the pocket battle lasted until 5 August 1941.
36. H.Gr. Mitte, Abt. Ia, Nr. 104/41 Geh.Kdos, of 1 July 1941, p. 3.
37. 4. Pz. Div. Abt. Ia, Anl. zum KTB, Nr. 71/42 geheim Beantwortung Fragebogen OKH betr. Erfahrungen Ostfeldzug, of 12 March 1942, p. 3.

Without the concentrated use of large panzer forces the moving pockets in Russia would not have been possible. When one thinks of Bialystock, Minsk, Kiev or Vyasma-Briansk, one has the impression of enclosed 'theatres of war' rather than battles of encirclement. When the heads of 1st and 2nd Panzer Army joined up near Lochviza,[38] the biggest battle of encirclement in history began. Four Russian armies with a total of 700,000 men were encircled in the area of Kiev-Cherkassy-Lochviza. Encircled by two panzer armies which formed a triangle with sides some 500 kilometres long; the area of encirclement was around 135,000 square kilometres.[39]

The enveloping operation near Kiev was perhaps the greatest victory achieved by German forces in Russia – a successful example of the encirclement tactics of large armoured elements. However, in order to close this 'superpocket', Hitler had the 2nd Panzer Army, which was only 350 kilometres from Moscow, roll south from Smolensk via Gomel and Pochep. Thus Panzer Army Guderian lost more than a month in the advance on Moscow. There is no argument about the battle of Kiev being a classic example of an encirclement battle. Equally, however, this is an example of how a tactical victory can place the greater goal of an operation in jeopardy or even make it impossible to achieve.

Unfortunately it is not possible, within the confines of this book, to examine in more detail how the tactical victory near Kiev caused a loss of time during the march on Moscow, and therefore had an influence on the result of the whole Eastern campaign.

---

38. 1st Pz. Army under Gen. von Kleist was subordinated to Army Group South, commanded by Field Marshal General von Rundstedt.
39. Cf. W. Haupt. *Kiew, die größte Kesselschlacht der Geschichte*, Bad Nauheim, 1964.

4
Armour and Infantry

4.1 Co-operation is Imperative

Normally a 'pure' commitment of larger armoured units only occurs in terrain where support from and co-operation with other arms is unnecessary. Such terrain is difficult to find in Europe, and thus it is no surprise when Rommel says of the North African theatre of war: 'Here were the only pure tank battles, with larger elements taking part.'[1] The so-called tank battles in European war theatres were pure combat scenes within actual battles, rather than battles in themselves.[2]

Purely armoured units are fully capable of breaking through linear defences from a movement and driving deep wedges into the enemy defence. However, as soon as it becomes a question not merely of gaining territory in the short term but of keeping it, co-operation with the infantry becomes a must. In the last chapter we also saw that even the typical panzer pocket can be closed but not cleared out without infantry.[3]

In the *Handbuch der neuzeitlichen Wehrwissenschaften* which appeared in 1937, we read: 'The question of co-operation between panzer units and the other arms is, at the moment, the most acute and intensely-discussed problem of many caused by the creation of the new arms.'[4]

After the experiences of the Polish and Western campaigns it became clear that co-operation between tanks and infantry had

---

1. J.L. Wallach, *Das Dogma der Vernichtungsschlacht. Die Lehren von Clausewitz und Schlieffen und ihre Wirkung in zwei Weltkriegen*, Munich, 1970, p. 402.
2. An example is the battle near Hannut on 10 May 1940, where the German 3rd Pz. Div. and the 3rd French Mech. Div. faced one another. Also, the pure panzer skirmishes in the Sinai peninsula during the Six Day War in 1967 should not be seen as tank battles from the point of view of the Second World War.
3. Cf. above pp. 35ff.
4. Franke, *Handbuch*, p. 393.

to be specifically trained. On 24 July 1940 General von Kleist ordered his Panzer Group: 'The Panzer Divisions are to attach a combined instruction unit to their infantry divisions until further notice . . . The task of the unit is . . . above all to impart the necessary knowledge of armour and the interaction between armoured and non-armoured forces to all branches of the service.'[5] In autumn 1940 the Army Commander-in-Chief issued the following order which applied to all combat units: 'Exercises in combined units encourage co-operation between the arms. This method of fighting is to be practised early and often as a preliminary stage for the closed panzer attack within the Panzer Division'.[6]

General Guderian, however, warned against a stereotyped 'combat group method' because this very often meant a shuffling-off of responsibility onto the lower command echelons, since: 'the unit is unable to fight in units of brigade size due to lack of training and facilities for training.'[7]

It is obvious that co-operation between armour and infantry should start not on the field of battle but before this, in other words during the advance itself:

> It is in the interests of the infantry that the Mobile Unit moves forward quickly and without hindrance. It is in the interests of the Mobile Unit that the infantry is not left too far behind later.[8]

> The infantry must understand the needs of the motorised units in front of them and not block their supply lines.[9]

So as not to get in each other's way, it was found to be necessary to allocate separate march routes to panzer and infantry units:

> There should not be any kind of advance in the Panzer Group's attack sector on the part of infantry or other forces. The infantry is to receive its own combat sector adjacent to that of the Panzer Group . . . Shared combat sectors . . . have proved to be a massive

5. Pz. Gr. von Kleist, Abt. Ia, Nr. 3,305/40 geheim of 24 July 1940, pp. 4–5.
6. OB d. H. /Gen.St.d.H. /Ausb. Abt. Ia, Nr. 3,000/40 geheim of 7 October 1940, p. 11.
7. Pz. Gr. Guderian, Abt. Ia, Nr. 502/40 geheim of 22 August 1940.
8. Pz. Gr. von Kleist, Chief of General Staff, Richtlinien für die Führung Schneller Gruppen, version of 20 October 1940, p. 32.
9. Ibid, Anl. B. zum KTB Nr. 3, Vorläufige Erfahrungen mit großen motorisierten Verbänden, of 10 August 1940.

hindrance upon both armoured and infantry divisions' advance and attack during the Western Campaign. For this reason they will not be tolerated.[10]

Advances by armoured units without worrying about whether the flanks are threatened can only be justified if the action is limited in time and space,[11] or if the enemy can be relied upon to keep his linear defence. In 1937 the Commanding General of Armoured Units wrote: 'The initial surprise of the tank break-through must be exploited with vigour (by the infantry).'[12] In the 'Instructions for the Command of the Panzer Division' (Richtlinien für die Führung der Panzerdivision) the need for co-operation is put across even more clearly: 'The tank attack won't be successful until the infantrymen have occupied the common objective. The most important task of the infantry bri-gade is to exploit quickly the achievement of the tank brigade.'[13]

On the endless Russian steppe it became more and more clear that a tank advance without infantry follow-up was like hitting at thin air.

Where there is no infantry follow-up, an armoured thrust is useless.[14]

A tank attack is only really worthwhile if there is an infantry unit to cover the flanks and to immediately clear the country once it has been passed through.[15]

As a result of Russian in-depth tactics,[16] there was indeed the danger, not to be underestimated, that Russian units would re-group after a German tank advance in order to engage the

---

10. Pz. Gr. Guderian, Abt. Ia, Nr. 133/40 Geh.Kdos.Chefs., of 2 October 1940, p. 2. Cf. Pz. AOK 3, Abt. Ia, Nr. 520/42 geheim of 10 February 1942, p. 31.

11. Cf. OKH, Gen.St.d.H./Ausb. Abt. Ia, Nr. 2,400/40 geheim of 20 November 1940, p. 2.

12. Besichtigungsbemerkungen des Kommandierenden Generals der Pz. Truppen im Jahr 1937, Kdo. der Pz. Trp. Id, Nr. 3,770/37.

13. Richtlinien für Führung und Einsatz der Panzerdivision, of 3 December 1940, p. 26.

14. AOK 6, Abt. Ia, Anl. zum KTB, of 4 October 1942. Cf. XV. Pz. Korps Abt. Ia, Nr. 210/40 geheim, undated, p. 4.

15. 24. Pz. Div. Abt. Ia, Nr. 365/42 geheim, of 6 November 1942, p. 9. Cf. O. Munzel, *Panzer-Taktik. Raids gepanzerter Verbände im Ostfeldzug 1941/42*, Neckargemünd, 1959, p. 45.

16. Cf. above, pp. 36.

Wehrmacht infantry, which had been left behind, with a full compliment. So as to put a stop to isolated tank tactics, the C-in-C of 6th Army issued the categorical order, on 29 October: 'I forbid panzer attacks without infantry and artillery support.'[17]

There were often problems in the relationship between armour and infantry because infantry commanders misjudged the performance of the panzers. For this reason Army High Command issued the following directive in November 1940: 'Putting the tanks under the command of the infantry divisions has not been a success. Co-operation between the arms in armoured attack can only be successful within the panzer division which is equipped for the task.'[18] Alongside technical and tactical weapons operation experience, personal contact, above all, is the best guarantee of good co-operation. In a report by one rifle regiment we read: 'The combination of the two arms has functioned exceptionally well. Good personal relations between the commanders, if possible also between the subordinate commanders, is vital to its success.'[19]

There were never any serious doubts about the necessity for co-operation between the armoured force and the infantry. However, the consequences of this co-operation seem to have been ignored for a long time.

4.2 Misuse of Armour or Overstretching the Infantry

Whereas armour was seen in Poland, France and Russia merely as a means of support for the infantry even at the beginning of the Second World War,[20] the ideas of Guderian and his staff, that the tanks be formed into independent groups, were put into effect in Germany. If armoured units are under the command of the infantry there is a danger that speed, a most important factor in armour, is completely forgotten. Guderian has this to say on the subject:

17. AOK 6, Abt. Ia, Nr. 4,257/42 Geh.Kdos., of 29 October 1942.
18. OKH, Gen. St.d.H./Ausb. Abt. Ia, Nr. 2,400/40 geheim, of 20 November 1940, p. 7.
19. 20. Pz. Div. Abt. Ia, Erfahrungsbericht des Sch. Rgt. 112, of 30 October 1941.
20. The views of the European army commands on the use of armour can be seen in Nehring, *Panzerwaffe*, pp. 107ff.

When new weapons are closely tied to old ones, the new ones sacrifice their best features.[21]

The panzer unit is no longer a back-up weapon for the infantry – one could almost say that the opposite was true.[22]

An extract from the 'Militär-Wochenblatt' of 29 April 1938 shows that Guderian was not alone in his beliefs about the use of tanks: 'Therefore the real sense of this kind of use of infantry tanks is the abandonment of the one-off, mechanised attack where tanks are used as a special weapon, like a cavalry charge.'[23] Indeed, the Wehrmacht's operational panzer units played a large part in halting the misuse of the armoured force. But this did not solve the problem of co-operation with the infantry. 'Non-armoured units advance at 30 km per hour.'[24]

This statement was based on the experience of the Western campaign, where the infantry forces in the panzer division could follow the advance of the tanks on lorries. The road conditions in Russia were portrayed as follows by the G.S.O.1 (Ia) of 4th Army: 'The great highway from the border to Moscow, the only road which could be described as such by Western standards was not yet finished. We were not prepared for the conditions, since our maps bore no relation to reality.'[25] Liddell Hart says of the Russian road network: 'If the Soviet regime had provided Russia with a road network comparable to Western countries, the Soviet Union would probably have been overrun in a short time.'[26]

It was almost impossible for riflemen to follow the tanks on wheeled vehicles over rough country. But they were completely overtaxed on the battlefield if this were the case: 'It is essential to stay close to the tanks.'[27] In reality it was clear that infantry

21. O. Munzel, *Die deutschen gepanzerten Truppen bis 1945*, Herford and Bonn, 1965, p. 229.

22. H. Guderian, *Achtung – Panzer. Die Entwicklung der Panzerwaffe, ihre Kampf-taktik und ihre operativen Möglichkeiten*, Stuttgart, 1937, p. 165.

23. Doege, 'Infanterie und Panzer', in *Militär-Wochenblatt* of 29 April 1938, Sp. 2,814.

24. OKH, Richtlinien für Führung und Einsatz der Panzerdivision, of 3 December 1940, p. 14.

25. B.H. Liddell Hart, *Jetzt dürfen sie reden. Hitlers Generale berichten*, Stuttgart und Hamburg, 1950, p. 329.

26. Ibid, p. 174.

27. OKH, Richtlinien für Führung und Einsatz der Panzerdivision, of 3 December 1940, p. 1.

simply cannot attack 'quickly'. Their attack is a protracted, laborious affair, alternately firing and moving. The reason for many failures lay in the fact that the pinning-down effect of the tanks could not be fully utilised by the riflemen left far behind:[28]

> During frequent co-operation with the tanks it has been seen again and again that the tanks drove away from the riflemen, and, therefore, that their success just could not be built upon.[29]
>
> Because the panzer attack is very fast, the infantrymen cannot follow on foot.[30]
>
> Because no riflemen kept up with us, we can take few prisoners.[31]
>
> Because our own infantry is too weak to follow the tank attack, the tanks must roll back in order to attack again.[32]

Armour tacticians had foreseen the almost insoluble problems faced by tanks and infantry in co-operation very clearly as early as 1935:

> To be quite frank, tactics expects the impossible from the foot soldiers. Tanks are immediately put under fire by the enemy machine guns en masse as soon as they appear, with such a high point of aim that the space behind the tanks is at least 500 metres deep. If the riflemen follow within this zone, most of them will no longer be alive. However, if the foot soldiers are more than 500 metres away, the effect of the attack will have fizzled out.[33]

If the panzer is not to be misused as a back-up weapon for the infantry, but if co-operation is still necessary, then the infantry must be as mobile on the march and almost as protected on the

---

28. Cf. OKH, Gen. St.d.H./Ausb. Abt. (II) Nr. 1,550/42 geheim, of 10 June 1942, p. 7.
29. 20. Pz. Div. Abt. Ia, Erfahrungsbericht des Sch. Regt. 59, of 5 November 1941, p. 2.
30. 4. Pz. Div. Abt. Ia, Anl. der Gef. Bericht zum KTB, Meldung der 5. Pz. Brig. of 6 September 1941.
31. Ibid, Meldung der 5. Pz. Brig. of 20 September 1941.
32. 7. Pz. Div. Abt. Ia, Morgenmeldung des Art. Regt. 78, of 26 August 1941, p. 2.
33. W. Brandt, 'Wie soll das Fußvolk den Tankangriff begleiten?' in *Militär-Wochenblatt* of 11 August 1955, Sp. 238. How the infantry was overstretched in co-operating with armour in Russia is described by General M. Fretter-Pico in detail in his book, . . . *Verlassen von den Sieges Göttern*, Wiesbaden, 1969.

battlefield as the tanks themselves. It is with this challenge that we arrive at the concept of the armoured infantry.

4.3 The Armoured Infantry

> *What we want is a modern, fast rifle unit with a lot of firepower, and which is specially trained, equipped and organised to work together with the tanks.*[34]

The armoured infantry (Panzergrenadiere) has only been in existence since 7 July 1972, but its roots can be traced back to the start of the motorisation of the German Army. In 1938, under the command of the 'Chef der Schnellen Truppen',[35] the mechanised cavalry was assigned to co-operate with the armoured force, and thus ten panzer regiments and ten rifle regiments went into the Polish campaign.[36] The name Panzergrenadier, however, up to 1941, was more of a concept than a realistic description, there being only one company in each rifle regiment of the panzer divisions equipped with lightly armoured personnel carriers (MTW).

Not until 1941, when the infantry accompanied the panzer attack in armoured troop carriers (SPW) could one speak of real co-operation between tanks and infantry, without the tanks being misused or the infantry being totally overstretched. General Nehring, in 1941 commander of 18th Panzer Division and Commander-in-Chief of 1st Panzer Army in the last months of the war, says: 'Close co-operation between armour and grenadiers in all forms of combat and in all kinds of terrain is essential.'[37]

4.3.1 *Simultaneous Advance in all Terrain*

Employment will be carried out from the march column.[38]

---

34. H. Guderian, *Achtung - Panzer*, p. 169.

35. On 20 November 1938 Guderian was promoted to General der Pz. Trp. and appointed as Chef der Schnellen Truppen.

36. Cf. F.M. von Senger und Etterlin, *Die Panzergrenadiere*, Munich, 1961, pp. 67–77.

37. H. Guderian, *Panzer-Marsch*, p. 163.

38. OKH, Richtlinien für Führung und Einsatz der Panzerdivision, of 3 December 1940, p. 16.

In a joint attack with the tanks, the riflemen are to be trained to stay close to the tanks and to quickly exploit their achievements.[39]

Although the first armoured troop carriers had many defects,[40] it was their use which made the above demands practicable.

It is necessary to equip all rifle units with the highly successful MTW . . . Only the MTW gives the riflemen the chance of maintaining contact with the panzers and of making use of their successes.[41]

The armoured troop carriers have proved themselves well in this battle. Only thanks to the tight co-operation between tanks and riflemen . . . was the enemy thrown out of his well-fortified position.[42]

Such achievements were only possible when the armoured infantry could follow close behind the panzers. Having infantrymen sit on the tanks themselves was not a success: 'An attack mounted on tanks can only be made as a last resort over short distances, since there is no way of transmitting orders to soldiers sitting on a tank, and the companies are difficult to command once they have dismounted.'[43]

In the armoured troop carriers the grenadiers could reach the combat area using the effect on morale of the tanks rushing forward, without having to worry about difficult terrain or heavy losses through enemy snipers. Infantry in lorries were faster than the tanks on good roads, but in difficult country they could only be employed on foot. Even if the armoured troop carriers did not fully live up to expectations,[44] they did make successful co-operation with the armoured force possible:

Never lose contact with the tanks.[45]

---

39. OB d.H./Gen. St.d.H./Ausb. Abt. (Ia) Nr. 3,000/40 geheim, of 7 October 1940, p. 12.
40. The first SPWs were a variation on the half-tracked vehicles which were extremely well-known at the time.
41. Pz. Gr. Guderian, Abt. Ia, Nr. 502/40 geheim of 12 August 1940, p. 3.
42. 20. Pz. Div. Abt. Ia, Gef. Bericht der Kampfgruppe Lützwitz, of 7 September 1941, p. 3.
43. Ibid, Erfahrungsbericht des Sch. Regt. 59, of 5 November 1941.
44. Before the Russian campaign it was thought that the SPW was capable of crossing any terrain in any season. Cf. H. Dv. Nr. 299/11d, Entwurf dated 1 March 1941, p. 3.
45. OKH, H.Dv. Nr. 299/11d, Entwurf dated 1 March 1941, Ziffer 128.

While the tanks conquer, the riflemen clear up and consolidate what has been gained.[46]

Failing other orders, you are to attack mounted.[47]

The troop carrier is the main combat aid of the riflemen.[48]

And after nine months of the eastern campaign the experience report by 4th Panzer Division noted that: 'The creation of further MTW companies is vitally necessary. They have been most successful.'[49]

There are basically five variations for combining tanks with armoured infantry:

1. The grenadiers follow the tanks mounted;
2. The tanks follow the mounted grenadiers;
3. The tanks follow the dismounted grenadiers;
4. Tanks and grenadiers attack from different directions;
4. Grenadiers attack alone under the covering fire of the tanks.

Especially in infantry terrain the grenadiers become essential to armour by clearing away any obstacles, so that the armoured attack does not lose its momentum. When tanks and armoured infantry attack at the same time, the troop carriers attack the enemy anti-tank weapons in particular, so that the tanks can gain ground quickly. The grenadiers follow the tanks mounted in tank country, in order to: 'exploit the inaction of the enemy, due to the tank fire, for a ruthless forward charge.'[50] Narrow formation echeloned in depth will thereby be the norm, so as to remove the unit from the effects of enemy artillery fire, and to be able to apply force from the depth when contact with the enemy is made.[51]

The mechanised grenadiers play a special role in pursuing the enemy as, thanks to their speed and cross-country mobility, they can stop the enemy erecting a rearward defence position, or, with the aid of the tanks, cut off any escape routes: 'Should

46. 18. Pz. Div. Abt. Ia, Nr. 55/40 geheim of 20 November 1940.
47. OKH, Richtlinien für Führung und Einsatz der Panzerdivision, of 3 December 1940, p. 22.
48. H. Div. Nr. 299/11d, Entwurf dated 1 March 1941, Ziffer 13.
49. 4. Pz. Div. Abt. Ia, Nr. 71/42 geheim, of 12 March 1942, p. 20.
50. OKH, H. Dv. Nr. 299/11d, Entwurf dated 1 March 1941, Ziffer 126.
51. Cf. Ibid, Ziffer 128.

the enemy give way, then he is to be made to break up by constant pursuit, even into the night, and he is to be annihilated.'[52]

4.3.2   The Price of Duty

We have already seen that there were extremely high losses of officers in the panzer units.[53] It is clear from the close co-operation of the two arms that 'leadership from the front' was necessary for the armoured infantry also. Many achievements made by the panzer force would have been impossible without the grenadiers. However, the price was high, sometimes too high. Thus 59th Rifle Regiment reported, after an attack of only two days, on 24 February 1942: 'Officer losses were especially high. In the battalion under the command of Feurer, all the officers fell except the commander himself.'[54] In four days a rifle battalion of 20th Panzer Division lost 249 men, about 60% of its complement.[55] The rifle regiment of the same division lost 172 men in a single day.[56]

4th Panzer Division, in answer to a questionnaire by Army High Command, reported on the employment of its armoured infantry: 'During this year's campaign, in some companies, four or five times (sometimes more) the platoon and group leaders have been killed or wounded in action.'[57]

52. Ibid, Ziffer 130.
53. Cf. above, p. 30.
54. 20. Pz. Div. Abt. Ia, Gef. Bericht des Sch. Regt. 59, of 24 February 1942, p. 4.
55. Cf. Ibid, Abt. Ia, Nr. 23/41 geheim Meldung des Schw. Bat., of 6 December 1941. Included in the figures are dead, wounded, missing and sick.
56. Cf. 20. Pz. Div. Abt. Ia, Gef. Bericht des Sch. Regt. 59, of 1 November 1941, p. 6. Cf. 7. Pz. Div. Abt. Ia, Morgenmeldung des Sch. Regt. 6, of 7 October 1941, p. 2.
57. 4. Pz. Div. Abt. Ia, Nr. 71/42 geheim, of 12 March 1942, p. 20.

5
Armour and Drawn Artillery

5.1 Waiting for the Artillery

As long as panzers and armoured infantry in troop carriers alone are used for counterattacks which are limited in terms of time and place, the tracked vehicles determine the speed and, above all, the manoeuvrability on the battlefield. If, however, other, non-mechanised units are also employed, which is the case in every large operation, then the tracked vehicles have to adapt to the mobility of the wheeled vehicles, for an army is, after all, only as fast as its slowest element! For this reason it is not at all surprising that the German Eastern Army took almost as long, to the day, to get from the River Bug to the area outside Moscow as Napoleon's 'Grande Armée' did 129 years before. Let us not forget that of 152 divisions committed in Operation Barbarossa, 119 were horse-drawn![1]

Even when one speaks of a panzer army, it should be remembered that only a small percentage of this army is actually equipped with tanks. Thus, for example, the 2nd Panzer Army under Guderian had, in 1941, only 930 tanks for a complement of 148,544 men. In planning the Eastern campaign, therefore, one should have considered that speed on the march and mobility in terrain would depend not on the tank units but on the infantry, horses and wheeled vehicles.

Surprise tactics, manoeuvrability on the battlefield and freedom from restrictions imposed by roads and weather are only possible if a unit is fully mobile across country. Only then can

---

1. Cf. H.A. Jacobsen, *1939–1945. Der Zweite Weltkrieg in Chronik und Dokumentation*, 5th revised ed., Darmstadt, 1961, pp. 39–40.
On 22 June 1941 the Germans employed the following against the Soviet Union: 19 panzer divisions; 15 motorised infantry divisions; 119 infantry and cavalry divisions; 3,580 tanks; 600,000 motor vehicles; 750,000 (!) horses.

one speak of mobile warfare, only then are large-scale blitz campaigns feasible.

Two years before the Polish campaign, it had been recognised that artillery support of a mechanised attack can be decisive: 'The support of tank warfare needs to be specially trained. The new training year will see more emphasis put on this. Support must never stop.'[2] In the 'Richtlinien für die Führung der Panzerdivision', which were brought out after the Western campaign, great store was laid by supporting artillery fire:

> The artillery must be very mobile and flexible according to the mobility of the panzer division. It must be able to support the fast-moving panzer attack constantly and effectively.[3]

> The artillery must be allotted a place so far forward in the columns that they are ready to fire at the right time when the battle begins.[4]

> Forward observers in armoured scout cars, which travel with the first waves of tanks, direct their battery's fire at targets in the way of the attack.[5]

With a view to Operation Barbarossa, there was a demand, during a map exercise by 2nd Panzer Army, that the artillery always be so far forward that enemy resistance could be broken 'from out of the column'.[6]

There was agreement that, in theory, the artillery was to keep up with the mechanised units, and, on the very good roads of France, this was no problem. Even during the first days of the Russian campaign there was no sign of conflict between theory and practice – the few roads were still passable for drawn artillery and the terrain was not too difficult.

> All the artillery in the division . . . is supporting the attack on the Dnjepr from positions west of the Prut.[7]

2. Kdo der Pz. Trp., Id, Nr. 3,770/37, Besichtigungsbemerkungen des Kommandierenden Generals der Pz. Trp. im Jahr 1937.

3. OKH, Richtlinien für Führung und Einsatz der Panzerdivision, of 3 December 1940, p. 8.

4. Ibid, p. 18.

5. Ibid, p. 29.

6. Cf. Pz. AOK 2, Abt. Ia, Planspiel, Nr. 16/41 Geh.Kdos., of 14 March 1941, Anlage 3, p. 2. Cf. LVII, Pz. Korps Abt. Ia, Besprechung mit den Divisionskommandeuren, from 21–26 April 1941, p. 7, 'Adapt the tasks to the characteristics of the tank battle – fight from the column, that applies also to the heavy artillery.'

7. 3. Pz. Div. Abt. Ia, Anl. Nr. 3 zum KTB Nr. 3, of 4 July 1941.

Kleemann's Group is attacking such that the offensive will be driven like a wedge into the enemy after the artillery has prepared the ground.[8]

It is a question of infantry and tanks entering battle and fighting together in order to make the best use of the effect of the artillery fire.[9]

Whenever there was artillery support for a panzer attack there were surprisingly good results. On 23 August 1941, Panzerregiment 6 of 3rd Panzer Division reported that:

the excellently laid artillery fire not only had a soul-destroying effect on the enemy but also caused him heavy human losses.[10]

Co-operation with the artillery was very good. As far as possible the wishes of II Bat. 6 Coy of the Panzer Regiment were put into effect, and the artillery was not afraid to take up position in front of the covering tanks.[11]

Without doubt, as long as the artillery could keep up with the panzers, they were extremely effective. Their bursts of fire forced enemy tank columns to turn back[12] or even put some tanks out of action: 'In the woods a scout patrol found four knocked-out Russian tanks which had seemingly been destroyed the day before due to surprise fire by an artillery unit.'[13]

On well-maintained roads the heavy field guns, which were drawn by tractors, could be moved fairly quickly. However, as soon as the panzers entered 'no man's land', where there were no roads or even tracks which could be used, a gap arose in the artillery support which had dire consequences. When, to cap it all, the mud period set in,[14] artillery fire often remained in the realms of fantasy. On 1 December 1941 4th Panzer Division only had 38% of its complement of lorries and reported that: 'The artillery tractors break down more and more often and,

---

8. Ibid, Abt. Ia, Anl. Nr. 32 zum KTB Nr. 3, of 13 July 1941.
9. Ibid.
10. 3. Pz. Div. Abt. Ia, Anl. Nr. 9 zum KTB Nr. 3, of 23 August 1941, p. 70.
11. Ibid, p. 3.
12. Cf. XXXXVII. Pz. Korps Abt. Ia, Tagesmeldung of the 18. Pz. Div. of 10 October 1941.
13. XXXXVII. Pz. Korps Abt. Ia, Anl. Nr. 41 zum KTB Nr. 3, Zwischenmeldung der 29. Inf. Div. mot. of 28 September 1941.
14. Cf. below, pp. 95ff.

therefore, also the field guns we urgently need for battle.'[15]

The attack by XXIV. Panzer Corps, planned for 1 November 1941, had to be postponed because it took several days for the artillery to catch up.[16] One motorised infantry division, which had to provide rear cover on a front of 90 (!) kilometres in the battle of Tula, could only commit four light and three heavy howitzers for the task.[17] The drawn artillery no longer existed: 'There is no artillery support, since the road situation remains difficult for vehicles and artillery.'[18]

Not until the field guns could follow the mechanised attack on self-propelled mounts, rather than having to be towed, was co-operation with the armoured force independent of terrain and weather possible. In August 1940, General Guderian has demanded: 'The self-propelled mount for light artillery is vital.'[19]

5.2 Direct Fire Against Tanks

To confine this chapter to the supporting role would be to underestimate the artillery. In numerous portrayals of the Second World War, there are descriptions of how unexpectedly good results were achieved by artillery units in direct fire against enemy tanks.[20] On this point we read the following:

The Army under von Kluge had found out that the light howitzer with steel grenades is very effective against French heavy 30-ton tanks.[21]

3 field guns of the 73rd . . . are brought into an open firing position

15. 4. Pz. Div. Abt. Ia, Anl. der Gef. Berichte zum KTB of 15 December 1941.

16. Cf. XXIV. Pz. Korps Abt. Ia, Anl. Nr. 281 zum KTB Nr. 8, of 1 November 1941.

17. Cf. Pz. AOK 2, Abt. Ia, KTB Nr. 1, p. 4, of 2 December 1941. Cf. Ibid, p. 5, of 3 December 1941. Cf. Ibid, p. 2, of 18 December 1941.

18. Pz. AOK 2, Abt. Ia, KTB Nr. 1, p. 6, of 15 December 1941.

19. Pz. Gr. Guderian, Abt. Ia, Nr. 502/40 geheim, of 22 August 1940, p. 11. Cf. K. Bühler, 'Auszüge aus den Erfahrungen über den Einsatz einer Panzerartillerieabteilung im Verbande einer Panzerdivision', in *Allgemeine Schweizerische Militärzeitschrift*, Heft 2, 1953, pp. 122–41.

20. Cf. Manteuffel, *7. Panzerdivision*. Cf. R.O.G. Stoves, *1. Panzerdivision, 1939–1945, Chronik einer der drei Stammdivisionen der deutschen Panzerwaffe*, Bad Nauheim, 1961.

21. Pz. Gr. von Kleist, Chef des Gen. St. an die Herren Chefs des XIV., XIX. and XXXXI. Armeekorps, of 19 May 1940.

and, despite machine-gun fire being directed at them, destroy 2 tanks, three others escaping.[22]

Both tanks are engaged and knocked out by the gun.[23]

The experience gained during the Western campaign was contained in the 'Richtlinien für die Führung der Panzerdivision', which appeared in December 1940: 'It is especially important to prepare to fire quickly. Direct fire will . . . often have to be used'.[24]

In the summer of 1941, German armour found the new Russian T-34 and KW-II tanks to be technically far superior. The chances of speedy and decisive victories disappeared for good.[25] Thus, for a time,[26] the strange situation arose in which anti-aircraft and artillery pieces were the only land-based weapons which could penetrate the heavy enemy tanks:

> Russian heavy tanks are difficult to fight because they mostly open fire at a distance of over 800 metres, so that only field guns of 8.8 cm Flak (anti-aircraft) and upward are able to engage them.[27]

> In addition to this, the Russians have many 52-ton tanks (the KW-II), against which all German defensive weapons except the 8.8 cm Flak and the 10 cm cannon are useless.[28]

During this period of technical inferiority, the German panzers sometimes took over the role of back-up weapons by trying to 'draw the enemy [Russian tank] along behind them by rolling back to one side, so that he comes into the line of fire of the 8.8 cm AA guns and the 10 cm cannon'.[29]

It seems almost unbelievable that an artillery unit had to be allotted to a panzer regiment in order for it to be able to roll into battle against enemy tanks:[30]

22. 1. Pz. Div. Abt. Ia, Gef. Bericht des Art. Regt. 73, of 12 June 1940.
23. Ibid, of 13 June 1940.
24. OKH, Richtlinien für die Führung und Einsatz der Panzerdivision, of 3 December 1940, p. 26.
25. Cf. below, pp. 150ff.
26. The 7.5 cm anti-tank gun, which was undergoing tests, was not built into the Panzer IV until 1942.
27. 4. Pz. Div. Abt. Ia, Nr. 71/42 geheim, of 12 March 1942, p. 19.
28. XXIV. Pz. Korps Abt. Ia, Anl. Nr. 237 zum KTB Nr. 8, of 8 October 1941.
29. 4. Pz. Div. Abt. Ia, Nr. 71/42 geheim, of 12 March 1942, p. 19.
30. Cf. 3. Panzer Div. Abt. Ia, Anl. Nr. 21 zum KTB Nr. 3, of 27 September 1941.

It is assumed that the regiment's batteries had a big part in throwing off the enemy attack, in that they prevented tank units from approaching in formation from a great distance at the start.[31]

The enemy puts in still more tanks, but they are being thrown back due to the well-placed artillery fire.[32]

Not surprisingly, the crews of the AA guns and artillery pieces very often had to endure heavy losses when fighting enemy tanks directly:

One field gun opens fire now and fires to the last shell. Then it is run over and crushed by a 52-ton tank.[33]

One gun of 3rd Battery, whose crew holds out under most heavy fire, shoots and hits the tank in the turret while it is moving, at 30 metres, so that the turret sticks and the tank can no longer fight.[34]

The tank fired at the emplacement with cannon and machine gun and rammed the first field gun . . . Then it ran over the fourth gun.[35]

The Russian tanks drive all over the place firing all the time.
   None of the crew leaves the gun. Some of the tanks are between 10 and 30 metres away. The artillery knocks out three tanks by shooting directly at them.[36]

Probably the greatest problem concerning the direct-shot method was getting the guns into position in time without being hit by enemy tanks. For this reason back-slope positions were very successful.[37] However, these tactics did not have much in common either with an attack or a blitz campaign.

5.3   The Smoke-Mortar Units

During the Western campaign of 1940, some German attack divisions were reinforced with smoke-mortar units. In 7th Panzer Division's war diary we can read the following on these

31. 7. Pz. Div. Abt. Ia, Morgenmeldung des Art. Rgt. 78, of 8 July 1941.
32. Ibid, Gef. Bericht des Sch. Rgt. 6, of 9 July 1941, p. 5.
33. 4. Pz. Div. Abt. Ia, Gef. Bericht des Art. Rgt. 103, of 24 September 1941.
34. 7.Pz. Div. Abt. Ia, Gef. Meldung des Art. Rgt. 78, of 18 July 1941.
35. 4. Pz. Div. Abt. Ia, Gef. Bericht des Art. Rgt. 103, of 24 September 1941.
36. Ibid, Gef. Bericht der Pz. Brig. 5, of 18 November 1941.
37. Cf. 4. Pz. Div. Abt. Ia, Nr. 71/42 geheim, of 12 March 1942, p. 19.

special artillery duties: 'Smoke was used from time to time during the Division's battles, for example while crossing the Meuse, breaking through the Maginot Line, during the advance on Cambrai and while crossing the La Bassée Canal.'[38]

It was to be expected that, protected by artificial fog, positions could be changed, obstacles could be overcome or bypassed and a safe distance from the enemy could be reached. The psychological effect the smoke-mortar units had was somewhat more surprising: 'In some case the smoke led to the enemy fleeing in panic. The effect of smoke on morale, especially when fighting to capture houses or bases, sometimes brought us surprising results.'[39] 18th Panzer Division reports on experiences obtained with the smoke-mortar unit in November 1941: 'Smoke makes desertion by the enemy possible because the officers and political commissars are unable to see and stop people deserting.'[40] Although the smoke-mortar units in the German panzer divisions were not equipped with armoured troop carriers until 1942, they were already undeniably successful: 'Seen as a whole, the smoke-mortar unit can already be looked upon as a valuable, modern artillery weapon, an addition to the artillery, especially in co-operation with the infantry regiments in motorised units and armoured forces.'[41]

38. 7. Pz. Div. Abt. Ia, Nr. 440/40 geh., of 14 July 1940, p. 4. Cf. ibid, Abt. Ia, Morgenmeldung des Inf. Regt. 239, of 2 August 1941.

39. OKH, Gen. St. des H./Ausb. Abt. (Ia) Nr. 2,400/40 geheim, of 20 November 1940, p. 9.

40. 18. Pz. Div. Abt. Ia, Anl. Nr. 62 zum KTB, of 4 November 1941.

41. 4. Pz. Div. Abt. Ia, Gef. Bericht des Art. Rgt. 103, of 8 August 1941, p. 2.

6
The Armoured Engineers

Obstacles, destruction and mines can make a tank advance so difficult that the success of the whole enterprise is seriously threatened. Impassable terrain, for example, places the highest demands on an armoured division's commander, since: 'It is extremely difficult to turn a panzer division which is 100 kilometres long in a different direction in such a short time.'[1] So as not to lose the pace of the attack, it will be the aim of every tank unit commander to bypass obstacles or to overcome them with the minimum possible loss of time.

6.1 Mined Advance Routes

The French had been content to lay mines on and on either side of the main roads. Therefore it was the exception rather than the rule to speak of the advance routes as being mined. We learn the following from the war diary of the German 7th Panzer Division on the subject:

> For this reason the unit was instructed to avoid main and minor roads if at all possible and to travel over fields, or use farm tracks where cattle had perhaps been driven before the division arrived.
> Tanks are always able to make new paths for all the division's wheeled vehicles, even through copses.[2]

In exceptional cases the artillery is perfectly capable of shooting a path through smaller minefields. However, the ammunition used up when clearing mines with artillery very soon puts limits on this method. 'To shoot a path through recognised minefields

1. 3. Pz. Div. Abt. Ia, KTB Nr. 3, of 3 July 1941.
2. 7. Pz. Div. Abt. Ia, Nr. 440/40 geheim, of 14 July 1940, p. 5.

of about 20 to 25 metres width and 100 metres depth, about 120 rounds of 21 cm mortar, or about 100 rounds of heavy field howitzer, or about 400 rounds of light field howitzer are needed.'[3]

A few days after the attack on Russia, the German armoured force had to face, in effect, a war of mines, a long, hard battle through almost endless minefields. According to the daily report by LVII. Panzer Corps of 12 July 1941: 'At this time we can only travel forward slowly, since the enemy has blocked all roads and paths with trees and mines.'[4] At the end of September XXXXVII. Panzer Corps reported to 2nd Panzer Army briefly:

All roads in the area of advance are mined.[5]

All bridges have been blown up.[6]

One panzer brigade dug up around 600 mines at a single ford,[7] and, according to a report by 3rd Panzer Division, in the town of Tula in November 1941, the following were mined:

1. The main street, with remote-control detonators;
2. All the town's bridges;
3. The railway station;
4. The town park;
5. The waterworks and the water towers;
6. All grocers' shops and bakeries;
7. All public buildings and corner houses.[8]

However, not only extensive minefields, but also tank traps, dug at right angles to the path of the advance, made it difficult for the tanks to move forwards: 'Half-finished tank traps run at right angles across the terrain, and in between there are aircraft

---

3. H. Dv. 470/7. Ausbildungsvorschrift für die Panzertruppe, of 1 May 1941, p. 101.
4. LVII. Pz. Korps Abt. Ia, Tagesmeldung of 12 July 1941. Cf. Ibid, Abt. Ia, Gef. Bericht der 20. Pz. Div., of 5 September 1941, p. 4.
5. XXXXVII. Pz. Korps Abt. Ia, Anl. Nr. 57 zum KTB 3, of 30 September 1941.
6. Ibid, Anl. Nr. 66, of 1 October 1941, Cf. Ibid, Anl. Nr. 177, of 13 October 1941.
7. Cf. 4. Pz. Div. Abt. Ia, Gef. Bericht der 5. Pz. Brig. of 21 August 1941.
8. 3. Pz. Div. Abt. Ia, Anl. Nr. 108 zum KTB Nr. 3, Feindnachrichtenblatt, of 30 November 1941.

bombs dug into the ground.'[9] Most of the tank traps were built as follows:

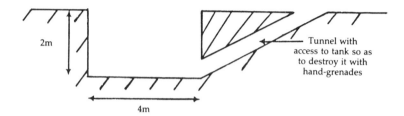

2m

Tunnel with
access to tank so as
to destroy it with
hand-grenades

4m

Figure 1 Tank-trap

If the belief had been held, after the Polish and Western campaigns, that nothing could stop the panzer divisions, then the conclusion had to be reached that, in Russia, well-planned obstacles and minefields could effectively stop tanks for a long period:[10]

> The large amount of mines will make it necessary to conduct the attack purely with infantry.[11]

> The tanks of 4th Division have not attacked due to being stuck in the firing line (in a minefield).[12]

These two quotations from the war diary of one panzer corps make it unmistakeably clear how much influence the laying of minefields can have on tank tactics.

9. 4. Pz. Div. Abt. Ia, Gef. Bericht, of 1 November 1941, p. 14. Cf. 3. Pz. Div. Abt. Ia, Anl. Nr. 50 zum KTB Nr. 3, of 8 July 1941.

10. At the beginning of October the following were built in the third defensive line before Moscow: 98 km of tank traps, 284 km of barbed-wire obstacles, 132 km of gradients, 8,063 km of trenches, 72 km of felled trees, 11,520 km of tank islands. Cf. A.M. Samsonov, *Die große Schlacht*, p. 68.

11. XXIV. Pz. Korps Abt. Ia, Anl. Nr. 253 zum KTB Nr. 8, of 18 October 1941, p. 4.

12. Ibid, Anl. Nr. 263, of 23 October 1941. As an addition to the minefields the Russians used 'mine-dogs'; they tied 2-kilogram bombs on their backs, and then set them against the German panzers. The commander of a German panzer regiment said concerning the use of dogs, 'I don't know of a case of this Red Army trick succeeding anywhere in our attack sector. We shot all the dogs.' Quoted in Manteuffel, *7. Panzer Division*, p. 226. Cf. Pz. AOK 3, Abt. Ia, Tagesmeldung der LVI. A.K. of 17 November 1941.

6.2   Mine Damage

Despite the commitment of armoured engineers and constant study of maps to see where minefields could be, the German armoured force suffered serious losses through mines:

A Panzer IV (weight 21 tons) ran onto a mine, was thrown into the air and was gutted by fire.[13]

The explosion, especially that of the last tank, was such that the hull was thrown 10 metres and the whole crew was killed.[14]

In three days, from 1 to 3 December 1941, no less than ten tanks of Panzer Regiment 21 were out of action due to mine damage:

38-ton tank No. 15 ran onto a mine. Damage: left hull side torn open, all rollers destroyed, write-off, 2 dead, 2 wounded.[15]

38-ton tank No. 2 ran onto 2 mines. Damage: whole rear end torn away . . . Ran onto another mine while being towed away. This time the front of the hull was torn open, write-off, 2 wounded.[16]

The mines, laid in numbers not seen before, very well-camouflaged and hardly recognisable under the snow, led in each case to the vehicle's immediate breakdown.[17]

What was merely a suppressed theory before the Russian campaign became grim reality for the panzer crews: 'Mines will often become obvious when the first tanks run onto them.'[18]

6.3   Armoured Engineers to the Head of the Attack

We will now consider the armoured engineers, this branch of the service whose task it is to make a path for the panzer units over obstacles and through minefields:

13. 19. Pz. Div. Abt. Ia, Gef. Bericht of 11 July 1941, p. 9.
14. 3. Pz. Div. Abt. Ia, Gef. Bericht of 16 July 1941, p. 3.
15. 20. Pz. Div. Abt. Ia, Bergungsbericht des Pz. Rgt. 21, of 4 December 1941.
16. Ibid.
17. Ibid, Abt. Ia, Gef. Bericht des Pz. Rgt. 21 of 6 December 1941.
18. H. Dv. 470/7, Ausbildungsvorschrift für die Panzertruppe, of 1 May 1941, p. 73.

> All other tasks are minor compared to that of clearing the way to the enemy for the tank brigade.[19]

> However, everything depends on getting over the obstacles quickly.[20]

Since 15 April 1940 the engineers in the German armoured divisions had been combined into one battalion. For technical reasons, however, only one company in each of these battalions could be equipped with armoured troop carriers, although experience from the Polish campaign showed clearly that: 'the extensive use of engineer battalions in particular makes the introduction of armoured engineer vehicles necessary.'[21] It is undeniable that only with the help of armoured troop carriers could the engineers follow the vanguard of the panzer attack and aid it when necessary. In the war diary of 1st Panzer Division we read: 'Here is proof of how vital it is to have engineers protected by armour, able to give covering fire themselves in their vehicles, travelling at the head of the panzer attack.'[22]

Because the work of the armoured engineers was so bound up with tank tactics, it was advisable to have them included in the panzer divisions even in peacetime, in order to train them to work together with the armoured force on a full-time basis.[23] 'It is more useful to equip the panzer division and the corps with their own engineers than to rely on the infrequent and therefore mostly delayed assistance of army pioneers.'[24]

To be sure, every panzer division must have its own engineers. This does not, however, guarantee the success of a mission. To be able to help the vanguard when it runs into obstacles or minefields without loss of time, the armoured engineers should be kept ready behind the first panzer unit. We can see from the experience report by 4th Panzer Division that ar-

19. OKH, Richtlinien für Führung und Kampf der Panzerdivision, of 3 December 1940, p. 22.
20. 'Pioniere im Panzerverband', in *Militärwochenblatt*, of 4 June 1936, Sp. 2,062.
21. XIX. Pz. Korps Abt. Ia, Erf. Bericht des Pi. Bat. 43, of 2 October 1939.
22. 1. Pz. Div. Abt. Ia, Gef. Bericht der Pz. Jäger Abt. 37, of 10 June 1940, p. 2.
23. Cf. Kdo. der Panzertruppen, Id, Nr. 3,770/37, Besichtigungsbemerkungen des Kommandierenden Generals der Panzertruppe im Jahr 1937, pp. 4 and 12.
24. Pz. Gr. von Kleist, Abt. Ia, Nr. 3,422/40 geheim, of 9 August 1940, p. 4.

moured troop carriers were necessary if the engineers were going to be effective: 'The inadequate equipment of 3rd Company of the Engineer Battalion, which is under the command of the Panzer Regiment, meant that they could only follow far behind the regiment in a few non-armoured personnel carriers.'[25] Because the armoured engineer battalion belongs at the front of the attack, there is no doubt where the commander's place should be:

> The engineer battalion commander belongs at the front of the first attack group, only then can he see what work is necessary and he can employ his engineers with the benefit of advance information.[26]

> There must always be a trained officer of the armoured engineer battalion travelling with the vanguard of the panzers.[27]

6.4 The Achievements of the Armoured Engineers

> The heavily fortified base, with its mines and barbed wire . . . fell as a result of an attack by 59 Armoured Engineer Battalion of 8th Panzer Division.[28]

The tasks of the armoured engineers were as difficult as they were dangerous. They often had to make paths for their tanks under extremely heavy enemy fire, clear minefields or build temporary bridges in the shortest time possible.[29] In the experience report made by one panzer division, we read the following concerning the commitment of the engineer battalion: 'The battalion had built 153 bridges on the 150th day of battle, which proves that repairing and building bridges and temporary bridges has to be more intensively trained than before.'[30] Perhaps more astonishing than the bridge-building achievements are those of clearing minefields: 'Our engineers have dug up 550 of these 50-kilogram bombs . . . on top of that 1,300 mines on and near the road, with regrettable human losses on

---

25. 4. Pz. Div. Abt. Ia, Nr. 71/42 geheim, of 12 March 1942, p. 21.
26. Ibid.
27. Ibid.
28. Pz. Gr. von Kleist, Abt. Ia, Tagesabschlußmeldung of 28 May 1940.
29. In order to avoid at least some of the enemy fire, they often worked under cover of darkness. Cf. 18. Pz. Div. Abt. Ia, Nr. 28/41 geheim of 17 January 1941.
30. 4. Pz. Div. Abt. Ia, Nr. 71/42 geheim, of 12 March 1942, p. 17.

their side.'[31] The same battalion dug up 546 aircraft bombs and 1,308 tin- or iron-box mines in a single day near Msensk, also filled up countless bomb craters and rebuilt three bridges which had been blown up.[32] In 2nd Panzer Army's war diary there is the following recognition of the achievement of one armoured engineer battalion:

> The battalion has, therefore, cleared the road between Msensk and Chern of mines and made it passable again. I would like to pay tribute to the battalion for this excellent work.
>
> C-in-C 2nd. Panzer Army.[33]

Finding and digging up wooden mines was extremely dangerous for the engineers, for the metal detectors used at this time were not finely-tuned enough to register them: 'Wooden mines must be searched for with a fork.'[34]

One could see from the way Russian armoured engineers were employed that the Red Army was very well trained in mine warfare. As a combat report by 4th Panzer Division says: 'When blocking roads with mines, the Russians also laid them on the steep slopes at either side so that they caused losses among the units clearing the roads during an aircraft attack.'[35] In February 1941, the Commander-in-Chief of the German Army had ordered that:

> All units must be proficient in:
> 1. The speedy crossing of rivers and boggy terrain using makeshift materials;
> 2. The removal of simple obstacles and temporary road repair.[36]

Even if a panzer division has a well-equipped engineer battalion, every tankman, or at least every armoured infantryman, should be trained in the taking up and transfer of mines.[37] For it is only theoretically possible to have an engineer battalion to

---

31. Ibid, Gef. Bericht des Pz. Pi. Bat. 79, of 4 November 1941.
32. Cf. ibid.
33. Pz. AOK 2, Abt. Ia, Anl. Nr. 70 zum KTB Nr. 1, of 17 November 1941.
34. 4. Pz. Div. Abt. Ia, Gef. Bericht of 2 November 1941.
35. Ibid.
36. OB d. H./ Gen. St. d. H. / Ausb. Abt. (Ia) Nr. 555/41 geheim, of 21 February 1941, p. 7.
37. Cf. OKH/Gen. St. d. H. /Ausb. Abt. (Ia) Anl. zu Nr. 1,550/42 geheim,

make a path for each panzer unit: 'The tanks could not cross the river because of a deep ditch. The tanks nearest to the crossing put their crews ashore, filled in the ditch and removed a large number of mines which had been laid between the ditch and the river.'[38] When there are man-made obstacles and minefields on the scale of those found during the Russian campaign,[39] then it is unthinkable to employ an armoured division without a well-trained engineer battalion. The following proved to be true over and over again during the co-operation between the armoured force and the armoured engineers: 'It is not granted to one single branch of the service to achieve victory. The secret of success lies in all branches of warfare working together.'[40]

Ausbildungsanweisungen nach Fronterfahrungen dated 28 June 1942, p. 5.

38. 20. Pz. Div. Abt. Ia, Gef. Bericht des Pz. Rgt. 21, of 1 September 1941, p. 3.

39. Cf. above, pp. 103f. In Stalingrad and the area to the south around 150,000 mines had been laid. Cf. A.J. Jeremenko, *Tage der Bewährung*, Berlin, 1961, p. 285.

40. W. Spannenkrebs, *Angriff mit Kampfwagen*, Berlin, 1939, p. 175.

7
The Perfect Pair – Tank and Aeroplane

7.1 Air Supremacy

The achievements of German armour in the blitz campaigns of 1939 to 1941 would not have been possible without the support of the Luftwaffe. Although the build-up of the Luftwaffe had delayed tank production, it was the air force squadrons which made both possible and easier the quick breakthroughs of the armoured spearheads led by Guderian, Hoth, Kleist or any other commander.

> Close and lasting co-operation with the Luftwaffe is still one of the foundations of the successful use of panzer divisions. Unified and co-ordinated march movements by divisions, especially through bottlenecks or rivers, were only made possible at all by shutting out the enemy air force at an early stage.[1]

> The operative use of large armoured and motorised units in conjunction with the Luftwaffe was characteristic of the French campaign and proved to be the decisive factor in modern mobile warfare.[2]

Because the 405 Polish planes had been almost totally destroyed by the German Luftwaffe while they were still on the ground, the latter could be committed in support of the ground forces without hindrance.[3]

After the Polish campaign the Army High Command issued the following order: 'It is the task of the light squadrons (of the

---

1. Pz. Gr. von Kleist, Abt. Ia, Nr. 3,422/40 geheim, of 9 August 1940, p. 3.
2. Ibid, Abt. Ia, KTB, Final remark after the end of the Western campaign, of 11 July 1940.
3. Cf. XV. Pz. Korps Abt. Ia, Nr. 4/39 geheim of 5 September 1939.

Luftwaffe) to escort the tanks, and they are indispensable for this task.'[4] And indeed, theory and practice were one and the same. During the Western campaign the German air force was at all times the master of the air and was, therefore, able to give effective support to the large-scale operations of Panzer Groups von Kleist und Guderian:

> Over Panzer Group von Kleist's sectors, the Luftwaffe had command of the skies. Sometimes there were no enemy planes at all to be seen.[5]

> Air supremacy was always complete, apart from in Flanders, due to the proximity of the British airfields.[6]

The Chief of the General Staff of Panzer Group von Kleist went into the question of co-operation between Mobile Units and the Luftwaffe in great detail. In the autumn of 1940 he wrote:

> It must be theoretically possible to ask for an air corps and an anti-aircraft unit to be put under the command of the motorised army group, for this particular combination has led to Panzer Group von Kleist's great victories. There were only problems when an army command got between air corps and group asking for special favours and demanding that the group should not be allowed to deal directly with the air corps.[7]

> Our air force must prepare and support the Mobile Unit's panzer attack ruthlessly. It must keep the enemy air force from making effective attacks on the Mobile Unit.[8]

Experience obtained during the blitz campaigns in Poland and France had showed that armoured forces could only be supported in time and in sufficient strength by the Luftwaffe when the panzer divisions had fighter squadrons allotted to them. This fact was recognised in December 1940 in the 'Richtlinien für

---

4. OKH, Gen. St. des H./Ausb. Abt. (Ia), Nr. 746/39 geheim, of 25 November 1939, p. 8.
5. Pz. Gr. von Kleist, Abt. Ia, KTB, of 17 May 1940.
6. Pz. Gr. Guderian, Abt. Ia, Nr. 502/40 geheim, of 22 August 1940, p. 4.
7. Pz. Gr. von Kleist, Abt. Ia, Chef des Gen. St., Anl. B zum KTB Nr. 3, Vorläufige Erinnerungen . . ., of 10 August 1940, p. 12.
8. Ibid, Abt. Ia, Richtlinien für die Führung Schneller Gruppen, version of 20 October 1940.

Führung und Einsatz der Panzerdivision': 'If the panzer division is assigned to a breakthrough or a task which is limited in a strategic sense, then it is necessary from the start to allot fighters to it.'[9] Also, during the first days of the Russian campaign, in the summer of 1941, the German Luftwaffe had almost complete control of the skies. As in the Polish campaign, most of the enemy air force had been destroyed on the airfields. On 22 June, according to Russian sources, about 800 planes had been blown up by bombers before they could go into action, on the 66 airfields in the border areas.[10] Without this air supremacy, the German armoured forces would scarcely have been able to penetrate so far into the Russian border districts:

> Our fighters were highly successful – they shot down more than 20 (Russian) bombers.[11]

> On 8 July, in particular, our fighter, bomber and dive-bomber squadrons made a great contribution to the speedy end of the 17th Panzer Division's crisis.[12]

> At around 1200 hrs . . . second dive-bomber attack on the enemy position. At the same time, at 1230 hrs, the Panzer Company advances over its own lines and throws the enemy back about 600 metres.[13]

Alongside the successes of the co-operation between armour and air force, we must also, however, consider the dangers involved. Because the German armoured units approached the enemy as quickly as possible most of the time and often ran into them earlier than expected, it happened, from time to time, that German column spearheads were fired at by their own fighters:

> At 1300 hrs 3rd Panzer Division attacked by own planes while advancing on Vlodova, south of Brest.[14]

---

9. OKH, Richtlinien für Führung und Kampf der Panzerdivision, of 3 December 1940, p. 7.

10. Cf. A. Nekrich and P. Grigorenko. *Genickschuß. Die Rote Armee am 22. Juni 1941*, ed. and intro. by G. Haupt, Vienna, Frankfurt am Main and Zürich, 1969, p. 172. G.K. Zhukov, *Erinnerungen*, p. 236.

11. 3. Pz. Div. Ia, KTB Nr. 3, of 30 June 1941.

12. Pz. AOK 2, Abt. Ia, Anl. Bd. 1 zum KTB Nr. 1, of 9 August 1941, p. 11.

13. 7. Pz. Div. Abt. Ia, Morgenmeldung des Sch. Regt. 6, of 23 July 1941.

14. XIX. Pz. Korps Abt. Ia, KTB Nr. 1, of 16 September 1939.

The unit had put out plenty of ground signals and had shot flares. Despite this, however, squadrons with visibly German markings continued their attacks. The consequence was a delay of several hours in crossing the river, building the bridge and, therefore, the advance of the whole division on Besançon. The unit suffered casualties, dead and wounded.[15]

Between 1200 and 1300 hrs German planes attacked their own tanks.[16]

Mistakes in distinguishing between friend and foe were not only made by the fighter pilots but also by the ground troops: 'In the last few days friendly planes were often mistaken for enemy ones and shot down or damaged when flying at low altitude.'[17] However, these incidents should not make us blind to the fact that the achievements of the German armoured force were only possible thanks to the excellent Luftwaffe support. General Guderian, after the war, described the success of the blitz campaigns of 1939 to 1941 as 'the result of air-ground co-ordination',[18] and we can say, with Eddy Bauer, that: 'Seen as a whole, armour has never been successfully employed by those who did not also have air supremacy.'[19]

7.2 If There is no Air Support

One can see from the dire consequences inevitably resulting from a lack of air support how important this is for the employment of large armoured units. While there was never a serious danger to German air supremacy during the Polish and French campaigns, the strength of the Russian air force should have

---

15. Pz. Gr. Guderian, Abt. Ia, Meldung an Gen. Kdo. II. Fliegerkorps, date burned. The 1. Panzer Division had to suffer more than most from air attacks by their own planes between 16 and 21 June 1940. Cf. 1. Pz. Div. Abt. IIa, Meldung des Art. Kommandeurs 101, of 16 June 1940. Cf. Ibid, Abt. IIa, Meldung der Pz. Jäger Abt. 37, of 17 June 1940. Cf. Ibid, Abt. IIa, Meldung des Kraftradschützenbat. 1, of 21 June 1940.
16. Pz. AOK 3, Abt. Ia, Tagemeldung des Gen. Kdo. LVI. A.K. of 5 December 1941.
17. LVII. Pz. Korps Abt. Ia, Anl. 1 zum Korpsbefehl Nr. 13, of 8 July 1941, p. 2.
18. H. Guderian, 'Armored Warfare', in *Armored Cavalry Journal*, vol. 1, 1949, p. 4.
19. E. Bauer, *Der Panzerkrieg*, Bonn, 1964, p. 9.

raised questions from the beginning about a long-term use of German armoured units in the depths of Russia. In 1936 it was known, in German military circles, that Russia had 4600 first-line and 1400 second-line tactical warplanes.[20] From these figures there was no doubt that Russia put great emphasis on her air force and fully recognised its importance in modern mobile warfare.[21]

Table 1 Aircraft production in Russia

Year	Employees	Factories	Aircraft produced
1928	20,000	18	500
1933	110,000	54	1,700
1936	200,000	74	8,000[21]

It was true that the German air force had been able to score a great surprise victory on 22 June 1941 by bombarding the Russian border airfields. But, on the other hand, thousands of fighters and bombers were waiting deep inside Russia. Thus, the further east German armoured divisions advanced, the more difficult it became to protect them from the air. After a few weeks of the Russian campaign, Luftwaffe support could only be counted upon in certain areas and for a limited period. Warplanes securely allotted to each attack division were already a dream left over from the Western campaign, as we can read in the war diaries:

> Strong enemy air superiority, many low-level strafes and bomber attacks, many casualties.[22]

> The dive-bomber attack asked for and agreed to by the Corps seems not to be taking place.[23]

---

20. Cf. Frhr. von Bülow, 'Die Luftwaffe Sowjetrußlands', in *Militärwissenschaft-liche Rundschau*, vol. 6, 1936, p. 801. The German air force comprised, on 22 June 1941: 1160 bombers; 710 scout planes; 720 fighters; 150 transport planes. Cf. H.A. Jacobsen, *1939–1945, Der Zweite Weltkrieg in Chronik und Dokumenten*, 5th enlarged and revised edition, Darmstadt, 1961, p. 40.
21. Cf. A. Guillaume, *Warum siegte die Rote Armee?*, Baden-Baden, 1950, p. 285.
22. LVII. Pz. Korps Abt. Ia, Tagesmeldung an Pz. AOK 3, of 27 July 1941.
23. 3. Pz. Div. Abt. Ia, KTB Nr. 3, of 27 August 1941.

No friendly air support.[24]

The effects on the morale of tankmen of being attacked for hours at a time by enemy low-flying planes should not be under-estimated, especially when there is no sign of their own fighters.

The Red air force is master of the skies. No fighter cover. Human and material losses due to bombing.[25]

Absolute enemy air supremacy. Up to midday a total of 69 bomber attacks.[26]

Very heavy enemy air attacks with great effect on our spearheads.[27]

Reports on how heads of mechanised columns were stopped by planes dropping explosives, fire bombs and phosphor bombs can be found over and over again.[28] How bitter it must have been for the German tank units, accustomed as they were to victory, to receive the following order, on 6 September 1941, from the Commander-in-Chief of the Army: 'The unit must . . . therefore be trained to fight enemy planes with their own weapons (machine-gun and rifle).'[29]

While the Wehrmacht's tank columns had to suffer more and more under the blows of the enemy air force, the latter found the perfect ally in the vast moorlands of Russia. The German 'panzer queues' often got stuck on one road, completely unable to escape the air attacks by splitting up. The rule 'march separately' was an important part of tank tactics, but the *'passages obligés'* made sure that this principle remained a theoretical concept. On 9 November 1941 the commander of XXIV. Panzer Corps reported to 2nd Panzer Army that his troops were becoming heavily damaged by constant Russian air attacks, both

24. XXXXVII. Pz. Korps Abt. Ia, Anl. Nr. 599 zum KTB Nr. 2, of 30 August 1941.
25. Ibid, XXXXVII. Pz. Korps Abt. Ia, Anl. Nr. 697 zum KTB Nr. 2, of 8 September 1941.
26. Ibid, Abt. Ia, Anl. Nr. 600 zum KTB Nr. 2, of 30 August 1941.
27. Pz. AOK 3, Abt. Ia, Zwischenmeldung zum AOK 9, of 4 October 1941.
28. Cf. XXXXVII. Pz. Korps Abt. Ia, Anl. Nr. 533 zum KTB Nr. 2, of 22 August 1941. Cf. ibid, Anl. Nr. 561, of 27 August 1941. Cf. ibid, Anl. Nr. 588, of 29 August 1941. Cf. LVII. Pz. Korps Abt. Ia, Zwischenmeldung of 29.10.1941. Cf. ibid, Zwischenmeldung of 4. November 1941.
29. OB d. H./Gen. St. d. H./Ausb. Abt. (Ia) Nr. 2,053/41 geheim of 6 September 1941.

in terms of matériel and morale. There were insufficient anti-aircraft guns, and the fighter base was too far away.[30] And still the armoured units moved eastwards, albeit slowly, the distance between them and the Luftwaffe bases becoming greater every day.

In March 1942 (what was planned as a blitz campaign had already lasted nine months), the Commander-in-Chief of the German Army had to admit that: 'The events of the last months have shown once again that attacks without air support have led to failure and thus to unnecessary losses.'[31]

7.3   The Reconnaissance Aircraft

Merely to consider the co-ordination of armour and aircraft from the tactical point of view would be to oversimplify matters. In the Balkan and, above all, the North African campaigns, Mobile Units were often only supplied by means of airlifts, a use of the air force which was, however, not fully feasible until after the Second World War, when wide-bodied aircraft were developed.

When we speak of tank tactics in the years 1939–41, we must also mention reconnaissance aircraft. It was they who constantly put the data needed to make decisions into the hands of the tank unit commander. They were the eyes of the armoured divisions:

> The speedy advance of the German tank wedge was made easier due to air supremacy, but especially due to extremely detailed air reconnaissance, whose reports reached the Corps daily.[32]

> During the French campaign ideal co-operation between reconnaissance and tanks. For example, on 19 May 1940, Panzer Group von Kleist received no less than 22 message drops on the enemy situation.[33]

> The tankmen are always pleased to see the reconnaissance plane . . . We regard it as our best friend.[34]

30. Cf. XXIV. Pz. Korps Abt. Ia, Anl. Nr. 290 zum KTB Nr. 8, of 9 November 1941.
31. OB d. H./Gen. St. d. H./Op. Abt. (II) Nr. 10,328/42 Geh.Kdos., of 23 March 1942.
32. XIX. Pz. Korps Abt. Ia, Akte V, Berichte der täglichen Luftaufklärung, of 10–31 May 1940.
33. Pz. Gr. von Kleist, Abt. Ic, Abwurfmeldungen des Koluft of 19 May 1940. Cf. ibid, Abwurfmeldungen des Koluft of 21 May 1940.
34. 4. Pz. Div. Abt. Ia, Gef. Bericht of 20 August 1941.

These 'Luftwaffe comrades' dropped regular, very detailed messages over the front panzer units concerning the traffic situation, the lie of the land, enemy defences and the situation of nearby units. In addition, the light planes sometimes took over the role of background noise by masking the noise of the tank motors as they approached, and thus contributing to the total surprise of the enemy.[35]

To have light aircraft squadrons allotted to panzer divisions is also indispensable for the co-ordination of reconnaissance and armoured forces. General von Manteuffel, one of the most outstanding German tank tacticians, even had this to say on the subject: 'The commander of a panzer division should very often give orders from the air. At the beginning of the Russian campaign the armoured units had their own aircraft squadrons . . . I would also recommend that the squadrons be trained together with the panzer divisions in peacetime.'[36]

---

35. 18. Pz. Div. Abt. Ia, Nr. 55/41 geheim of 20 November 1941, p. 3.
36. Liddell Hart, *Jetzt dürfen sie reden*, p. 159.

8
Tank Versus Tank

In the last four chapters we have seen the tank in conjunction with other arms. The next pages will show the tank as it fights other tanks: 'The most dangerous opponent of a tank is an enemy tank. If it cannot be beaten, the breakthrough can be seen as a failure, as the infantry and the artillery will also fail to get through.'[1]

8.1   There is no Ideal Tank

The technical details of tank construction cannot be dealt with in the confines of this book. However, we must briefly consider a few basic principles. Every tank represents a compromise. Thus, to compare tanks in the form of a table will never be satisfactory, except when the tanks have been specifically designed for the same use, in the same terrain and against the same potential enemy. I will briefly list some of the main factors which determine the combat efficiency of a tank:

1. Fire power;
2. Manoeuvrability;
3. Armour thickness;
4. Range;
5. Shape;
6. Ammunition capacity.

From this (admittedly incomplete) listing it can already be seen that all factors depend on one another to such an extent that to emphasise one would inevitably weaken one or more of the

---

1. Guderian, *Achtung-Panzer!*, p. 176.

others. When designing a tank, certain main features will be determined and thus, correspondingly, certain disadvantages must be taken into account.[2] For example, thicker armour which is too heavy will lead to less manoeuvrability and a smaller range, while extra fuel tanks on the outer hull increase the danger of the tank being set on fire. A high ammunition capacity makes a well-designed, flat turret impossible. In a conversation with Liddell Hart, General von Manteuffel, Commander of the 5th German Panzer Army in 1944/45, voiced the following opinion: 'Manoeuvrability has developed into a weapon, and is often considered to be as important as fire-power and armour.'[3]

This is certainly true, but one can also ask oneself the question: what is the use of superior manoeuvrability in a light tank when it can outflank the enemy tank, but cannot destroy him because its gun cannot penetrate his armour? It must be reiterated that every tank represents a compromise, planned and constructed with a conception of the way war will be fought in the future.

8.2 Successes in the West in 1940

The German armoured force had come through its acid test during the Polish campaign of 1939. The high expectations set by Guderian had not only been fulfilled but exceeded. We cannot go into the panzer battles during this month-long blitz campaign in more detail for two reasons. Firstly, there is such a dearth of source material that any attempt to give a description would be inconsistent with the title of this book.[4] Secondly, the Polish armoured force, divided in dribs and drabs among eighteen infantry and eleven cavalry brigades, hardly made an appearance. The only four armoured battalions were reserves,

2. Such advantages and disadvantages can be found in all modern tanks. It is difficult to determine the combat efficiency of individual tanks because there are often very different opinions on the value of certain factors. Cf. R. Knecht, *Kampfpanzer Leopard*, Munich, 1972; B. Perrett, *NATO Armour*, London, 1971; C.F. Foss, *Armoured Fighting Vehicles of the World*, London, 1971.

3. Liddell Hart, *Jetzt dürfen sie reden*, p. 161. General Bayerlein, who had served under Guderian as Ia (G.S.O. 1) and under Rommel as Chief of Staff, held the same opinion as Manteuffel.

4. Cf. above, pp. xiii/xivff.

and spent most of the time during the September battles moving from place to place on administrative marches.[5]

We have already discussed the general reasons for the defeat of France in the Western campaign of 1940.[6] Now we can look at the following question in more depth: Why was the German armoured force able to achieve such astoundingly good results against the French tanks, although they were inferior both in numbers and in performance?

In a panzer duel, in other words, in a head-to-head battle, the German tanks had no chance against the French 'char B' and Somua tanks. In combat reports by 1st Panzer Division we read:

> The immediate fire opened by both regiments had no visible effect on the enemy who defended bitterly for a long time. Our armour-piercing weapons are fairly ineffective against the well-armoured B2.[7]

> Our two panzer regiments are being taught a lesson by a few French tanks . . . in any case these few enemy tanks are holding up a whole armoured divisions for hours on end.[8]

> It is becoming more and more noticeable that the 3.7 cm anti-tank gun is totally ineffective against the B2 tank. The cases in which there have been good results can be seen as the exception.[9]

In the light of such statements, it is hard to imagine why the German armoured divisions could not be effectively stopped. We have already spoken about the lack of esprit de combat among the French tank crews.[10] However, there are other, more telling reasons for the achievements of the German tanks, although they were often far inferior to the French models; for the tactical side, the actual use made of the tank on the battlefield is as decisive as the combat efficiency of the tank itself. While the German army commanders put their tanks into the battle en masse, in order to break through enemy front sectors with

5. Cf. above, pp. 4ff. Cf. Stoves, *1. Panzerdivision*, p. 74.
6. Cf. above, pp. 6ff.
7. 1. Pz. Div. Abt. Ia, Gef. Bericht der 1. Pz. Brig. of 10 June 1940, p. 2. Cf. ibid, Gef. Bericht des Art. Regt. 73, of 12 June 1940.
8. Ibid, Gef. Bericht des Sch. Rgt. 1, of 10 June 1940.
9. Ibid, Gef. Bericht der Pz. Jägerabt. 37, of 10 June 1940, p. 2.
10. Cf. above, pp. 25ff.

hammer-blows, the French had their 1800 or so tanks divided into 'splinter units':[11]

> The fragmented commitment of the French tanks was obvious.[12]

> The tank battles which we expected have seldom taken place. The reason – fragmented employment of the enemy tanks.[13]

> Lack of will to attack and dissipated commitment of the French tanks make up for our less-effective anti-tank guns.[14]

Because the French tanks often only appeared in groups or platoons against German armoured regiments, their combat efficiency could not have any effect. 'Although the number of enemy tanks is here, as everywhere, not very large, they are well hidden in positions near woods, so that they are not easy to recognise.'[15]

Jean Marot writes the following about the 4th division cuirassée (armoured division) commanded by General de Gaulle:

> The officers . . . were ill-prepared for commanding tanks. The lieutenants, all from Saint-Cyr (officer training academy) had never had to command an armoured unit. The tank leaders were nearly all from cavalry units and knew almost nothing about how to drive a tank. They had no experience of living and fighting in a tank, apart from what they had had to gain on the field of battle.[16]

When tank commanders climb into a tank for the first time immediately prior to the battle one can scarcely apply the term 'armour tactics' any longer! 'His tank commanders, good Saint-Cyr graduates to a man, climbed into a tank for the first time on the 17th of May.'[17]

Training at a famous military academy is doubtless very valuable; however, combat technique is, of course, learned on

---

11. Cf. above, Chapter 1, notes 28 and 29, p. 7.
12. Pz. Gr. Guderian, Abt. Ia, Nr. 502/40 geheim, of 22 August 1940, p. 2.
13. Ibid, p. 3.
14. Ibid, p. 7. Cf. E. Frhr. von Jungenfeld, *So kämpften Panzer*, Berlin, 1941, p. 55.
15. 1. Pz. Div. Abt. Ia, Gef. Bericht der Sch. Brig. of 10 June 1940.
16. J. Marot, *Abbéville 1940, Avec la division cuirassée de Gaulle*, Paris, 1967, p. 44.
17. L. Saurel, *La tragédie de juin 1940*, Paris, 1966, p. 78.

the battlefield. A tank company without iron firing discipline has no right to call itself a company. It is merely an uncontrolled mob of field guns on tracks, which will more than likely open fire at the wrong moment. Knowing when to open fire is, however, the most important factor in the panzer battle, as we can see from the experience of the successful German armoured units:

> The enemy tanks were mostly far superior to ours regarding the thickness of their armour. By opening fire early on meeting the enemy and quickly going to selective fire from the right position, we mostly succeeded in beating down the stronger enemy tanks.[18]

> In the few places where enemy tank confronted our panzer regiments in greater numbers, it has been shown time and again that those tanks which open fire first, even while still moving, and then fire at the target while stationary are the victors.[19]

In the files of Panzer Group Guderian we read for 22nd August 1940:

> In the struggle between the tank units, our panzers were in a superior position after a short fire-fight. The reasons for this were:
> 1. Our weapons' great accuracy of fire.
> 2. High firing rate which partly made up for the lack of penetration.
> 3. Hits from tanks Type III and IV had such an effect on morale, even if the enemy tanks were not penetrated, that crews often showed the white flag in surrender.
> 4. Our panzers are faster and have greater manoeuvrability.
> 5. Our leadership, training and the crews' morale are superior.
> 6. Radio contact, therefore easier to command and more manoeuvrable.[20]

We should concentrate on this last point, that of command by radio, because only thanks to the excellent means of contact were the achievements of the blitzkrieg possible. It is difficult to transmit orders to large armoured units because:

18. 7. Pz. Div. Abt. Ia, Nr. 440/40 geheim, of 14 July 1940, p. 3.
19. Ibid, p. 15.
20. Pz. Gr. Guderian, Abt. Ia, Nr. 502/40 geheim of 22 August 1940.
21. Pz. Gr. von Kleist, Abt. Ia, Chef d. Gen. St., Anlage B zum KTB Nr. 3, Vorläufige Erfahrungen mit großen motorisierten Verbänden, of 10 August 1940, p. 3.

1. they travel so quickly;
2. staff often change their posts;
3. commanding officers often have to be at the front, separated from their staff;
4. the chain of command is mostly very long;
5. the roads are mostly crowded or even full.[21]

On 10 May 1940, for example, Panzer Group von Kleist consisted of five tank divisions, three motorised infantry divisions and several army units. It had 42,000 motor vehicles and a marching length of about 400 kilometres on four routes next to each other.[22] On 25 September 1940, General Guderian had the following report sent to the signals regiment of his Panzer Group: 'As I have already said, thanks to the outstanding performance of the regiment, I was able to command the units under me at all times.'[23]

In the course of this book we have seen several times that the Polish and French High Commands contributed greatly to the success of the German armoured units with their outdated ideas of warfare. However, the blitz campaigns could only be carried out because the favourable conditions created by the Poles and the French were extremely well exploited by the German tank commanders. They avoided a division of forces, and the units at the head, perfectly trained for their job and eager for battle, broke through enemy fronts and thrust deep into the enemy hinterland without fear of leaving the flanks unprotected. It cannot be emphasised enough that expert knowledge of all available means of communication was a prerequisite for the smooth running of these operations.

What had been demanded by the Commanding General of the German armoured forces in 1937 proved to be correct in the blitz campaigns of 1939/40: 'A tank unit commander can only really lead his unit if he knows the radio terms of command inside out.'[24]

---

22. Cf. ibid.
23. Pz. Gr. Guderian, Abt. Ia/IIa, Meldung an Nachrichtenabteilung 80, of 25 September 1940. Cf. Pz. Gr. von Kleist, Abt. Ia, KTB, of 17 May 1940. Cf. Nachrichtenabteilung 80, Abt. Ia, Erfahrungsbericht, of 5 July 1940, p. 3.
24. Kdo. der Panzertruppen, Id. Nr. 3,770/37, Besichtigungsbemerkungen des Kommandieren Generals der Panzertruppen im Jahre 1937, p. 7.

8.3 Crisis in the East in 1941

While German tank tacticians were discussing the idea of mass commitment of armour on the battlefield before the outbreak of the Second World War, mass production of tanks became a reality in Russia. In 1939, Guderian had visited a Russian tank factory in which, at that time, 22 Christie-Russkij tanks a day were being produced.[25] Before the war he wrote: 'The numbers of tanks, about 10,000, plus 150,000 tractors and over 100,000 army vehicles, puts the Red Army at the head of the world's armies in respect of motorisation.'[26]

Why did Hitler believe that a blitzkrieg was possible against an armoured force at least three times as large as his own? Without doubt the tremendous results achieved during the Western campaign had intoxicated the amateur military leader and had prevented him from making a realistic appraisal of the situation. Thus it seemed not to worry him that the Balkan campaign had delayed Operation Barbarossa by about five weeks – five weeks which were lost at the start of the autumn mud period during the Russian campaign . . . In August 1941, Hitler is reported as saying to Guderian: 'If I had known that the numbers of tanks you mentioned in your book were actually correct, then I don't think I would have begun this war.'[27] However, not only Hitler but also many tank leaders made a grave error: 'At the start of the war against Russia we believed that we could count on having a technical advantage over the Russian tanks which would have almost made up for the well-known gigantic Russian superiority in numbers.'[28]

Thus the realisation, in the summer of 1941, that the technical superiority of the new Russian tank was equal to their numerical superiority, was a bitter one!

25. Cf. H. Guderian, *Erinnerungen*, p. 129.
26. H. Guderian, *Die Panzertruppen und ihr Zusammenwirken mit den anderen Waffen*, 4th enlarged edition, Berlin, 1943, p. 18. Cf. Moritz, 'Die Einschätzung der Roten Armee durch den faschistischen Generalstab von 1935–1941' in *Zeitschrift für Militärgeschichte*, no. 2, 1969, pp. 154–70, here p. 160.
27. Guderian, *Erinnerungen*, p. 172.
28. Ibid, p. 129.

8.3.1 Hopeless Struggle Against Russian Tanks

We have already spoken about the fact that the German anti-aircraft and artillery guns were the most effective ground-based weapons in the fight against Russian tanks.[29] On 28 June 1941, in the first week of the campaign, LVII. Panzer Corps reported: 'During the course of the day the enemy pushed forward heavy tanks of a type not seen before. 5 cm anti-tank guns cannot penetrate them.'[30]

Suddenly to have an enemy tank in front of you, one which you don't know and cannot stop, must be very demoralising for tank crews:

> Completely unknown type of tank before us. We opened fire immediately but the armour was not penetrated until the range was 100 metres. Armour-piercing grenades stuck in the armour plating at 200 metres.[31]

> Around midday two enemy 52-ton tanks attack, which cannot be destroyed even using special ammunition.[32]

> Half a dozen anti-tank gun fire shells at him [a T-34] which sound like a drum-roll. But he drives staunchly through our line like an impregnable prehistoric monster.[33]

Two months before the Russian campaign, the new training manual for the German armoured force was published, and it contained the following statement: 'It is always important to open fire from a good position in front of the enemy.'[34]

At the beginning of July 1941, a detachment of 6th Panzer Regiment lost twenty-one tanks, more than 50% of its strength, in a single battle against a few T-34s. The Russian tanks were hidden in barns and behind houses, and they didn't open fire until the range was 30(!) metres: 'There was firing from all around, but there was no enemy tank to be seen.'[35] The

---

29. Cf. above, pp. 52f.
30. LVII. Pz. Korps Abt. Ia, Tagesmeldung of 28 June 1941.
31. Pz. AOK 2, Abt. Ic, Meldung der Pzj. Abt. 42, of 8 July 1941.
32. 7. Pz. Div. Abt. Ia, Morgenmeldung der Pzj. Abt. 42, of 3 September 1941.
33. Schmidtgen, 'Unser erstes Gefecht mit schweren russischen T-34 Panzern' in *Die Panzertruppe*, vol. 6, 1942, p. 92.
34. H. Dv. 470/7, Ausbildungsvorschrift für die Panzertruppe, of 1 May 1941, p. 13.
35. 3. Pz. Div. Abt. Ia, Anl. Nr. 1 zum KTB Nr. 3, of 6 July 1941.

situation became especially critical for the armoured infantry, whose anti-tank rifles could only 'knock' on the enemy tanks with their ammunition, although they had learned, before the war, that they could destroy tanks up to a range of 300 metres.[36]

> Heavy Russian tanks have broken through the main combat line at 3rd Batt. 7th Coy . . . The heavy tanks cannot be beaten by our weaponry, they roll around 3rd Batt. 7th Coy's position . . . The men have almost no ammunition left and are being run down by Russian tanks.[37]

> At about 1400 hrs, four 52-ton tanks appeared but did not attack. The infantrymen retreated at the sight of the tanks.[38]

In a telephone conversation on 20 December 1941, Field Marshal von Kluge pointed out the following fact to the Army's Chief of General Staff: 'it should be clear to us that the infantry, at this time, runs away from every Russian tank because they have no defence against them.'[39] Well, the crews of the Types III and IV tanks were not having much more luck than the grenadiers with their anti-tank rifles. They had learned, before the Russian campaign, that: 'Quick action and sudden fire from all available armour-piercing weapons at an effective range, if possible from a hidden position and an unexpected direction, is the way of gaining the upper hand.'[40]

However, reality in the struggle against Russian tanks looked like this:

> It is remarkable that Lieutenant Steup's tank made hits on a T-34, once at about 20 metres and four times at 50 metres, with tank

36. Cf. Merkblatt für Gliederung und Kampfweise der Schützenkompanie zu 12 Gruppen, of 13 October 1939.
37. 7. Pz. Div. Abt. Ia, Morgenmeldung des Sch. Rgt. 7, of 14 October 1941, pp. 1–2.
38. 7. Pz. Div. Abt. Ia, Morgenmeldung der Pzj. Abt. 42, of 7 September 1941.
39. H. Gr. Mitte, Abt. Ia, Tel. conversation with General Halder, of 20 December 1941. After Field Marshal von Kluge had given a very serious description of the situation, Hitler allowed the use of hollow grenades, on 22 December 1941. The Führer had forbidden the employment of these new grenades for fear that the Russians would be able to copy them.
40. H. Dv. 470/7, Ausbildungsvorschrift für die Panzertruppe, of 1 May 1941, p. 73.

Grenade Type 40 (calibre 5 cm), without any noticeable effect.[41]

The T-34s came nearer and nearer although they were constantly under fire. The grenades did not penetrate but sprayed off to the side.[42]

The advance party is being prevented from moving since two 52-ton tanks are blocking the advance route and are making it impossible to continue at the moment.[43]

When the enemy's tanks are so technically superior, it becomes difficult to speak of tank tactics any longer. The German panzer crews had a small chance of success if they could outmanoeuvre the Russian tanks and attack them diagonally from the rear: 'Hits against the rear drive-wheel are often successful, along with chance hits on the turret rim.'[44] Therefore, getting the enemy in the right shooting position was already a difficult trick in itself. The following quotation shows how high the cost of underestimating the Russian armoured force had become: 'It is useless to waste tank grenades on heavy Russian tanks standing 800 metres away . . . Occasionally we obtained good results by avoiding fire altogether, especially at night. Russian tanks are neutralised by placing 3-kilogram charges onto them on foot.'[45] It had come to this. German panzer crews were recommended to climb out of their vehicles, creep up to the enemy tanks on foot and blow them up!

The fighting morale of the German armoured units was splendid during the Polish and Western campaigns. In May 1941 this was reflected in the following training principle: 'Special emphasis is to be placed on toughness, courage, dash and on training esprit de corps.'[46] A few lost battles would not have shaken this faith in the tank crews. What made this principle a theory, however, was the recognition that their tanks were technically

---

41. 3. Pz. Div. Abt. Ia, Anl. Nr. 156 zum KTB Nr. 3, of 16 November 1941, p. 3.
42. Ibid, p. 5.
43. 4. Pz. Div. Abt. Ia, Gef. Meldung der Pz. Brig. 5, of 5 October 1941. Cf. Gef. Bericht der Pz. Brig. 5, of 8 October 1941.
44. Pz. AOK 2, Abt. Ic, Bericht des Pz. Rgt. 25, of 8 July 1941.
45. 4. Pz. Div. Abt. Ia, Gef. Bericht des Pz. Rgt. 35, of 18 February 1942. This Combat Report was presented to the General der Schnellen Truppen as well as to the Oberbefehlshaber des Heeres.
46. H. Dv. 470/7, Ausbildungsvorschrift für die Panzertruppe, of 1 May 1941, p. 7.

inferior to the Russian tanks in every situation. In his memoirs Guderian writes about the commander of 5th Panzer Brigade: 'For the first time during their exhausting campaign, Eberbach looked worn out, and it was not physical but psychological shock. It made one think to see that our best officers had been affected in such a way by recent battles.'[47]

Up to the summer of 1941, German armour had brought fear and desperation to the enemy lines. In the struggle against the Russian tanks they had to learn how to take punishment as well as give it:

> Time and again our tanks have been split right open by hits from the front and the commander's cupolas on the Type III and IV tanks have been completely blown off, proof that the armour plating is inadequate and that the fastening on the cupolas is faulty, and also proof of the great accuracy and penetration of the Russian (T-34) 7.62 cm tank cannon.[48]

> The former pace and spirit of the attack will die down and will be replaced by a feeling of inferiority, since the crews know that they can be knocked out by enemy tanks while they are still a great distance away.[49]

8.3.2 Was the T-34 a Decisive Weapon during the Second World War?

> If the defender succeeds in bringing out a gun which can penetrate all the attacker's tanks . . . the success of the tanks will either have to be bought at the cost of lives or . . . it will be jeopardised.[50]

The Russians, with the T-34, had such a weapon, and, for the first time, the achievements of armour, which up till then had been taken for granted were placed in jeopardy.

Without becoming too involved in technical details,[51] we must, together with General von Mellenthin, assert that the Wehrmacht had no tank in 1941 which could have borne com-

47. H. Guderian, *Erinnerungen*, p. 213.
48. 4. Pz. Div. Abt. Ia, Nr. 814/41 geheim of 22 October 1941. Cf. 3. Pz. Div. Abt. Ia, Anl. Nr. 43 zum KTB Nr. 3, of 8 October 1941.
49. 4. Pz. Div. Abt. Ia, Nr. 816/41 geheim, of 22 October 1941, p. 2.
50. H. Guderian, *Erinnerungen*, p. 34.
51. Cf. A.S. Antonov and B.A. Artamonov, *Der Panzer*, Berlin, 1959. Cf. V. Mostovenko, 'L'histoire du T-34' in *Revue Militaire Soviétique*, vol. 3, 1967, pp. 36–7, Cf. B. Perrett, *Fighting Vehicles of the Red Army*, London, 1969, pp. 31–8.

parison with the new Russian model.[52] In the report by 4th Panzer Division we read the following facts about it: 'Very wide track, therefore good cross-country mobility, good fording capacity, superior speed. Better armour due to angled surfaces, excellent diesel engine, better cannon (7.2 cm), very good sighting mechanism.'[53] One cannot help wondering in what way this new Russian tank was not superior to the German models. Thanks to its extremely wide tracks it could attack in places where the Wehrmacht tanks became hopelessly stuck: 'In a tremendously bitter struggle against Russian elite units and numerous tanks (T-34s), whose mobility in deep snow is far superior to that of our tanks, which are dependent upon cleared paths.'[54]

The T-34 is rightly called the first successful tank in the history of war by many books about armour.[55] General von Kleist, commander of 1st Panzer Army in 1941, has this to say: 'Their T-34 tank was the best in the world.'[56]

On 18 November 1941, the Special Committee on Tanks of the Heeres-Waffenamt (Army Ordinance Office) met in the headquarters of 2nd Panzer Army in Orel.[57] Using latest combat experiences as a guide, measures had to be taken against the absolute superiority of the T-34. The front officers suggested that the Russian tank be copied immediately.[58] However, the German armaments industry was evidently not in a position to build the T-34's aluminium diesel engine in good time. As a stop-gap measure, the unit demanded that a more effective gun be built into the Panzer IV,[59] leaving out thicker armour, the machine gun and even the commander if necessary. What the

---

52. Cf. F.M. von Mellenthin, *Panzer-Schlachten. Eine Studie über den Einsatz von Panzerverbänden im Zweiten Weltkrieg*, Neckargemünd, 1963, p. 64.

53. 4. Pz. Div. Abt. Ia, Nr. 71/42 geheim, of 12 March 1942, p. 30.

54. 20. Pz. Div. Abt. Ia, Beitrag zur Erinnerungsschrift 'Winterfeldzug des Pz. AOK 4, 1941/42', p. 11. Cf. Manteuffel, *7. Panzerdivision*, p. 260.

55. Cf. D. Orgill, *The Tank*, p. 189; C.F. Foss, *Armoured Fighting Vehicles*, p. 82; Halle und Demand, *Illustrierte Geschichte*, p. 89.

56. Liddell Hart, *Jetzt dürfen sie reden*, p. 401.

57. Cf. 4. Pz. AOK 2, Abt. Ia, Anl. Nr. 16 zum KTB Nr. 1, of 18 November 1941.

58. Cf. 4. Pz. Div. Abt. Ia, Nr. 816/41 geheim of 22 October 1941.

59. Cf. Pz. AOK 2, Abt. Ia, Anl. Nr. 16 zum KTB Nr. 1, pp. 2–3, of 18 November 1941. In 1942 the short cannon L/24 was replaced by the longer L/48. This new cannon enabled the Panzer IV to be used successfully against all tank types known at that time up to a range of 1,000 metres.

panzer crews wanted, in the autumn of 1941, was simply a tank which could beat the T-34, and not only by making a chance hit diagonally, from behind, from a range of less than 100 metres! So as not to keep halting tank production for countless improvements, the unit asked for a new tank design as a long-term project, with the following features: 'Stronger, thicker armour, better suspension and a wider track, a more powerful motor, whereby care should be taken that the power-to-weight ratio should make it possible to drive for long periods across country and along bogged tracks.'[60]

These demands were largely met by the new Panther and Tiger tanks in the years 1942–45. However, while the Russian armaments industry could raise tank production levels almost month for month, the reserves of the German war machine began to dry up. Thus the total of 6,296 panzers built in Germany was but a small fraction of the mass production of the Soviet T-34, which reached almost 40,000 by the end of the war.[61]

Not until 1943 did the German armoured force, with their Panthers and Tigers, manage to beat down the T-34s in a head-to-head conflict.[62] Thus we must ask the following question; why was the Red Army not able, in 1941, to put a stop to the advance of the inferior German panzers with their T-34 tanks?

On 22 June 1941, there were, according to Russian sources, only 957 T-34s in action.[63] Is this the answer to the question we have just asked? Not really. We will not find the answer in a comparison of tank numbers. There were 3,580 German panzers as against 10,000 or so Russian tanks.[64] Rather, we must look at Russian tactics in 1941. Andronikov and Mostovenko write, in their book on the history of the Soviet armoured units:

60. Cf. Pz. AOK 2, Abt. Ia, Anl. Nr. 16 zum KTB Nr. 1, of 18 November 1941, p. 3.
61. Cf. Knecht, *Leopard*, p. 22/23. Cf. Halle und Demand, *Illustrierte Geschichte*, pp. 96–7. Only 1,350 'Tiger I' tanks could be produced up to 1945.
62. In answer to these new Wehrmacht tanks, the Russians developed the T-34/85, the last tank in the T-34 series. It had an 85 mm cannon, which made it the worthy opponent of all German tanks. The T-34/85, produced until 1964, is still used in some Warsaw Pact countries. On the battlefield it was present in the Sinai campaign in 1967 and until 1972 in Vietnam.
63. Cf. A. Nekrich and P. Grigorenko, *Genickschuß*, pp. 88ff. Up to the end of the year, 2,810 T-34s are said to have been produced, and from 1943 to 1945 around 10,000 annually.
64. Cf. Jacobsen, *1939–1945*, p. 40. Cf. above, p. 78.

'It must be admitted that great mistakes were made in armour commitment at the start of the war. The tanks were committed in small groups, and sometimes they were even thrown into battle singly, which caused a division of power.'[65]

We will now look at the effects of this dissipation of the Russian armoured forces from the viewpoint of German war diaries:

Advance by 4 enemy tanks.[66]

Attack by infantry battalion supported by 5 tanks.[67]

Enemy attacking with 5 to 6 tanks.[68]

Russians mostly attacked in a strength of about a battalion, supported by a few tanks.[69]

Russian infantry is always accompanied by a few tanks.[70]

Because the Russian tanks were assigned in dribs and drabs, their technical superiority could not come to the fore. 'Supporting' and 'accompanying' was obviously the task of the T-34s, a fairly unfitting role for what was, at the time, the best tank in the world.

No doubt the concentrated use of T-34 regiments would have made the advance of the German armoured spearheads very difficult, but tactical concentration was not a well-known concept in Russia in 1941. From experience reports by 20th Panzer Division we can see that:

Larger units, such as a tank company in the German Army, did not attack in our sector. The Russians used their tanks mostly as accompanying vehicles for the infantry.[71]

The Russians did not know how to commit their tanks correctly en

65. J.G. Andronikov and W. Mostovenko, *Die roten Panzer*, p. 50. Cf. Zhukov, *Erinnerungen*, p. 237.

66. XXXXVII. Pz. K. Abt. Ia, Anl. Nr. 659 zum KTB Nr. 2, of 5 September 1941.

67. Ibid, Anl. Nr. 777, of 20 September 1941.

68. Ibid, Anl. Nr. 4 zum KTB Nr. 3, of 23 September 1941.

69. Pz. AOK 2, Abt. Ia, KTB Nr. 1, of 12 December 1941.

70. Ibid, p. 3, of 10 December 1941. Cf. ibid, p. 4, of 14.12. and p. 5, of 17 December 1941.

71. 20th Pz. Div. Abt. Ia, Erfahrungsbericht der Pzj. Abt. 92, of 25 October 1941.

masse and in depth. The tanks mainly fight singly, and in close contact with their infantry.[72]

The Russian commitment of armour, in dribs and drabs, did not bring them any great results.[73]

At this point we can attempt to answer the question of whether the T-34 was a decisive weapon in the war. There is no argument about the fact that this new Russian tank changed the face of armour, both during the Second World War and in the following years. And it could have changed the course of events in 1941. But because the Soviet commanders dissolved the newly-formed mechanised corps after the successful surprise attack by the German Wehrmacht, probably for reasons of training and command, and frittered away the excellent T-34s on infantry units, the Germans faced these rather than tactical armoured units.[74] Even the best tank loses its value when it is used as a single weapon, without a tactical purpose and strategic goal.

The legend has held for too long that the German Wehrmacht was beaten in Russia, not by the Red Army, but above all by 'General Winter'. Certainly the endless Russian terrain, the mud period, difficulties with supplies and not least the hard winter played a great part in the German defeat. Just as important, however, was the tough resistance of the Red Army, which, had they employed their T-34s strategically in 1941 and not just from the spring of 1942, may not have had to rely on the help of the Russian winter.

As a result of an outdated set of tactics, the excellent T-34 tank could not play a decisive role in the defensive battle against German armour in the summer of 1941. However, the war diaries are clear enough, and so we can say, together with H. Kissel: 'Looking back, it must, however, be said that the T-34 made a great contribution to the Russian victory.'[75]

72. 20th Pz. Div. Abt. Ia, Nr. 267/41 geheim, of 31 October 1941, p. 16.
73. Ibid, Abt. Ia, Erfahrungsbericht des Sch. Rgt. 59, of 5 November 1941, p. 14.
74. In the Soviet magazine *Voennyi Vestnik*, in vols. 5 and 6, 1967, appeared an article by Major-General A. Ryazansky, an excellent analysis of the tactics employed by the Soviet armoured force during the Second World War. Cf. the German translation, *Truppendienst*, vol. 6, 1967, pp. 519–22.
75. H. Kissel, 'Die ersten T-34' in *Wehrwissenschaftliche Rundschau*, vol. 3, 1955, p. 132.

9

Armour Faced by Natural Obstacles

Because the tank against tank battle is the climax or the end of every tank mission, we have gone into this in great detail. However, we must not forget that the actual combat phase is often very short. The phase of approach is usually very much longer, especially when there are natural obstacles to be overcome before the battlefield is reached.

Portrayals of tank battles during the Polish and Western campaigns, which appeared in 1939/40, bear witness, almost without exception, to a boundless optimism, an unshakeable trust in the new armoured force and its ability to overcome all obstacles. 'Nothing can halt the German tanks – they can overcome any obstacle on the way to the target.'[1]

Once again we must make it clear, from the following pages, that emotionally coloured reports, to say nothing of out-and-out propaganda,[2] have very little to do with reality, as we can see from armoured units' war diaries.

9.1 Built-up Areas

> *One thing, however, is sure and fundamental to the issue: it is a risky business to attack an able opponent in a good position.*[3]

Densely built-up areas can be made into strong defensive positions in a relatively short time and without too much effort. As

1. H.W. Borchert, *Panzerkampf im Westen*, caption to photo Nr. 31. Cf. Guderian, *Panzer in Ost und West*; F. Hess, *Der Sieg im Osten*, Berlin, 1940; E. Kabisch, *Deutscher Siegeszug in Polen*, Berlin, 1940; Ch. von Imhoff, *Sturm durch Frankreich*, Berlin, 1941.
2. Cf. OKH, *Kampferlebnisse aus dem Feldzug in Polen 1939*, Berlin, 1941; OKH, *Kampferlebnisse aus dem Krieg an der Westfront*, Berlin, 1941; OKH, *Kampferlebnisse aus dem Feldzug gegen Sowjetrußland 1941/42*, Berlin, 1943.
3. C. von Clausewitz, *On War*, p. 535.

soon as the most important roads leading through the town or village are blocked by means of obstacles, mines, and firing on top of these, the mechanised attacker is slowed down and is forced to carry out his attack metre by metre, even from house to house, a method which is costly in terms of time and manpower.

> Tanks should not be used in towns . . . When the defence is good (for example from cellars, as has often happened) the tank falls prey to this defence.[4]

> At the beginning of the campaign tanks and armoured scout cars were employed in street warfare. The losses on our side were very heavy, since the villages and gardens made it possible for the enemy to set up well-camouflaged guns and some cannon, which often did not open fire until a range of 50 metres.[5]

> According to experience, the capture of a town or village, when it runs smoothly, causes a loss of about 60 men.[6]

> Experience shows that it is only possible to approach a village at night.[7]

When we speak of densely built-up areas, we must leave out villages, which mostly consist of wooden buildings, since their obstacle value for attacking tanks is very limited, as we can see from the reports of the Polish and Russian campaigns:

> Because the lightly built Polish villages could easily be shot on fire by a few shots from the (Panzer IV's) 7.5 cm gun. The Poles were forced to evacuate the village due to the flames, and were caught in the fire of the tanks' machine-guns.[8]

> The best means of combat – shoot the village on fire. In the warm season the Russians are mostly dug in in front of or to the side of the village. Even then a burning village is valuable for the attacker (dazzling effect, destruction of the vehicles, effect on morale).[9]

Any panzer leader will, however, try to give built-up areas as

---

4. XIX. Pz. Korps Abt. Ia, Erfahrungsbericht der 3. Pz. Div. of 4 October 1939. Cf. Ibid, Erfahrungsbericht des Pz. Rgt. 5, of 1 October 1939.
5. 7. Pz. Div. Abt. Ia, Nr. 440/40 geheim, of 14 July 1940, p. 6.
6. 20. Pz. Div. Abt. Ia, Lagebeurteilung, of 31 January 1942, p. 2.
7. Ibid, p. 4.
8. XIX. Pz. Korps Abt. Ia, Erfahrungsbericht des Pz. Rgt. 5, of 1 October 1939.
9. 4. Pz. Div. Abt. Ia, Nr. 71/42 geheim, of 12 March 1942, p. 7.

wide a berth as the task and the terrain will allow: 'The division, therefore, very soon resorted to avoiding villages altogether, especially during daytime attacks, and to bypassing the villages, with the panzer companies going left and right, so that the infantry regiments could follow.'[10] An order issued on 20 November 1940 shows that German Army High Command was of the same opinion: 'If possible, the attack should go around villages and woods. While pushing past, the edges facing the unit when under attack must be held down using high explosive and smoke.'[11]

This is the end of the problem for the armoured spearhead as it travels past, but not for the infantry which is following on behind. On this point we read in a document by Panzer Group von Kleist: 'Obviously having taken into account German armour commitment up to now, the French are concentrating their defence solely on the edges of the villages, which they bitterly defend as tank-proof islands, even against the infantry following in the rear of a tank breakthrough.'[12]

And it was precisely this infantry which was the constant stumbling block during larger operations. Because so many defended islands had been left out by the tanks as they rushed forward, they had to wait around for the infantry, which had been saddled with the exhausting task of clearing the enemy from country which the tanks had merely passed through:[13] 'Again the success of the panzer attack could not be capitalized upon, since the infantrymen following behind were held up by the struggle for the outskirts of the villages.'[14]

To summarise, we must keep in mind that built-up areas are a great obstacle to tank operations, even if they can be bypassed.

9.2   Advance Through Woods

> *In Russia and Poland, on the other hand, vast tracts of land are almost completely covered by forests; if an attacker is not strong*

10. 7. Pz. Div. Abt. Ia, Nr. 440/40 geheim, of 14 July 1940, p. 6.
11. OKH, Gen. St. d. H./Ausb. Abt. (Ia), Nr. 2,400/40 geheim, of 20 November 1940, p. 8.
12. Pz. Gr. von Kleist, Abt. Ia, KTB, of 5 June 1940.
13. Cf. above pp. 61ff.
14. Pz. Gr. von Kleist, Abt. Ia, KTB, of 6 June 1940.

> *enough to get to the far side, he will be in a most difficult situation.*[15]

This statement is valid for any attacker, but especially for a mechanised one. In his memoirs, General von Arnim, in 1941 Commander of 17th Panzer Division and in April 1943 Commander-in-Chief of Army Group Africa, writes: 'The attempt to thrust through the woods south of Briansk had failed, just as in 1915 near Augustov. Armoured divisions in particular are totally unsuitable for fighting in woods; the only alternative is to swerve around them, especially when the units are so mobile.'[16] Without doubt any mechanised unit will try to find ways around woods as long as there are only limited wooded areas in its attack sector. In order to make it easier for subsequent elements, it sometimes also happens that armoured units and their grenadiers will clear such small obstacles as copses themselves: 'Surround the woods with tanks. Infantry (i.e. the unit's own armoured infantry) is to be pushed through in a wide front.'[17]

However, the situation of an attacking armoured unit becomes difficult when not just small areas but large expanses are completely covered in forest. Then the question arises of how to push through the zone without too great a loss of manpower and matériel. In the war diary of XV. Panzer Corps, we read in the entry for 18 September 1939:

'In the woods, where it is hard to see and impossible to drive, our superiority in terms of matériel could not be exploited.'[18]

Forest warfare is characterised by the fact that the battlefield is very broken, and the operational range of the heavy weapons is reduced to a minimum of about 50 to 100 metres, two very serious disadvantages for tanks. Just as in urban warfare, the lone infantryman has a good chance against the strongest enemy tank, because the latter cannot make use of his advantages. 'In heavy forest fighting the division battled its way up to the enemy position. The enemy in front of 6th Panzer Division fought grimly and made good use of the wooded terrain.'[19]

15. C. von Clausewitz, *On War*, pp. 543–4.
16. Generaloberst von Arnim, *Lebenserinnerungen*, Part VII, p. 5.
17. XIX. Pz. K. Abt. Ia, Erfahrungsbericht des Pz. Rgt. 8, of 3 October 1939.
18. XV. Pz. K. Abt. Ia, KTB, of 18 September 1939. Cf. ibid, Erfahrungsbericht of 29 September 1939.
19. Pz. AOK 3, Abt. Ia, Zwischenmeldung des Gen. Kdo. XXXXI. Pz. K. of 3 December 1941.

Without extremely close co-operation with the armoured grenadiers, a panzer advance through wooded areas is inconceivable.
On this point we read in the combat reports of various armoured
divisions:

> Forest warfare puts high demands on the infantry. In hand-to-hand
> fighting, which often occurs, the number of fighters is of great
> importance because of the limited range of weapons.[20]

> In a struggle for wooded terrain, only by co-operating very closely
> with the infantry can the mission be successful.[21]

> Tanks without infantry . . . are unusable in forests, since they see
> too little and are unable to make much use of their weapons.[22]

It would be the safest thing, and therefore always preferable, to
be able to comb through the woods along their whole width.
Only in a very few cases, however, will this be possible, because
of lack of manpower. Mostly, therefore, individual shock units
will try to go through the woods along paths or aisles without
immediate contact with one another. In a guide to forest warfare, the German Army General Staff wrote, on 20 November
1940: 'If an attack must be made through forests, it is best to
carry out the attack sector by sector; to be more exact, thrusts are
made into the woods along and on either side of the paths and
aisles running in the direction of the attack.'[23]

In answer to a questionnaire by Army High Command on the
experiences of the Eastern campaign, 4th Panzer Division reported,
on 12 March 1942:

> While advancing along roads through the woods, the unit should
> shoot itself space forward with howitzers and artillery, covering their
> deep flank by forming in depth on both sides of the path . . .
> Sweeping the sides with fire about 50 metres on either side shocks
> the enemy in most cases . . .
>   When the enemy is persistent, use thrusts by the infantry, which
> has arrived in the meantime, and which combs the edges of the
> woods on either side to a depth of 200 metres . . . Sweep the treetops

---

20. 4. Pz. Div. Abt. Ia, Nr. 71/42 geheim, of 12 March 1942, p. 6.
21. 20. Pz. Div. Abt. Ia, Gef. Bericht des Pz. Rgt. 21, of 26 November 1941.
22. 4. Pz. Div. Abt. Ia, Gef. Bericht, of 2 November 1941, p. 4.
23. OKH, Gen. St. d. H./Ausb. Abt. (Ia), Nr. 2,400/40 geheim, of
20 November 1940, p. 8.

with machine-gun and anti-tank guns against snipers, attack each enemy with shouts of 'Hurra'.[24]

The report by 12th Panzer Division, however, shows that the opposite tactic also brought good results: 'Avoid paths and aisles, there are always pockets of resistance. Do not advance in a narrow, deep line, but widely-spread and with the outer edges in echelons behind a creeping barrage.'[25]

How armoured units are to pass through woods, if there is no way round, seems not to be completely clear, even to judge by the experiences of battle-hardy tank divisions. However, any panzer leader knows that wooded country can delay or even prevent a tank advance if it is large enough.

9.3   River Barriers

> 'A major river that cuts across the line of attack is a great inconvenience to the attacker. Having crossed it he is usually limited to a single bridge, so unless he stays close to the river his actions will be severely hampered.'[26]

I do not wish to go into too much detail about river-crossing campaigns by mechanised units. It must, however, be said that large rivers are a barrier to attacking armour which are not impassable, but which always cause some degree of loss of time. For this reason any panzer leader will be eager to gain possession of the bridges in his attack sector by surprise actions, at the right time and above all without damage to the bridges themselves: 'The important thing for von Kleist's Group, on 19.5., is to win possession of the bridges on the Canal du Nord west of the line running from Cambrai to Peronne. This waterway is decisive in that it is the last body of water and the last tank obstacle before the coast.'[27]

On the other hand, the defender will try to make the water obstacle more difficult by destroying all bridges and fords,

24. 4. Pz. Div. Abt. Ia, Nr. 71/42 geheim, of 12 March 1942, p. 6.
25. 12. Pz. Div. Abt. Ia, Erfahrungsbericht, of 24 January 1942, p. 2. Even today crossing woods with armoured units is one of the most difficult phases of an attack operation. Cf. B. Grouzdev, 'Le franchissement des bois et marais par les chars', in *Revue militaire soviétique*, vol. 1, 1972, pp. 20–2.
26. C. von Clausewitz, *On War*, p. 532.
27. Pz. Gr. von Kleist, Abt. Ia, KTB, of 19 May 1940.

mining the march routes to these and aiming fire at possible crossing places. In a document from LVII. Panzer Corps we read:

> Next to the ruins of a wooden bridge there was a woodstore. In the correct assumption that this wood would be used to repair the bridge, the Russians had laid mines between the wood-piles.[28]

> A bridge had been blown up by the Russians, purposely using so much explosive that a larger crater was formed. The edge of the crater and the immediate vicinity were mined, so that vehicles which wanted to drive around the edge ran onto the mines.[29]

There can be no doubt that a mechanised attack over water will always be a risky undertaking, despite long planning and thorough preparation, and that secrecy, deception and the use of special detachments will play an important role in this. The mission and the enemy situation will dictate whether the crossing will take place at several points at once, or if all forces are to be concentrated on one point.

On 21 May 1941, General Hoth, commander of 3rd Panzer Army, told his Commanding Officer, concerning river crossings in Russia: 'Do not cross a wide front, but rather at particular points. Anything else is dissipation of power. Take hold of the enemy bank where the bridge is, and concentrate everything you have on that!'[30] So as to avoid bridgeheads, which serve to delay rather than speed up the advance of the armoured force, he went on to demand: 'Only a small bridgehead, and then advance quickly forwards . . . 3 divisions at a time, thus win space at the front. When halt at the front, keep on crossing regardless. (Turn or deploy). Vital to cross without delays.'[31] General Hoth held the same opinion in his book *Panzer-Operationen*, which appeared in 1956: 'As soon as the bridge is ready, the division's panzer regiment rolls across first . . . and thrusts further in the direction ordered without stopping in a bridgehead.'[32]

---

28. LVII. Pz. K. Abt. Ia/Pi, Nr. 237/41 Geh.Kdos., of 30 September 1941, p. 2.
29. Ibid.
30. Pz. AOK 3, Abt. Ia, Kriegsspiel 'Barbarossa', of 20/21 May 1941.
31. Ibid.
32. H. Hoth, *Panzer-Operationen. Die Panzergruppe 3 und der operative Gedanke der deutschen Führung, Sommer 1941*, Heidelberg, 1956, p. 81.

The assertion that bridgeheads are a sign of reluctance to exploit fully the power and speed of the tanks is taking things a little too far.[33] On the other hand, it is indeed important to make a deep thrust with the first wave of the attack after crossing the river, so as to prevent the enemy from directing his fire at the crossing place.

March discipline, discipline while firing, everywhere in the field of tank tactics one encounters the term 'discipline', and thus it is no surprise to see it again when overcoming river obstacles: 'Strictest bridge discipline, not just at the bridge, but also long before and after.'[34]

To summarise, then, we can keep the following in mind: rivers are no impassable obstacle for a mechanised attacker. But they are barriers in the hand of the defender, which he can, by destroying bridges and means of crossing the river, close again and again, not just in front of the attacker, but also between him and his supply columns . . .

On 12 March 1942 4th Panzer Division reported to Army High Command:

'Rivers mean loss of time. Travel to and from military bridges more difficult in Russia than elsewhere, often only possible near the wrecked bridge.

One-lane bridges badly delay the advance and supply services . . . On the bridge at Propoisk a unit en route to a mission had to wait for 16 hours, although the traffic was moving over the bridge constantly. Remedy – double-lane bridges.'[35]

33. Cf. ibid.
34. Pz. AOK 3, Abt. Ia, Kriegsspiel 'Barbarossa', of 20/21 May 1941.
35. 4. Pz. Div. Abt. Ia, Nr. 71/42 geheim, of 12 March 1942, pp. 2 and 10. Recent articles in military journals show that even today rivers have not lost their value as obstacles. Cf. K.A. Hansen, 'Zusammenwirken mit Pionieren beim Überwinden von Gewässern', in *Kampftruppen*, vol. 4, 1972, pp. 113–17. Cf. H.J. Hartung, 'Forcieren oder Überwinden von Gewässern', in *Kampftruppen*, vol. 4, 1972, pp. 123–4.

10
Tanks in Mud and Snow

I have already pointed out in this book that factors such as terrain and climate had a greater influence upon tactics because of motorisation and mechanisation.[1] Perhaps the most impressive examples of this are the 'mud period' and the onset of winter, which hit German armour just as hard, in the autumn of 1941, as did the arrival of the previously-unknown T-34 tanks. 'The suitability of the terrain for tanks is the prerequisite for the panzer attack.'[2]

10.1 Roads are no longer Roads

On 9 August 1940, Panzer Group von Kleist's war diary contained the following entry: "The unexpectedly long distances achieved on the march, also that of the purely tracked units, must, however, be partly attributed to the good weather and the excellent road system.'[3] While the armoured force had been able to drive to success in France on extremely good roads, 3rd Panzer Army, on the other hand, was fighting against great road difficulties as early as the first week of Operation Barbarossa.[4]

On 30 June 1941, at the best time of the year, the staff officer responsible for supervising the march of 3rd Panzer Army wrote in his report: 'Most of the roads aren't roads at all, but rather the worst kind of country track.'[5] Not until they got to the area of

1. Cf. above, pp. 12ff.
2. OKH, Richtlinien für Führung und Einsatz der Panzerdivision, of 3 December 1940, p. 22.
3. Pz. Gr. von Kleist, Abt. Ia, Nr. 3,422/40 geheim, of 9 August 1940, p. 2.
4. Cf. Pz. AOK 3, Abt. Ia, Tagesmeldung of 24 June 1941; Ibid, Zwischenmeldung an H. Gr. B, of 25 June 1941; Ibid, Tagesmeldung an H. Gr. B, of 26 June 1941.
5. Pz. AOK 3, Abt. Ia, Bericht des Stabsoffiziers für Marschüberwachung, of 30 June 1941.

operations did the panzer leaders find that their road maps bore no relation to reality. Added to this was the fact that in Russia only a very few roads were metalled or had a solid base. Most of them were merely narrow natural tracks, whose fine black dust immediately became sticky mud when mixed with rainwater.[6] 'Everything which was described as a road on the map turned out to be unmade, unmaintained sand-tracks.'[7]

Who could have imagined, before the summer of 1941, that a rainstorm could hold up a tank advance for several hours? Well, on 2 July 1941 the armoured reconnaissance battalion of 7th Panzer Division reported that it had halted the advance: 'because the prescribed routes have become totally boggy and impassable due to heavy rain.'[8] And what occurred in the summer months as an exception became the rule after the autumn rains. On 3 September, XXXXVII. Panzer Corps had to conclude that: 'All roads are bogged down. With the exception of a few highly-mobile cross-country vehicles, all traffic is at a standstill.'[9] There are any number of examples of how the onset of the mud period put an end to the already faint hopes of an early end to the planned blitz campaign in Russia:

> As a result of continual rainfall in the last few days, the paths have become quagmires. The divisions had travelled 20 kilometres in 10 hours.[10]

> Heavy delays in the march due to muddy roads.[11]

In the rules for the command and commitment of the armoured division, written after the Western campaign, it said that tracked vehicles could travel up to 200 kilometres per day, wheeled vehicles up to 300 km per day.[12] In the autumn of 1941, the reality was somewhat different:

---

6. Cf. F.M. von Senger und Etterlin, 'Der Marsch einer Panzerdivision in der Schlammperiode', in *Wehrkunde*, vol. 3, 1955, p. 87.

7. Pz. AOK 3, Abt. Ia, Nr. 250/42 geheim, of 10 February 1942, p. 5.

8. 7. Pz. Div. Abt. Ia, Meldung der Pz. Aufkl. Abt. 37, of 2 July 1941.

9. XXXXVII. Pz. Korps Abt. Ia, Anl. Nr. 642 zum KTB Nr. 2, of 3 September 1941.

10. 18. Pz. Div. Abt. Ia, Gef. Bericht of 7 September 1941.

11. XXXXVII. Pz. Korps Abt. Ia, Anl. Nr. 651 zum KTB Nr. 2, of 4 September 1941.

12. Cf. OKH, Richtlinien für Führung und Einsatz der Panzerdivision, of 3 December 1940, p. 30. Cf. above, p. 12.

The daily distance achieved by the Mobile Units on the road falls constantly.[13]

Movements are heavily delayed because of impassable roads. The column's speed at the moment is about 2 kilometres per hour![14]

It was recognised, with growing concern, that it was indeed the slowest, least mobile and most susceptible vehicles which determined the speed of a Mobile Unit on the march. It should not be forgotten that panzer spearheads were often only delayed because the wheeled sections of the Panzer Divisions got stuck in the Russian mud:[15] 'The roads can only be used by tracked vehicles.'[16]

Since wheeled vehicles sank up to the axles in the mud, and could only be pulled out by horses and vehicles with caterpillar tracks, many armoured units received totally unusual operational orders which had nothing more to do with blitz campaigns.[17] On 30 October 1941, XXIV. Panzer Corps sent 4th Panzer Division the following orders: 'From this moment 4th Panzer Division will take charge of road repairs, technical and tactical traffic control and towing on the track from Msensk to Chern.'[18]

10.2 Mud Dictates Tactics

The state of the terrain should be considered in any tactical decision made by a panzer leader to at least as great an extent as the enemy situation. However, during the mud period, it was not so much a question of tacticians considering the ground conditions as conditions basically dictating tactics.

13. 3. Pz. Div. Abt. Ia, Anl. Nr. 9 zum KTB Nr. 3, of 22 September 1941.

14. XXXXVII. Pz. Korps Abt. Ia, Zwischenmeldung an Pz. AOK 3, of 9 October 1941.

15. In 1941 the ratio of tracked to wheeled vehicles in a German panzer division was about 10:1.

16. XXXXVII Pz. Korps Abt. Ia, Anl. Nr. 659 zum KTB Nr. 2, of 5 September 1941. Cf. Manteuffel, 7. *Panzer Division*, pp. 185–6, 'Only by using one tank to pull two trucks each did we get our vehicles through . . . For 127 kilometres we needed 5 days.'

17. Cf. Hoth, *Panzer-Operationen*, p. 136, 'It is not the Russian winter but rather the autumn rains which are bringing the German advance to a standstill.'

18. XXIV. Pz. Korps Abt. Ia, Anl. Nr. 275b zum KTB Nr. 8, of 30 October 1941. Cf. ibid, Anl. Nr. 278, of 31 October 1941.

It was true that large-scale encircling operations were still being carried out, for example the pocket near Smolensk at the beginning of October, but the pockets could no longer be completely closed because the Mobile Units were simply not mobile enough.[19]

Marching and operational orders issued by higher command echelons were seen by armoured units more and more as recommendations, which needed to be scrutinised in terms of feasibility:

> The Corps orders that a large reconnaissance unit is to be pushed to the south tomorrow. The Division considers this to be impossible due to the bad weather.[20]

> General Guderian explained that the intentions laid down in the last tactical order were impracticable due to the weather conditions, because the state of the roads made any movement of motorised units impossible without metalled roads.[21]

It was no longer wise to speak of large armoured attacks coordinated in terms of time and place, since any long period of rain could make nonsense of prepared march tables:

> The designated departure time of 0300 hrs has had to be constantly postponed due to heavy rain and the roads which are becoming worse and worse as a result.[22]

> Because of constant rain and completely soaked roads 19th Panzer Division's attack on 29.8. is not possible.[23]

> The division's advance route from . . . to . . . has been changed via . . . because of bogged roads.[24]

On 1 November 1941, XIV. Panzer Corps reported that its planned attack would not be taking place because the artillery could not be towed away in time, the roads were impassable and the corps was being attacked from the air the whole time.[25]

---

19. 3. Pz. Div. Abt. Ia, Anl. Nr. 50 zum KTB Nr. 3, of 14 October 1941.
20. Ibid, KTB Nr. 3, of 14 October 1941.
21. XXIV. Pz. Korps Abt. Ia, Anl. Nr. 247 zum KTB Nr. 8, of 14 October 1941.
22. 7.Pz. Div. Abt. Ia, Meldung des Art. Rgt. 78, of 2 July 1941.
23. LVII. Pz. Korps Abt. Ia, Zwischenmeldung of 28 August 1941. Cf. Ibid, Zwischenmeldung of 29 August 1941 and Tagesmeldung of 7 September 1941.
24. 7.Pz. Div. Abt. Ia, Morgenmeldung des Pi. Bat. 58, of 4 October 1941.
25. Pz. AOK 2, Abt. Ia KTB Nr. 1, of 9 November 1941, p. 2.

XXXXVII. Panzer Corps was not having it any better: 'All the corps's movements are being made on foot.'[26] One day later, two divisions reported that their attack was unfeasible, since they could not close ranks due to the muddy country.[27] By way of answer they received an order wondrous in its simplicity, which had almost nothing to do with tank tactics: '17th Panzer Division is to be brought into the area . . . on foot, if necessary.'[28]

In the autumn of 1941, there was not much to be seen of surprise attacks, front breakthroughs, pocket warfare and tactical pursuit. The mud proved to be an extremely insidious enemy which could not be matched by mechanised units, still less motorised ones. After the war General Guderian wrote: 'If the state of the armoured corps was serious after the rigours of the mud period, then that of the infantry corps must be seen as hopeless and hardly feasible.'[29]

A mere 100 kilometres from Moscow, German armour missions got literally stuck in the mud in the autumn of 1941. During the successful blitz campaigns in Poland and France, this would have been a normal day's march. But now, outside Moscow, armoured units were stuck far apart, occupied with repairs on bogged roads, towing and skirmishes along the advance route.[30] The mud had brought the already exhausted German front to a standstill. Tank tactics became merely an empty phrase!

Around 110 years before the unsuccessful German blitz campaign against Russia, General von Clausewitz had written: 'Quagmires, that is, impassable terrain only crossed by a few dams, present some difficulties to the tactical attack. The strategic consequence of this is that one tries not to mount an attack there, but rather to circumvent them.'[31]

Hitler attacked Russia on 22 June, only two months before the

26. XXXXVII. Pz. Korps Abt. Ia, Anl. Nr. 464 zum KTB Nr. 3, of 8 November 1941.
27. Cf. Pz. AOK 2, Abt. Ia, KTB Nr. 1, of 9 November 1941, p. 2.
28. Ibid, of 9 November 1941, p. 5. Cf. 3. Pz. Div. Abt. Ia, Anl. Nr. 54 zum KTB Nr. 3, of 22 October 1941, 'The condition of the roads means that all infantrymen must attack on foot.'
29. H. Guderian, 'Der Vorstoß auf Tula 1941', in *Allgemeine Schweizerische Militärzeitschrift*, vol. 10, 1949, p. 749.
30. Cf. Pz. AOK 2, Abt. Ia, KTB Nr. 1, of 1 November 1941, p. 5. Cf. ibid, of 3 November 1941, p. 4, and of 4 November 1941, p. 1.
31. C. von Clausewitz, *On War*, pp. 653f.

onset of the annual autumn rains, which turn large parts of this country into almost endless quagmires.

10.3 *Passages Obligés* Help the Defender

It would be assuming too much to say that the Red Army felt fully at home during the mud period:[32] 'Tanks seem to have landed in boggy terrain. Russians can be seen trying to give the tanks some grip with the aid of planks and boards.'[33] Despite this, there can be no doubt that the Russian units had far fewer problems with the weather conditions and their consequences than the Germans. They knew what was going to happen and were prepared for it. We need only look at the T-34 tank, which, thanks to its wide tracks, could continue to attack where the Wehrmacht's panzers got stuck in the deep mud.[34]

We can see from the *passages obligés* created by the mud period that it is, to a great extent, the defender who benefits from difficult terrain rather than the attacker. While the general lack of roads had forced whole Wehrmacht divisions to use one single march route, the mud period played its part, in that it 'nailed' these columns to the tracks, as deep quagmires made any movement to the side impossible: 'These problems put a high level of strain on the divisions. They were marching in a column which was becoming longer and longer because of heavy vehicles getting stuck, without any means of deployment, so that even weak enemy resistance meant a long delay.'[35]

As a result of the mud, the Russians did not have to mine wide areas of terrain. A mined stretch of road was enough to neutralised an enemy tank division for hours: '6th Panzer Division's attack on 2.12. had to be cancelled, since . . . the advance routes are completely mined and the land either side of the road is marshy.'[36]

32. Cf. A. Phillipi, 'Das Pripjetproblem', Beiheft 2 der *Wehrwissenschaftlichen Rundschau*, 1936, p. 21.
33. 7. Pz. Div. Abt. Ia, Morgenmeldung des Art. Rgt. 78, of 2 August 1941, p. 2.
34. Cf. 4. Pz. Div. Abt. Ia, Nr. 71/42 geheim, of 12 March 1942, p. 30.
35. Pz. AOK 3, Abt. Ia, Nr. 520/41 geheim, of 10 February 1942, p. 5.
36. H. Gr. Mitte, Abt. Ia, Ferngespräch des Chefs mit General Reinhardt, of 3 December 1941.

A small force is enough in these *passages obligés* to halt a numerically superior opponent, because he is unable to deploy his fire-
power and therefore cannot commit it: 'At the same time the
regiment got an order from the division to send a strengthened
panzer company forward to . . . . . It is difficult to carry out this
order, since it is impossible to bring the company forward due to
the narrow roads.'[37] The *passages obligés* had especially serious
consequences for the supplies vital to the German divisions, and
a blocked supply line means nothing less than the paralysis of a
fighting unit: 'A single KW-II (52-ton Russian tank) blocked the
whole supply line of one division for more than 24 hours!'[38] The
situation became critical when not just one but several divisions
advanced on the same route, one after the other. In this case the
Russians, defending grimly, achieved results by means of: 'prepared artillery fire, combined with several rows of mines and air
strikes.'[39]

Co-operation between panzers and armoured infantry was also
mostly theoretical, for what use is covering fire for an armoured
regiment whose tanks are advancing in single file? 'As a
result of the marshy terrain, only one tank was able to travel at
the front with infantry support, with one exception. The battles
were merely a painful crawl forward along narrow boggy paths
or corduroy roads, resulting in many losses.'[40]

The Russians, in the autumn of 1941 far inferior in terms of
armour tactics, could gain great advantage from the fact that the
Germans were limited to single file, because the more effective
German armour strategy could no longer come into play. Thanks
to the *passages obligés*, the defenders always knew where to
expect the German armoured units. There was no longer the
surprise typical of panzer attacks.

During the mud period, German armour had to learn to its
cost that weather and the resulting difficulties in terrain can be
enemies as persistent as the opposing tanks. Against all the
rules of armoured warfare, tanks could not roll over hollows
which could give the enemy cover, and tactically worthless

37. 7. Pz. Div. Abt. Ia, Morgenmeldung des Sch. Rgt. 6, of 3 October 1941.
38. E. Raus, 'Die Panzerschlacht bei Rossienie', in *Allgemeine Schweizerische
Militärzeitschrift*, vol. 2, 1952, p. 146.
39. 4. Pz. Div. Abt. Ia, Anl. der Gef. Berichte zum KTB, 'Osterfahrungen', of
2 November 1941.
40. 12. Pz. Div. Abt. Ia, Erfahrungsbericht of 24 January 1942.

villages had to be taken in bloody struggles, while attacks had to be carried out on hills or along the edges of forests. If a tank column can no longer move away from the advance route because of the mud, then the consequences will be dire: 'Thus tank after tank rolls into the enemy line of fire which is becoming heavier all the time . . The first German panzer gets stuck, the second runs onto a mine, and the next three are destroyed by the Russian tanks.'[41] Out of the thirteen tanks which had to attack in single file, only three came back. In a few minutes, twenty-two officers and men, two platoon leaders and the company commander were killed.

For 2 November 1941, we read in the situation report issued by 12th Panzer Division: 'This struggle is above all a problem of roads and traffic as well as a problem of terrain.'[42]

10.4   Frost, a Faint Ray of Hope

Normally cold snaps are feared by the tank units because marching speed is reduced by frost and black ice. However, the situation was totally different for the German armoured units, which were stuck fast somewhere in the Russian mud. The frost was, to them, often the only way of regaining their lost mobility.

Roads and paths frozen, good to drive on.[43]

The destroyed vehicles straggling behind must be brought back to their units. This is only possible during frost. Thus every hour of frost is to be used, even at night.[44]

Using the frost, 10th Motorised Infantry Division marched into the area.[45]

Even rivers and lakes lost their obstacle value when they were covered by a 25-cm-thick layer of ice.

41. *Geschichte der 3. Panzerdivision*, p. 127.
42. 12. Pz. Div. Abt. Ia, Lagebeurteilung of 2 November 1941.
43. 7. Pz. Div. Abt. Ia, Morgenmeldung des Sch. Rgt. 6, of 15 October 1941, p. 3.
44. XXXXVII. Pz. Korps Abt. Ia, Anl. Nr. 360 zum KTB Nr. 3, of 21 October 1941.
45. Ibid, Anl. Nr. 451, of 6 November 1941. Cf. ibid, Anl. Nr. 487, of 11 November 1941.

While large bodies of water are an almost impassable obstacle in summer, they become passable when they freeze. Indeed, they can even be used as roads.[46]

According to the prisoners' statements, an enemy regiment is travelling across the ice of the reservoir north of Koslova.[47]

Driving across water on such ice roads became dangerous when, for some reason, the water level had sunk, or had been drained on purpose. 'Water level sunk 20 cm. Ice hollow, impossible to drive on it. Division blasting a channel and building eight-ton ferry.[48] The German panzer crews saw an ally in the frost also because mines no longer exploded as soon as the covering layer was frozen hard.[49]

One thing is certain – the cold snap following the mud period gave German armour a valid ray of hope – and new illusions, as we can see from the files of LVII Panzer Corps: 'Now that the frost has set in, it is possible, in my opinion, to start afresh and to reach the goal set for the corps – Moscow.[50] Did they not know that the frost was merely the foretaste of the hard, snowy Russian winter to come?

10.5 Minus 30 Degrees Centigrade Without Winter Equipment

Because the German leadership just thought in terms of blitz campaigns, High Command did not think it necessary even to take precautions for a winter war in Russia.[51] On 24 November 1941, 2nd Panzer Army had its liaison officer report to the Army Chief of General Staff: 'Winter clothing had not yet fully arrived at the unit. Some of the men were wearing fatigue trousers in temperatures of – 26°C and an icy wind, and wearing torn or

46. Pz. AOK 2, Abt. Ia, KTB Nr. 1, of 20 November 1941, p. 4.

47. Pz. AOK 3, Abt. Ia, Zwischenmeldung an Pz. AOK 4, of 14 December 1941.

48. 10. Pz. Div. Abt. Ia, Fernschreiben an XXXXVI. Pz. Korps, of 26 November 1941.

49. Cf. OKH, Merkblatt für alle Waffen, Flußübergang, Feldbefestigung und Minenverwendung bei strengem Frost.

50. LVII. Pz. Korps Abt. Ia, Chefbesprechung, of 24 October 1941, p. 2.

51. Cf. above, pp. 12f.

even no underwear.'[52] Ten days later Army Group Centre received a similar report from 3rd Panzer Army:

> Winter clothing is only partly available, and in too small a quantity. On 5.12. alone, in one division (the 6th Pz. Div.) there were 129 cases of frostbite . . . The war has thus become a struggle for shelter . . . If no new village is reached in an attack, then the attacking unit has to be taken back to its former billets.[53]

If no heated billets could be found, the soldiers were not allowed to sleep, because each had to observe the other for signs of frostbite.[54] The average strength of the companies dropped to between 35–40 men,[55] in some divisions it even dropped to 20![56]

> Due to the sudden cold snap and lack of clothing, sharp rise in colds, up to 400–500 men daily (in 2nd Pz. Army).[57]

> Thus the number of sick and frostbite cases is constantly increasing.[58]

> Winter clothing was delivered much too late. Several hundred cases of frostbite in 4th Panzer Division alone as a result.[59]

> The breakdown of frost damage shows 103 third-degree cases of frostbite. Therefore, one man in six in the battalion (marching-out strength 620 men) may have to have an amputation.[60]

Before the great cold snap in November 1941, General Nehring, the commander of 18th Panzer Division, was of the opinion that: 'A winter campaign is not pleasant, but it is feasible, like many things which did not seem feasible before.'[61] Doubtless this front-line officer still thought the unit would be equipped with at least the basic winter kit. But, in December 1941, German armoured units were not so much fighting against Russian T-34 tanks but rather against the Russian winter.

---

52. Pz. AOK 2, Abt. Ia, KTB Nr. 1, of 24 November 1941, p. 4.
53. Pz. AOK 3, Abt. Ia, Tagesmeldung an H. Gr. Mitte, of 5 December 1941.
54. Cf. XXXXVII. Pz. Korps Abt. Ia, Anl. Nr. 683 zum KTB Nr. 3, of 7 December 1941.
55. Cf. Pz. AOK 2, Abt. Ia, KTB Nr. 1, of 24 November 1941, p. 3.
56. Cf. ibid, of 23 November 1941, p. 4.
57. Ibid, of 24 November 1941, p. 5.
58. 4. Pz. Div. Abt. Ia, Gef. Bericht of 15 December 1941.
59. Ibid, Abt. Ia, Nr. 71/42 geheim, of 12 March 1942, p. 25.
60. 20. Pz. Div. Abt. Ia, Gef. Bericht des Sch. Bat. of 10 January 1942.
61. 18. Pz. Div. Abt. Ia, Nr. 044/41 geheim of 19 September 1941.

Now the winter has arrived at full force. It brings with it many problems and privations, which are almost harder to overcome than the enemy.[62]

The weather is becoming more and more the greatest enemy of our unit.[63]

Indeed, while the frost had given the bogged-down German armoured force new mobility, it also left them open to attack from the Russian air force: 'Russian planes interfered constantly with the ground battle fought by 18th Panzer Division and caused considerable losses, since our units cannot dig in because of the frost and because there are no anti-aircraft guns.'[64]

Some units suffered so much from the cold that they could no longer carry out their combat tasks. For example, from one Panzerjäger (anti-tank) unit we read: 'Members of Panzerjäger-Abteilung 10 sawed down telegraph poles carrying the most important lines to the division, in order to use them for firewood.'[65] Russian soldiers, on the other hand, wore skeepskin coats, warm hats and felt boots.[66] They knew about winter warfare and were prepared and properly equipped for it. On 1 January 1942, the Russian Lieutenant Goncharov wrote in his diary: 'Today a captured "Fritz" was brought in. Despite my contempt for him as a person, I have to feel sorry for him. Badly dressed, covered in lice, with frostbitten legs . . . And Hitler sends such poor creatures to take Moscow.'[67]

10.6 Re-equipment With Sleds

On the Eastern front winter equipment for the vehicles was missing just as it was for the men. Even small but vital things were simply not there. For example, no anti-freeze was delivered, something which put a tremendous strain on the already scarce

---

62. Pz. AOK 2, Abt. Ia, KTB Nr. 1, of 9 December 1941, p. 8.
63. LVII. Pz. Korps Abt. Ia, KTB Nr. 2, of 26 December 1941.
64. XXXXVII. Pz. Korps Abt. Ia, Anl. Nr. 516 zum KTB Nr. 3, of 15 November 1941. Cf. ibid, Anl. Nr. 590, of 25 November 1941.
65. Pz. AOK 2, Abt. Ia, KTB Nr. 1, of 7 November 1941, p. 3.
66. Cf. Guillaume, *Warum siegte die Rote Armee?*, p. 109.
67. B. Martin, 'Tagebuch eines sowjetischen Offiziers', in *Wehrwissenschaftliche Rundschau*, vol. 6, 1967, p. 353.

fuel reserves. To save fuel, the panzers were sometimes 'warmed up'[68] with a fire under the hull, which could then lead to an explosion![69]

At temperatures of as low as minus 40 degrees C, the turret gear and the sights of the tanks froze solid, all the rubber seals and gaskets became brittle, and many field guns were unusable because of stoppages.[70] Tracked vehicles which had not been moved for more than one night were often frozen so strongly to the ground that they had to be blown up to prevent them falling into the hands of the enemy.

> Immovable panzers and field guns have had to be left behind after having been blown up . . . Until now around 20 tanks, including several Panzer IV . . have had to be destroyed.[71]

> Tank drivers who have brought their vehicles through Poland, the Western campaign and now the Eastern campaign unharmed, now have to look on in despair as their tanks are destroyed.[72]

The soldiers and tanks of the Red Army, on the other hand, were equipped for winter warfare. On 5 December 1941, General Guderian reported to Army Group Centre: 'Our tanks fail while the Russian ones, obviously having better oil, seem to be better fitted for the winter.'[73] We can clearly see from the following quotations that tactics are often dictated by technical details:

> Panzer employment is strongly limited by the lack of ice-studs.[74]

> Due to thick ice the tanks of Panzer Regiment 18 cannot get over the bridge.[75]

68. Cf. Pz. AOK 2, Abt. Ia, KTB Nr. 1, of 4 December 1941, p. 9.
69. Cf. 4. Pz. Div. Abt. Ia, Gef. Bericht, of 15 December 1941, p. 11.
70. Cf. Pz. AOK 2, Abt. Ia, KTB Nr. 1, of 13 November 1941, p. 4.
71. Pz. AOK 3, Abt. Ia, Tagesmeldung des LVI. Pz. Korps of 7 December 1941.
72. 4. Pz. Div. Abt. Ia, Gef. Bericht, of 15 December 1941, p. 11. Cf. Pz. AOK 2, Abt. Ia, KTB Nr. 1, of 6 December 1941, p. 4.
73. H. Gr. Mitte, Abt. Ia, Meldung des Generaloberst Guderian, of 5 December 1941. 'Thanks to the very wide tracks the specific pressure on the ground exerted by the Russian tanks was much lower than that of the German models.' Cf. Andronikov and Mostovenko, p. 237.
74. Pz. AOK 2, Abt. Ia, KTB Nr. 1, of 13 November 1941, p. 3.
75. Ibid, of 19 November 1941, p. 6.

Panzer Regiment 6 now has six operational tanks, for which there are no ice-studs available.[76]

The tanks will not go further without ice-studs.[77]

Simply because German tanks had no ice-studs, the smallest snowdrifts, slightly sloping roads covered with snow and bridges covered with ice became insurmountable obstacles.[78]

Often bombed or mined stretches of road could not be bypassed, or made lengthy repair work necessary only because the smooth stud-less tank tracks slipped on the sides of the road. As in the mud period, armour tactics were limited more and more to one question: how could the tanks be made to move at all? One answer, if an unusual one for armoured units, can be found in an order issued by XXXXVII Panzer Corps: 'The unit must generally look after the roads it has to use. Black ice must be removed by very careful gritting, and also with the aid of pickaxes (if possible down to the earth layer).'[79] However, when the snowdrifts were over 50 cm high, even the ice-studs, which a few units received in early December, did not help a lot. 'On the way to . . . the tanks often get stuck, since the snow is very high and there is only a narrow sled-path.'[80]

Because the tanks could no longer fulfil their tasks, other means had to be sought. At the beginning of November 1941, one panzer corps issued the following order: 'It will be necessary to set up sled units in each division for patrol, reconnaissance and fighting work.'[81] The – until then – motorised infantry regiment of 18th Panzer Division was ordered to stand by as a foot, ski or sled unit, and a whole division was laconically told: 'Should the enemy move away from the division front, then you should follow immediately, on foot if necessary.'[82] The situation

76. 3. Pz. Div. Abt. Ia, Anl. Nr. 11b zum KTB Nr. 3, of 14 December 1941, p. 2.

77. 4. Pz. Div. Abt. Ia, Gef. Bericht of 15 December 1941.

78. Cf. Pz. AOK 2, Abt. Ia, KTB Nr. 1, of 10 December 1941, p. 5. Cf. ibid, of 13 December 1941, p. 3.

79. XXXXVII. Pz. Korps Abt. Ia, Anl. Nr. 663 zum KTB Nr. 3, of 4 December 1941.

80. 20. Pz. Div. Abt. Ia, Gef. Bericht der Kp. Hudel, of 1 March 1941.

81. XXXXVII. Pz. Korps Abt. Ia, Anl. Nr. 435 zum KTB Nr. 3, of 2 November 1941.

82. XXIV. Pz. Korps Abt. Ia, Nr. 295/41 geheim of 12 November 1941.

became especially critical for the supply units, which also had to be re-equipped with sleds:

> Transport of supplies by lorry was almost impossible. Small hand sleds have proved to be successful.[83]

> Delivery of supplies using other methods (sleds etc.) can only be carried out with great difficulty.[84]

> Supply services have been partly diverted onto sleds.[85]

Many mechanised and motorised units were either merged or disbanded.[86] Thus 18th Panzer Division received the order to convert most of the units into sled units. Effective tank obstacles could be made from walls of snow,[87] field guns had to be drawn on runners by hand, and supplies to tank divisions were at least partly kept up by pack-horses and dog-sleds.[88] On 18 December 1941, the C-in-C of 2nd Panzer Army ordered: 'All elements still behind the front are to be concentrated on foot.'[89] The panzer armies now differed only in name from the infantry!

10.7 Tanks in Position Warfare

After the successes in the Western campaign, the training department of German Army High Command had demanded that recruits be trained to fight in mobile warfare, and above all to attack.[90] The secret of attack is initiative and mobility – two things which are closely connected with armour. The aim of a Mobile Unit, as well as its own safety, lies in being constantly mobile. And this is equally true in defence!

Counter-attack and counter-blow are the tasks of the panzer

---

83. 20. Pz. Div. Abt. Ia, Gef. Bericht des Sch. Rgt. 59, of 6 December 1941.

84. Pz. AOK 3, Abt. Ia, Zwischenmeldung an Pz. AOK 3, of 25 December 1941.

85. 18. Pz. Div. Abt. Ia, Meldung an XXIV. Pz. Korps, of 22 February 1942, p. 5.

86. Cf. XXXXVII. Pz. Korps Abt. Ia, Anl. Nr. 637 zum KTB Nr. 3, of 30 November 1941.

87. Cf. 4. Pz. Div. Abt. Ia, Gef. Bericht, of 17 November 1941, pp. 3–4.

88. Cf. H. Gr. Mitte, Abt. Ia, KTB Nr. 1, of 10 November 1941, p. 7.

89. Pz. AOK 2, Abt. Ia, KTB Nr. 1, of 18 December 1941.

90. Cf. OKH, OB d. H./Gen. St. d. H./Ausb. Abt. (Ia), Nr. 1940/40 geheim of 29 September 1940.

units in defence, and, the weaker the defender, the more effective the commitment of mobile forces, because otherwise the
stronger attacker will make use of the space by playing the
advantage with flanking manoeuvres:[91] 'The Russians have
pushed back parts of 161st Infantry Division. 7th Panzer Division is to make a counter-thrust from the north to engage and
dislodge the enemy.'[92]

The assumption that German armour was totally halted by the
onset of winter during the Eastern campaign is only partly true.
Certainly there were extremely difficult problems which had not
been encountered before. However, had the tank units been
equipped in time for the winter, and had the supply organisation not collapsed,[93] they could have been committed successfully even after 6 December 1941, when the Russians started
their great counter-offensive.

The following war diary entries, written in the autumn and
winter of 1941, show that, even under the worst weather conditions, the employment of mobile forces in defence can lead to
good results:

The commander does not want to use the panzers as a defensive
weapon, whose effects are limited, but rather to use their power in
attack or counterthrust.[94]

The backbone of the defence was always the [Russian] tanks,
which also attacked recklessly.[95]

By means of counterattacks the situation was brought back
under our control.[96]

Breakthroughs can only be cleared up by counterattacking.[97]

Even when units are weakened, counterattack seems to be
the best form of defence.[98]

91. Cf. B.H. Liddell Hart, *Strategie*, Wiesbaden, undated, p. 353.
92. 7. Pz. Div. Abt. Ia, Meldung der Pz. Abt. 101, of 23 August 1941.
93. Cf. below, pp. 95ff.
94. 7.Pz. Div. Abt. Ia, Morgenmeldung des Sch. Rgt. 7, of 20 October 1941.
95. 20. Pz. Div. Abt. Ia, Gef. Bericht des Pz. Rgt. 21, of 20 October 1941, p. 7.
96. Pz. AOK 2, Abt. Ia, KTB Nr. 1, of 22 December 1941, p. 7, Cf. ibid, of 25
December 1941, p. 5.
97. Ibid, of 21 December 1941, p. 5. Cf. XXXXVII. Pz. Korps Abt. Ia, Anl. Nr.
698 zum KTB Nr. 2, of 8 September 1941.
98. Pz. AOK 2, Abt. Ia, KTB Nr. 1, of 23 December 1941, p. 4.

Hitler's opinion that attack was the best form of defence was correct. But his belief that static resistance was the second-best form had fatal consequences for tactics. On 1 December the Commander-in-Chief of Army Group Centre informed High Command that: 'Army Group is, at this moment, stretched over a distance of nearly 1,000 kilometres, with only one weak division as reserve to the rear.'[99] From the autumn of 1939 to the onset of winter in 1941, Germany's military commanders were almost exclusively concerned with the tactics of offensive warfare. When, in December 1941, they had to go on the defensive for a time, they faced hitherto unknown problems.

Because Hitler saw ignominious retreat in any tactical shortening of the front, which would have avoided unnecessary losses and given the German units room to mount new operations,[100] he could only give the stereotyped order to hold ground, even when there was no longer any ground to hold. Positions which were now valueless and over-extended fronts also had to be held by armoured units (!), just because territory, once gained, could not be left to the enemy. Thus 54 bunkers, 30 machine-gun emplacements and 185 foxholes were dug into the ground, which was at that time frozen to a depth of 60cm, by 3rd Panzer Division, between 14 and 20 December 1941.[101] The idea of trench warfare was not yet dead, even for the German High Command. The few tanks still in operation were no longer committed en masse, but in dribs and drabs in support of the infantry:[102] 'The panzer company is divided among individual villages in a strength of 1 to 2 tanks along a sector of over 14 kilometres.'[103]

In 1938 there was agreement in German military circles about the role of the armoured force in the event of a defensive battle, more or less. In the book *Taschenbuch der Tanks*, in any case, one could read as one of the tactical principles: 'Even in defence, the panzer attack, at the right time and in the right place, is always

---

99. H.A. Jacobsen, *1939–1945*, p. 208.

100. Cf. C. Wagener, *Moskau 1941, Der Angriff auf die russische Hauptstadt*, Bad Nauheim, 1965, p. 193.

101. Cf. 3. Pz. Div. Abt. Ia, Anl. Nr. 12 der Gef. Berichte zum KTB Nr. 3, of 20 December 1941. Cf. XXXXVII. Pz. Korps Abt. Ia, Anl. Nr. 680 zum KTB Nr. 3, of 6 December 1941.

102. Cf. 3. Pz. Div. Abt. Ia, Anl. Nr. 119 zum KTB Nr. 3, of 10 December 1941, p. 2.

103. 20. Pz. Div. Abt. Ia, Gef. Bericht des Pz. Rgt. 21, of 12 January 1942, p. 2.

more effective than static fire, and is therefore to be aimed at.'[104]

It can be no surprise that General Guderian, the creator of the strategic armoured force, was not in agreement with the inflexible defence ordered in the winter of 1941. On 17 December, therefore, he had the following report sent to Army Group Centre: 'There can be no holding of ground if the unit is thereby threatened with destruction.'[105] A statement by the Commander-in-Chief of 3rd Panzer Army shows that Guderian was not alone in his opinion:

Armour is entering the most difficult period of its existence. The commanders must recognize that retreat is a form of warfare, where they can determine the pace, rather than a calamity forced upon them by the enemy. Thus it is a mistake that this form of warfare is looked upon with contempt in German Army training. Leadership from the rear was unknown to everyone.[106]

Hitler had other ideas, and was not willing to entertain any notion of a mixture of attack and defence, to say nothing of local retreats. On 18 December 1941, the Führer ordered that the whole Eastern front must be held at all costs.[107] Three days later, General Guderian urgently tried to convince his superiors once again that to hold out in unsuitable positions would be futile: 'If no new men are sent to 2nd Panzer Army, the static defence will mean that it will be a matter of days before the front breaks down.'[108] In the knowledge that he could be court-martialled, he took some of his units back to the best available defensive positions on his own authority.[109] He reported to his immediate superior, the Commander-in-Chief of Army Group Centre, in the following telephone conversation on 25 December: 'Under these unusual circumstances, I will command my

104. *Heigl's Taschenbuch der Tanks*, Part III, p. 263.
105. Pz. AOK 2, Abt. Ia, KTB Nr. 1, of 17 December 1941.
106. Pz. AOK 3, Abt. Ia, Nr. 520/42 geheim, of 10 February 1942, p. 50/51.
107. Cf. OKH, Gen. St. d. H./Op. Abt. III, Nr. 1736/41 Geh.Kdos. Chefs. of 18 December 1941.
108. Pz. AOK 2, Abt. Ia, KTB Nr. 1, of 21 December 1941, p. 3. In the files of 3. Panzerarmee is the following about the order to halt given by Hitler, 'Just to order "Halt" means nothing. Both the unit and the commanders must also be given the means to do so.' in Pz. AOK 3, Abt. Ia, Nr. 520/42 geheim, of 10 February 1942, p. 53.
109. Cf. H. Gr. Mitte, Abt. Ia, Ferngespräch zwischen G.F.M. von Kluge and Gen. Oberst Guderian, of 24 December 1941.

army according to my conscience.'[110] However, such command methods seemed to be unacceptable to Field Marshal von Kluge, and he told Army High Command: 'He [Gen. Guderian] is a fantastic commander but he cannot take orders.'[111] Hitler took no notice of the opinions of his best panzer tacticians. On 26 December 1941, he gave an order which no responsible tank leader could follow with a clear conscience: 'In defence, every foot of ground is to be fought for to the last. Each unit, no matter which branch of the service, is bound at all costs to defend these fortified positions to the last man.'[112] For armour this meant position warfare. And for its creator the order meant removal from the command of 2nd Panzer Army: 'By order of the Führer, General Guderian is relieved of command of 2nd Panzer Army with immediate effect, and joins the Officer Reserve of Army High Command.'[113]

110. H. Gr. Mitte, Abt. Ia, Ferngespräch zwischen G.F.M. von Kluge und Gen. Oberst Guderian, of 25 December 1941.

111. H. Gr. Mitte, Abt. Ia, Ferngespräch zwischen G.F.M. von Kluge und Gen. Oberst Halder, of 25 December 1941.

112. OKW, W.F. St./Op. Abt. (H), Nr. 442,277/41 Geh.Kdos.Chefs of 26 December 1941.

113. Pz. AOK 2, Abt. Ia, KTB Nr. 1, of 26 December 1941.

11
Armoured Divisions Without Supplies

Superior enemy tanks, an opponent who is greater in number and who fights grimly, natural obstacles and an unpredictable climate – these were all factors which made the crisis facing German armour worse in the autumn of 1941. But as long as no mention is made of the breakdown of the German lines of communication, then the main factor in the failure of Operation Barbarossa has not been recognised.

The rear services and supply organisations remain in the shadow of the fighting units. Although they are seldom if ever mentioned, it is they who provide the basis for any operation involving Mobile Units. If they fail, then armour tactics become meaningless. 'The smooth functioning of the rear services is just as vital for the success of a mission as the performance of the fighting units themselves.'[1]

11.1 Longer Supply Lines by the Day

> *These arteries [supply lines], then, must not be permanently cut, nor must they be too long or difficult to use. A long road always means a certain waste of strength, which tends to cripple the army.*[2]

> *All attackers find that their strength diminishes as they advance.*[3]

---

1. XIX. Pz. Korps Abt. Ia, Befehl Guderians an alle Divisionen und Korps-truppen, of 15 September 1939.
2. C. von Clausewitz, *On War*, p. 345.
3. Ibid, p. 469.

After the Polish campaign in the autumn of 1939, the German Wehrmacht High Command let it be known: 'Yes, German supply support was one of the great miracles of this war! On any terrain, in all weather – German supply support was always there and functioned with clockwork precision.'[4] However, if one takes a short look at German tank units' war diaries, one gets the impression that Clausewitz's lines are more realistic than those of Wehrmacht High Command . . .

> During the unimpeded thrust which was tactically feasible, there were, naturally, supply problems for the units which grew larger by the day . . . Finally, the supply lines reached their maximum length, over 350 kilometres. Since the command echelons obviously did not believe that such territorial gains by motorised units were possible, it was clear that the supply organisation, although sufficient for foot soldiers, would thus be inadequate.[5]

> The ammunition reports required to be sent by the unit according to Army Service Reg. 90 did not all arrive once during the whole campaign. The reason for this was the extremely speedy advance of the units.[6]

> The necessary daily supply of 600 cubic metres was never reached, since the columns were no longer in a position to cover the distance from the unit to the destination in East Prussia – between 350 and 370 km each way.[7]

The successful blitz campaign in the West in 1940 pointed out very clearly, as did the Polish campaign, the supply problems of large-scale tank operations: 'The grouping, for the first time, of 8 armoured and motorized divisions sets great new tasks for command and supply organisations.'[8] In the war diary of Panzer Group von Kleist, we read under 5 June 1940: 'After beating down 65 enemy tanks and 4 enemy batteries, the armoured brigade continues its fight until the onset of darkness, without communication to the rear. After firing its last ammunition, down to one grenade per gun, and with no hope of getting

---

4. OKW, *Der Sieg in Polen*, Berlin, 1940, pp. 142–3.
5. XIX. Pz. Korps, Quartiermeister, Nr. 061/329 Geh.Kdos. of 3 October 1939.
6. Ibid, p. 2.
7. Ibid, p. 11–12.
8. Pz. Gr. von Kleist, Abt. Ia, Nr. 207/40 Geh. Kdos. of 14 March 1940.

more that night, the brigade returns . . . to the infantry front line.'[9]

From 10 May to 30 June 1940, supply columns of XIX Panzer Corps, commanded by General Guderian, drove on average 6,350 kilometres, which represents a mean daily distance of 160 km. The following amounts were shipped:

262 tonnes of ammunition;
1,600 tonnes of fuel;
160 tonnes of food supplies;
140 tonnes of captured matériel;
60 tonnes of prisoners;
= 2,222 tonnes in total.[10]

Although the transport companies could follow the panzers on well-metalled roads, there was often a serious shortage of fuel. On 14 June, 1st Panzer Division reported: 'Fortunately the complete lack of fuel supply can be made up for by drawing sufficient quantities from the captured fuel dump near Donjeux.'[11]

Some tank unit commanders had doubts about Operation Barbarossa as early as the summer of 1940. How could one expect the supply organisation to function in Russia when there had been difficulties in supplying fuel and ammunition in the French campaign which had only lasted six weeks? On this point, we read in the files of Panzer Group Guderian:

> Furthermore, we must consider the particular conditions of the area of operation (France), especially the availability and condition of railway lines and roads. Therefore the number of transport vehicles needed for supply purposes in the East will have to be greater than in the West.[12]

Their use will largely depend upon the condition of the roads.[13]

---

9. Ibid, Abt. Ia, KTB, of 5 June 1940.
10. Pz. Gr. Guderian, Meldung des Nachschubführers 419, of 2 July 1940.
11. 1. Pz. Div. Abt. Ia, Gef. Bericht der Gef. Gruppe Krüger, of 14 June 1940, p. 4.
12. Pz. Gr. Guderian, Abt. Qu. Nr. 01,200/40 geheim, of 6 September 1940. p. 2.
13. Ibid, p. 4.

Based on the experience obtained during the French campaign, the German High Command published guidelines for the operation of the Panzer Division in December 1940, which included the following: 'Fuel replenishment, maintenance and repair of vehicles often have a decisive influence upon the command of the division on the way to and during combat. Any movement and any employment of the panzer division demands careful preparation and timely execution.'[14] It appears that the highest echelons of command had realised that moving a panzer division is mostly a question of supply support. Therefore one cannot help but wonder why Operation Barbarossa was launched although the Wehrmacht had been suffering from fuel shortage from the first day of the campaign.[15]

After the limited blitz campaign in the West, General Nehring had demanded: 'Stay as remote as possible! Use the engine! Think motorised!'[16] During the Eastern campaign perhaps they stayed a little too remote and thought a little too motorised. In any case, it is clear that too little thought was given to supplies, because as soon as mechanized units are sent into enemy territory they need a great number of well-equipped bases to provide supplies, replenishment and repair support. However, such bases were lacking in the Russian campaign from the very first day since: 'it was not possible to set them up due to the constant rush forward'.[17] As early as 25 July 1940, the German Army High Command noted with growing alarm that: 'The number of [supply] trains is not yet commensurate with the needs of a large-scale operation.'[18] And the attack operations grew larger in scale every day, and the lines of communication grew longer from day to day!

Only a small percentage of the supplies could be shipped by rail because the Russian railway tracks first had to be changed to the German gauge. Thus the lion's share of the burden lay with the transportation companies which, however, ran into prob-

14. OKH, Richtlinien für Führung und Einsatz der Panzerdivision, of 3 December 1940, p. 37.
15. Cf. H. Greiner, *Die Oberste Wehrmachtführung 1939–1943*, Wiesbaden, 1951, pp. 337–8.
16. 18. Pz. Div. Abt. Ia, Nr. 90/40 geheim, of 28 November 1940.
17. OKW, KTB vom Wehrwirtschafts- und Rüstungsamt, Wi. Rü. Amt/Stab, of 29 December 1941, p. 2.
18. Halder, KTB, vol. 3, p. 118, of 25 July 1941.

lems in the first days of the campaign because of the lack of roads: 'The supplies could not be brought up on time because 4th Panzer Division, which was following 3rd Panzer Division, was blocking the road.'[19] Despite this, it is astounding that many transportation companies accumulated an unbelievable mileage by the autumn of 1941. For instance, in only eight weeks, the supply vehicles of one panzer division travelled: 303,982 kilometres hauling ammunition:[20] 199,385 kilometres hauling fuel; 63,073 kilometres hauling spare parts, etc.[21] However, as the planned blitz campaign began to drag on and the supply line for some front-line units varied between 500 and 1,000 kilometres,[22] it finally became clear that the combat and support elements had to form one indivisible unit.[23]

German logistics were totally over-taxed after the onset of the mud period and during the hard winter months. The distance covered by the trucks dropped almost to zero, and:

kilometre-long corduroy roads had to be built to move the scarce supplies forward to the units.[24]

Units cannot go further away from the railheads than can be reached by horse and sled.[25]

Constant replenishment of ammunition is not feasible with the trucks at our disposal because of the great distance from the distribution point.[26]

On 24 November 1941, the liaison officer of 2nd Panzer Army to Army High Command briefed the Chief of General Staff on the supply situation in the Panzer Army. He explained:

19. 3. Pz. Div. Ia, Anl. Nr. 17, II/30 to KTB Nr. 3, of 27 June 1941.
20. 'A single tank battalion (Pz. IV and V, the author) required 31 4.5-ton trucks to load 40 tanks with ammunition.' Quoted from Guderian, *Panzer-Marsch*, p. 80.
21. Cf. Temmelsfeld, 'Der Nachschub (mot.)', in *Die Panzertruppe*, vol. 11, 1941, p. 173.
22. The distance from the Polish demarcation line to the River Dnjepr was about 500 kilometres, to Smolensk about 700 and to Moscow about 1,000 kilometres.
23. Cf. Guderian, *Panzer-Marsch*, p. 79.
24. Guderian, 'Der Vorstoß auf Tula 1941' in *Allgemeine Schweizerische Militärzeitschrift*, No. 10, 1949, p. 749.
25. Pz. AOK 2, Abt. Ia, KTB Nr. 1, of 10 November 1941, p. 7.
26. XXXXVII. Pz. Korps Abt. Ia, Anl. Nr. 699 zum KTB Nr. 3, of 5 December 1941, p. 3.

> The matériel and human fighting power of the units . . . does not permit major operations.
>
> The Army is living merely from hand to mouth. It is impossible to make a cache of rations either in winter (snowdrifts on roads and rail lines etc.) or in spring (road impassable). Living off the land is only possible to a very limited extent.[27]

The German supply lines not only grew longer day by day but also worse because of the weather. General Thoma was right when he said: 'In modern mobile warfare the main thing is no longer tactics. The deciding factor is the organisation of supplies in order to keep things moving.'[28]

11.2 Partisans Against Supply Convoys

> *The main weak points of an attack that penetrates deeply are, of course, the long lines of communication.*[29]

> *Overall (attack) strength is depleted: . . . By the invading armies' need to occupy the area in their rear so as to secure their lines of communication and exploit its resources.*[30]

Although the priority in mobile warfare is not so much the gaining of ground as the destruction of the enemy, the areas not physically occupied by the tanks but only run through command the closest attention. Through these areas run the lines of communication, and along these lines vast amounts of supplies for the armoured units have to be moved. 'To use tanks against partisans is a luxury which one can seldom afford.'[31] On the other hand, for the Russians it was no luxury to use partisans against supply convoys en route to the armoured units. When German transport companies had to travel hundreds of kilometres to supply front-line units, security on the road became impossible. For example, if only a few panzers had been used to cover the convoys, there would have been only infantry divisions left to fight on the Eastern front!

27. Pz. AOK 2, Abt. Ia, KTB Nr. 1, of 24 November 1941, p. 3.
28. Liddell Hart, *Jetzt dürfen sie reden*, p. 300.
29. C. von Clausewitz, *On War*, p. 476. Cf. ibid. pp. 345f.
30. Ibid, p. 527.
31. Guderian, *Panzer-Marsch*, p. 154.

During the Polish campaign, and in the West, there was little partisan activity against German supply convoys. One reason why this activity increased from the very beginning of the Russian campaign can be found in the files of Army Group Centre:

> While the encircled enemy, in the West and also in the Polish war, usually gave up at the end of the battle, and let themselves be taken prisoner almost to a man, the situation here [in Russia] will be very different. A high proportion of the Russians are still at large in wide areas of terrain, some of which have still to be combed, in woods, in cornfields, in marshes and so on.
>
> In this connection, whole bands of armed partisans will continue to pose a threat to the rear areas for some time.[32]

Because, in the summer of 1941, German panzer divisions had thrust deep into Russia along a very few routes, stragglers from Red Army units and organised partisan groups[33] had almost unlimited room to manoeuvre. As early as the second day of the campaign, 3rd Panzer Army reported: 'There was an increase in resistance by enemy stragglers in some areas to the rear of the Panzer Corps.'[34] On 3rd July 1941, LVII. Panzer Corps sent a message to 3rd Panzer Army which read as follows: 'In the rear area there are unknown numbers of Russians lurking in the woods, who cannot be captured by the Corps with its present manpower, but who pose a serious threat to supply convoys.'[35] Even attacks by small bands of partisans, because of the element of surprise, were so effective that some armoured units had their entire crews guarding the tanks at night.[36]

During the mud period and the subsequent winter, the threat of partisan attack increased, for what would have been more tempting for them than to attack almost-immobilised tank convoys, and especially supply convoys? 'XXXXVII. Panzer Corps

---

32. H. Gr. Mitte, Abt. Ia, Nr. 86/41 Geh.Kdos. of 29 June 1941.

33. Cf. B.S. Telpuchovski, *Die sowjetische Geschichte*, p. 103, 'The objective is to create intolerable conditions for the German invaders, to disorganise their communication system, their supply support and the units themselves.' Cf. J.J. Minz et al, pp. 60–2.

34. Pz. AOK 3, Abt. Ia, Tagesmeldung an AOK 9, of 23 June 1941.

35. LVII. Pz. Korps Abt. Ia, Fernspruch an Chef Pz. AOK 3, of 3 July 1941.

36. Cf. 3. Pz. Div. Abt. Ia, Anl. Nr. 11b zum KTB Nr. 3, of 14 December 1941.

reports an increase in partisan activity.'[37] Almost daily, in the rear of the German tank units, roads were mined, and bridges and railway lines blown up.[38] It seemed at times that it was the tanks who were encircled, as the often poorly armed partisans cut off the supply lines so essential to their mission:

> The supply route to the division appears to be under serious threat from fresh enemy forces arriving from the north.[39]

> Supply support is seriously threatened by partisans. Whole regions are completely controlled by them.[40]

We cannot go into greater detail on this subject within the confines of this book,[41] but it is worth mentioning that women and children had an important part in many partisan attacks:

> At 2015 hrs, we picked up a boy aged between 13 and 15, carrying on him low level codes, instructions on the use of radio sets and on signalling with lamps. He was trying to get into the encircled areas. Having been proved guilty beyond doubt, he was shot.[42]

> One partisan band was led by Maria D . . . This group filled several wells with earth, destroyed important bridges and cut telephone wires. On one occasion they succeeded in capturing two German motorcycle messengers. From them they learned that a convoy carrying spare parts for tanks was due to pass by that night. The group went into hiding. The convoy was attacked in the early hours of the morning on a narrow forest road. Eight trucks were destroyed and the spare parts were thrown into the marsh.[43]

Small children often worked closely with Red Army units as scouts and agents, thus inflicting heavy losses upon German transportation companies.

> Recently, a partisan group of children, led by two 12-year-old-boys, carried an explosive charge under a bridge. Under cover of darkness,

37. Pz. AOK 2, Abt. Ia, KTB Nr. 1, of 20 November 1941, p. 2.
38. Cf. ibid, KTB Nr. 1, of 13 December 1941, p. 2, and ibid, of 17 December 1941, p. 4.
39. Ibid, of 4 December 1941, p. 3.
40. OKW, KTB of Wehrwirtschafts- und Rüstungsamt, Wi. Rü. Amt/Stab, Geh.Kdos. of 29 December 1941.
41. Cf. E. Hesse, *Der Sowjetische Partisanenkrieg*.
42. 7. Pz. Div. Abt. Ia, Morgenmeldung des Sch. Rgt. 6, of 10 October 1941.
43. E. Hesse, *Der Sowjetische Partisanenkrieg*, p. 112.

also making use of the fact that the sentries had dozed off, they placed the charge in the correct position, lit the fuse and disappeared into the woods just as the bridge exploded.[44]

On this occasion Eugen Zelinski, 13, and his friend Paul Tropko discovered the position of German units and gave the necessary information to the commander of a Soviet tank platoon. The platoon wasted no time in attacking and destroying the enemy troops.[45]

During the Eastern campaign the German armoured force found to their cost that they could be fought most effectively without being involved in open battle:

Fighting on and close to the road. Enemy troops not completely neutralised in the area between routes of advance; will pose threat to flanks and supply convoys.[46]

Command in the East is mainly a problem of supply support.[47]

11.3   The Fuel Supply Determines the Mission

Each driver is responsible for replenishing his vehicle's fuel tanks in good time.[48]

A motorised unit's fuel supply must be planned in advance. This is the responsibility of all tactical commanders.[49]

These guidelines may be justified on the training ground, but, on the other hand, somewhere in Russia, tank drivers and their commanders could not be expected to make sure that fuel was replenished in good time. The Commander-in-Chief of 1st Panzer Army is supposed to have said: 'No Russians in front of us and no supplies behind us!'[50]

There will always be short-term supply problems when large armoured units are advancing. Even in a successful blitz campaign

44. Ibid, p. 111.
45. Ibid, p. 112.
46. 4. Pz. Div. Abt. Ia, Nr. 71/42 geheim, of 12 March 1942, p. 1.
47. Ibid, p. 18.
48. H. von Manteuffel, 'Marschtechnik motorisierter Verbände', in *Die Kraft-fahrkampftruppe*, vol. 6, 1938, p. 221.
49. Kdo. der Panzertruppen, Id, Nr. 3,370/37, Besichtigungsbemerkungen des Kommandierenden Generals der Panzertruppen im Jahre 1937, p. 5.
50. E. Bauer, *Der Panzerkrieg*, p. 222.

such as in Poland, panzer corps suffered temporary fuel shortages. On 14 September 1939, for example, XIX. Panzer Corps reported to Army Group North: 'The fuel situation had been very tense, both yesterday and today, as a result of the long lines of communication, and is a cause of great concern.'[51] Two days later the situation was even described as critical: 'Major elements of each division immobilised by the lack of fuel.'[52] After the six-week-long campaign in France the Chief of General Staff of Panzer Group von Kleist noted this in a draft on the operation of Mobile Units: 'The success of Mobile Unit commitment depends on a constant supply of fuel.'[53]

While the shortage of fuel, in the campaign against Poland and France, was a result of minor slip-ups, it remained a major problem for the German armoured units throughout the Russian campaign. To provide better understanding of the fuel supply problems, I will give a few figures. On good roads a German Panzer Mark III or IV consumed 300 litres of fuel per 100 kilometres,[54] therefore the consumption of the 200 or so tanks in a division was already 60,000 litres! This figure must be multiplied by two or three during cross-country operation. 'For each armoured division one must assume a fuel consumption rate of about 200 cubic metres. This represents the capacity of four large fuel convoys.'[55]

As we have seen, the mud period in the autumn of 1941 reduced the average speed of such convoys to as little as two kilometres per hour[56] and the supply lines, threatened by partisans, grew longer each day!

The war diaries of the armoured units record the consequences of the disastrous fuel situation:

5th Panzer Brigade's attack had to be postponed because there was no fuel available.[57]

---

51. XIX. Pz. K. Abt. Ia, Abendmeldung of 14 September 1939.

52. Ibid, Meldung an H. Gr. Nord of 16 September 1939.

53. Pz. Gr. von Kleist, Abt. Ia, Chef d. Gen. St., Richtlinien für die Führung Schneller Gruppen, outline of 20 October 1940, p. 46.

54. Cf. H. Dv. 470/7, Ausbildungsvorschrift für die Panzertruppe, of 1 May 1941, p. 80.

55. Pz. Gr. Guderian, Abt. Qu. Nr. 01,200/40 geheim, of 6 September 1940, p. 23.

56. Cf. above, p. 173.

57. 4. Pz. Div. Abt. Ia, Gef. Bericht, of 11 August 1941, p. 6.

The combat trains cannot move fuel forward to the artillery and tanks. Apart from this, the division, even after re-allocation of fuel among the units, can only travel about 20 or 30 kilometres before coming to a complete standstill.[58]

However, division elements that have arrived in Kalinin have no tank support because tanks have been immobilised by the lack of fuel.[59]

The leading tank had been hit by anti-tank fire and the others were put out of action because of shortage of fuel.[60]

All companies are immobilised now because of lack of fuel.[61]

At the beginning of October 1941, the commander of XXIV. Panzer Corps reported to 2nd Panzer Army that the state of the roads at that time would be favourable to an advance, but 'that only the lack of fuel is making any further advance by the Corps impossible'.[62]

XXXXIX. Panzer Corps let it be known, on 6 November, that the attack could not under any circumstances be continued until 12 November, because of the supply situation.[63]

It became more and more clear that the tactical and strategic situation of the German armoured units could be dictated just as much by the shortage of fuel as by terrain and weather conditions, or by the enemy situation. 'The enemy situation on the east flank still seems so favourable that we have freedom of operation. It is merely a question of fuel as to whether we can exploit this freedom.'[64]

In many units, lack of oil had an effect no less disastrous than lack of fuel. Thus, during 4th Panzer Division's thrust towards Kiev, around 50% of the tanks went out of action simply because of inadequate oil deliveries.[65] Because the tanks had to be driven in first gear, often for days at a time, because of the difficult terrain, the engines began to 'drink' oil!

---

58. 20. Pz. Div. Abt. Ia, Meldung an LVII. Pz. Korps of 2 September 1941.
59. Pz. AOK 3, Abt. Ia, Tagesmeldung des XXXXI. A.K. of 21 October 1941.
60. 4. Pz. Div. Abt. Ia, Gef. Bericht of 1 November 1941, p. 6.
61. 4. Pz. Div. Abt. Ia, Gef. Bericht der Pz. Brig. 5, of 4 November 1941, p. 7.
62. XXIV. Pz. Korps Abt. Ia, Anl. Nr. 232 zum KTB Nr. 8, of 5 October 1941.
63. Cf. XXXIX. Pz. Korps Abt. Ia/Op. Nr. 11/41, of 6 November 1941.
64. Pz. AOK 2, Abt. Ia, Meldung des XXIV. Pz. Korps, of 19 November 1941, p. 2.
65. 4. Pz. Div. Abt. Ia, Nr. 71/42 geheim, of 12 March 1942, p. 18.

Already (on 6 August 1941) many vehicles are consuming 20 to 30 litres of oil per 100 kilometres instead of the normal $\frac{1}{2}$ litre of oil.[66]

The 2nd Company of the Regiment is forced to leave several vehicles behind at the present position due to lack of oil.[67]

A report by 3rd Panzer Army of 17 October shows that Mobile Units could not possibly be supplied with fuel and oil by means of airlifts in the winter of 1941: 'The average amount of fuel supplied daily by the Luftwaffe is 30 to 50 cubic metres, and the consumption of a single panzer division (3rd Panzer Army, at that time, comprised 4 panzer divisions and 3 motorised infantry divisions) is 220 cubic metres!'[68] In November 1941 Guderian's 2nd Panzer Army received about 300,000 litres of fuel. Over 1,000,000 litres were necessary.[69] The war diaries are quite clear on this point – large mechanised units can only achieve outstanding results when there is also outstanding fuel supply support.

11.4 Breakdowns Due to Lack of Spare Parts

Fuel and ammunition supplies are essential for any Mobile Unit operation. On the next pages we shall see that these supplies are by no means the only ones which are essential.

The German armoured force lost only a few tanks during the Polish campaign as a result of enemy action.[70] Thus the report of the Quartermaster of XIX. Panzer Corps must seem all the more critical: 'The complete failure of the supply services to deliver spare parts had a noticeable effect on all tracked vehicles, that is, tanks and tractors. The very high number of breakdowns . . . would have been avoided if there had been a planned, regular supply support.'[71]

As early as the second day of the Western campaign (road and weather conditions were good, enemy resistance very light),

---

66. LVII. Pz. Korps Abt. Ia, Anl. Nr. 429 zum KTB Nr. 1, of 6 August 1941.
67. 4. Pz. Div. Abt. Ia, Gef. Bericht der Pz. Brig. 5, of 30 August 1941, p. 7.
68. Pz. AOK 3, Abt. Ia, Morgenmeldung an AOK 9 zur Weiterleitung an H. Gr. Mitte, of 17 October 1941.
69. Cf. Pz. AOK 2, Abt. Ia, KTB Nr. 1, of 16 November 1941, p. 5.
70. See above, p. 4.
71. XIX. Pz. Korps Abt. Qu, Nr. 061/39 Geh.Kdos, of 3 October 1939, p. 14.

Panzer Group von Kleist reported to Army Group A: 'temporary tank breakdowns due to heavy strain.'[72] Technically advanced weapons remain available for commitment only if they are always treated with the necessary care. For the tankman that means that after every journey, even short ones, a maintenance stop is carried out.[73] Should daily or weekly stops be omitted for weather reasons, the consequences will be dire. On 1 June 1940, after only three weeks' mission, the war diarist of Panzer Group von Kleist noted: 'Only 50% of the tanks in the Panzer Divisions are available for assignment as there has been no real time for rest and maintenance.'[74]

Even during what are termed blitz operations or even blitz campaigns, tank units have to be given time to overhaul their vehicles properly. During Operation Barbarossa this time was missing from the beginning! This had much more negative effects here than in the two blitz campaigns of 1939 and 1940 because road and weather conditions in Russia ate away at the wheeled and tracked vehicles in a manner not seen before. On 16 July 1941, 10th Panzer Division reported to XXXXVII. Panzer Corps:

During the last 100 kilometres, 24 tanks have broken down, their engines irreparable, because of a build-up of dust which has sprung up from nowhere.

This dust, which cannot be kept out by air filters, has such an abrasive effect, in conjunction with motor oil, that there is a sharp drop in power and the engines are no longer able to propel the tanks forward.[75]

Worse still was the position of 18th Panzer Division, as a situation report of 20 July shows:

Marching-out strength: 210 = 100% (tank strength)
Total write-offs: 37 =   18%

---

72. Pz. Gr. von Kleist, Abt. Ia, Meldung an H. Gr. A, of 11 May 1940.

73. A tank unit needs 45 minutes during the day and 75 minutes during the night to prepare for combat after a march. Cf. 18. Pz. Div. Abt. Ia, Nr. 55/40 geheim, of 20 November 1940, p. 10.

74. Pz. Gr. von Kleist, Abt. Ia, KTB, of 1 June 1940. Cf. ibid, Tätigkeitsbericht des Ia dated 12 July-30 September 1940.

75. 10. Pz. Div. Abt. Ia, Meldung an XXXXVI. Pz. Korps of 16 July 1941.

Available for assignment
with reservations: 47 = 22%
In need of repair: 126 = 60%[76]

Because Hitler was convinced that the campaign against Russia would be over in a matter of weeks, he urged the tank wedges to charge forward without rest, although in the guidelines for the operation of panzer divisions it said: 'After 4 to 5 days of a mission, the armoured units must be given the necessary time to prepare for action once again.'[77] We can see where disregarding this important order led to when we look at an entry in the war diary of Army Group Centre from 22 August 1941: 'The armoured units are so battle-weary and worn out that there can be no question of a mass operative mission until they have been completely replenished and repaired.'[78] As, to cap it all, the mud period set in, the supply of spare parts began to dry up.[79] Breakdowns due to lack of spare parts assumed hitherto unknown proportions. For example, 18th Panzer Division lost 59 tanks due to enemy action and accident, but 103 tanks because of shortage of spare parts![80] Thirty tanks were still fully operational, about 12% of total strength.[81] And they described such an outfit as an armoured division![82]

As early as mid-September 1941, the armoured divisions of 2nd Panzer Army had only the following operational strength:

3rd Pz. Div.   20%
4th Pz. Div.   29%
17th Pz. Div. 21%
18th Pz. Div. 31%[83]

Because one could no longer talk of a 'panzer army' under those circumstances, General Guderian requested permission to form

76. 18. Pz. Div. Abt. Ia, Zustandsbericht, of 20 July 1941.
77. OKH, Richtlinien für Führung und Einsatz der Panzerdivision, of 3 December 1940, p. 33.
78. H. Gr. Mitte, Abt. Ia, KTB Nr. 1, of 22 August 1941.
79. Cf. 18. Pz. Div. Abt. Ia, Anl. Nr. 1 zum Zustandsbericht der Div. Nachsch. Fü 88, of 31 October 1941.
80. Cf. 18. Pz. Div. Abt. Ia, Zustandsbericht des Div. Ingenieurs, of 4 November 1941.
81. Cf. ibid.
82. Cf. General von Arnim, *Lebenserinnerungen*, Part VII, p. 6.
83. F. Halder, KTB, vol. 3, p. 231, of 14 September 1941.

one full division from the four decimated ones, and to send the other three divisions home for repair and replenishment.[84] Army High Command, however, would hear nothing of such proposals, and thus there were armoured units still on the Eastern front which now barely deserved the name. On 12 November, Panzer Company 100 had 5 tanks for a mess strength of 720 men.[85] 18th Panzer Division had 18 tanks ready for action.[86]

Why did breakdowns due to shortage of spare parts occur during the Russian campaign in any case? One cause was, without doubt, the great variety of vehicles used by the Germans. In one armoured division, there were no less than 96 different types of personnel carrier, 111 types of truck and 37 types of motorcycle, truly a desperate situation for the repair-shop company.[87] In addition to this, most of the technical defects only became apparent after a phase of increased strain such as the advance on Moscow.[88] From 22 June to the November of 1941, German tanks had travelled a distance of about 4,000 kilometres.[89] 4,000 kilometres under the toughest terrain and climatic conditions, without the rest periods necessary for repair and maintenance work on the worn-out vehicles.

At the beginning of 1942, German Army High Command sent questionnaires to all divisions in order to gain insight into why the blitz campaign against Russia failed. In view of the disastrous amount of breakdowns due to lack of spare parts, the command staff of 4th Panzer Division made their point very clearly:

> The higher command echelons became used to acknowledging appeals for help from units concerning spare parts for vehicles and so on, without taking any steps, because our luck continued to hold regardless and the Division achieved what was supposed to be impossible.

84. Cf. Pz. AOK 2, Abt. Ia, KTB Nr. 1, of 11 November 1941, p. 5.

85. Cf. ibid, of 12 November 1941, p. 4.

86. Cf. 18. Pz. Div. Abt. Ia, Meldung an XXIV. Pz. Korps, of 22 February 1942, p. 4.

87. Cf. ibid, Abt. Ia/V, Anl. Nr. 3 zum KTB Nr. 3, of 3 November 1941, p. 7.

88. For example, a) torsion rod failure; b) cranskshaft failure; c) tearing away of shock-absorbers; d) suspension-spring failure; e) rust attack on cylinders; f) breaking of caterpillar-track links.

89. Cf. 18. Pz. Div. Abt. Ia, Zustandsbericht des Div. Ingenieurs of 4 November 1941, p. 3.

This led to the fact that on 5 December 1941 (the day before the start of the withdrawal), the Division had at its disposal only: 15% of its tanks; 30% of its personnel carriers; 34% of its trucks; 10% of its motorcycles.[90]

90. 4. Pz. Div. Abt. Ia, Nr. 71/42 geheim, of 12 March 1942, p. 3.

Conclusion

The blitz campaigns carried out by the German Wehrmacht against Poland and France during the period 1939–40 are rightly seen as milestones in military history.

While the Polish and French High Commands, in an outdated reliance upon linear defences, utterly wasted their armoured forces on supporting roles for the infantry, German armoured divisions were committed as the strategic factor in modern mobile warfare. Using the advantage of surprise characteristic of mechanised operations, German panzer wedges penetrated the enemy lines, which were prepared for position warfare. Realising that the surprise raid was more suited to the nature of armour than the planned and executed attack, German tank leaders rolled deep into the enemy's hinterland at the head of their units; independent of their infantry and without fear of leaving their flanks open, they forced the enemy to fight with reversed front. Large-scale envelopment, battles of encirclement and, on the part of those being attacked, confusion, sometimes mass flight and often completely demoralised soldiers were the visible signs of these new armour commitments, based as they were on Guderian's ideas.

After the six-week-long blitz campaign against France the German Wehrmacht had, in 1940, gained experience in the use of large armoured units which no other army in the world possessed. But because the French High Command had fought a war of missed opportunities, the German armoured force had been spared many difficult situations.

For this reason Hitler above all seemed to have lost sight of the limits of mechanised operations and of what could be achieved. On 18 December 1940, he issued Directive No. 21 under the code-name 'Barbarossa'. Russia was to be conquered in a blitz campaign, as were France and Poland.

On 22 June 1941, however, it was not the German Wehr-macht's third blitz campaign which was launched, but rather a war of attrition, which lasted years. It was true that, at the beginning, the brilliantly-led German armoured divisions pene-trated deep into the enemy's border areas, but, after only a few weeks, the results of faulty assessment of the situation became apparent. Surrounded by the dangerous aura of invincibility, the German High Command had underestimated the strength of the Red Army and had not sufficiently considered the condi-tions of climate and terrain in the Eastern theatre of war when preparing for the campaign.

The vastness of Russia, advance routes full of mines and later on, supply routes full of mud, as well as natural obstacles in hitherto-unknown numbers – all these proved to be just as per-sistent enemies as the technically superior Red Army tanks for German armour, accustomed as it was to victory.

The fact that the German infantry was left far behind, and the artillery was stranded in the mud; the lack of air support; the fact that the supply routes became longer each day; an inadequ-ate supply of fuel, breakdowns due to shortage of spare parts and, finally, the need to change tank companies into sled companies; these and other similar problems played a large part in determining German armour tactics.

German armour had to pay dearly for Hitler's unsuccessful attempt to defeat an enemy who was superior in terms of matériel, without preparing carefully enough, with limited means on limitless terrain.

Appendixes

Appendix I

Extracts from war diaries; Pz. AOK 2; AOK: Orel

Portrayal of the events of 21 December 1941

XXIV. Pz. Corps

The Commander-in-Chief of 2nd Pz. Army makes the following statement concerning the war of rigid defence ordered by the Führer, the directive saying that all units are to remain in position and defend to the last man.

The Army and the subordinate units are imbued with a desire to make a stand, and are utterly convinced of the need to do so. Any further withdrawal will lead to a loss of matériel and horses, and will sap the strength of the units to a greater or lesser extent, depending on how bad weather conditions, i.e. cold and snow, will be, without at the same time weakening the Russians, due to their greater winter mobility.

If, however, the order is carried out inflexibly, we run the considerable risk of failure. Our front is stretched to the limit, and we have no reserves. The Russians have advantages over us. They are close to their good rail network. They can move both strategically and tactically, thus concentrating their effort when and where they choose.

This must lead to penetrations and breakthroughs. These can only be cleared up by launching a counterattack. We do not have the manpower to do this on a front which is under attack, where one weak division has to hold a section averaging 25 km in width. When there is no manpower available to launch a counterattack, the only alternative is a local withdrawal, together with counterthrusts, so as to bring the situation back under control.

We are, at the moment, forced by the Führer's order, strictly interpreted, to face the enemy attacks in positions which are totally unsuitable for defence, although there are far more favourable sectors in the rear, some of them tank-proof.

The consequences of an over-strict interpretation must surely be encirclement and, therefore, the destruction of the encircled elements which, due to lack of reserves, can neither have a path cut through for them nor be received once they have broken through. Also, the Army could be destroyed before the expected reserves arrive. Thus, for example, if there were breakthroughs near 9th Pz. Div. and along the whole loose line of 95th Inf. Div., it would be impossible to hold the present line, which cannot be called a position; the encirclement of these elements would be inevitable even if they fought with the highest bravery.

In full awareness of my responsibility, I hereby point out the consequences of an inflexible, literal execution of the Führer's order and request permission to interpret it according to the above explanation.

Source: Pz. AOK 2, Abt. Ia, KTB Nr. 1 dated 21 December 1941 (RH 21-2/v.277)

Appendix II

Extracts from war diaries; Pz. AOK 2 AOK: Orel Weather: Snowstorm

Portrayal of the events of 26 December 1941

Final occupation and further fortification of the Susha-Oka line.

Further enemy advance into the gap between 2nd Pz. Army and 4th Army; Lichwin is abandoned. Command of 2nd Pz. Army passes from Gen. Guderian to Gen. der Trp. Schmidt. 04.35: By order of the Führer General Guderian is relieved of command of 2nd Panzer Army with immediate effect, and joins the Officer Reserve of Army High Command.

General der Panzertruppen Schmidt takes over command of 2nd Pz. Army, retaining command of 2nd Army until Gen. Frhr. von Weichs returns.

LIII. Army Corps

10.15: The subordinate corps are informed by radio that, according to the report by the Air Corps' weather station, a drop in temperature to as low as −35°C is expected.

XXIV. Pz. Corps

4th Pz. Div's advance into the area around Belev has been delayed due to heavy snowdrifts. During the day the Div., together with the leading motorised units, reached the area 14 km north-west of Belev. Further advance is rendered impossible because of snowdrifts up to 1 metre in height.

Source: Pz. AOK 2. Abt. Ia, KTB Nr. 1 dated 26 December 1941 (RH 21-2/v.277)

Appendix III

Extracts from war diaries; 4th Panzer Division Div. Command Post, 12 March 1942; Ia Nr. 71/42 geheim

Answers to questionnaire OKH concerning experiences Eastern campaign in command, training and organisation. (extracts)

I. Command and Training

Question 1: Influence of the Russian Terrain:

a) Shortage of roads often forced whole divisions onto a dirt road mostly consisting of bad patches. Thus the march was delayed, the column had to stop time after time, and thus the unit lost the calm vital to the operation.

Delayed mission.

Supply support problems (especially when there were several motorised divisions on one road).

Little opportunity to deploy the motorised divisions. Anti-aircraft guns inadequate, since one march route especially under threat.

At defiles a small enemy force was enough to hold up the march. Only in exceptional cases was it possible to chase and encircle the enemy.

Infantry and tanks had to fight separately for a long period until the infantry had established bridgeheads or had crossed marshy areas.

Fighting on and close to the road on both sides. Enemy in the intermediate area not completely neutralised and later posed a threat to the flanks and supply support.

The Division's sectors of combat were often too large because another advance route for the adjacent divisions was a greater distance away.

High degree of wear and tear of machinery. Time was needed for repairs and maintenance work. Since there was no time allowed for this, the result was a fall in the number of tanks still operational in the panzer regiments to a fraction of their marching-out strength, as well as a partial collapse of matériel strength in the other motorised arms.

Question 2: Experiences concerning the operation of larger units:

a) Panzer divisions are units which rely on the weather not being too bad. Where there are more than 15 degrees of frost or rainstorms which turn roads into quagmires, technical breakdowns occur which far outstrip any small achievements made in spite of this. If the unit is forced to retreat under such circumstances, there will be possibly catastrophic losses of matériel. In order to avoid this, the higher command echelons should think in a more technical way. For example, they should consider carefully whether it is worthwhile committing armoured divisions in bad weather, or else take them out well before the bad weather starts.

(b) Attack is the nature of the Panzer Division. If there is a standstill and the enemy has time to ascertain the positions of individual fighting units, there will be problems. Therefore there should only be a deep forward thrust if it is certain that further forces can be brought through the gap breached by the Panzer Division. Here one must also take road and weather conditions into account.

After the enemy has been encircled the Pz. Div. should be pulled out as soon as possible and made available for other tasks.

As long as the tanks are moving forward, breakdowns can be tolerated, because then immobilised vehicles can be taken in for repair. Every backward movement, however, causes extremely high losses in vehicles and weapons, thus strengthening enemy morale.

It should be up to the commanders to avoid putting the Panzer Division through such difficult withdrawals.

The higher command echelons became used to acknowledging cries for help from the units concerning spare parts and so on without taking steps to help, because our luck continued to hold regardless and the Division achieved what was thought to be impossible.

This led to the fact that on 5 December 1941 (the day before the start of the withdrawal) the Division had at its disposal only: 15% of its tanks; 30% of its personnel carriers; 34% of its trucks; 10% of its motorcycles.

Question 5: Experience in fighting under special conditions:

b) Combat in town and villages:
1. The best means of combat – shoot the village into flames. In the warmer months the Russians are mostly dug in in front of or to the side of the village. Even then the burning village is almost always valuable to the attacker (dazzling effect, destruction of vehicles, effect on morale).

2. Employment of armour to bring riflemen (if there is no enemy anti-tank fire) and to bypass the village. In the village itself tanks are at a disadvantage against an already dug-in enemy (see Combat in woods).

3. In a large built-up area it is better to defend than to attack. This is particularly true of tank-to-tank combat.

4. Villages and towns must be cleared of enemy forces much more thoroughly than has been the case up to now. Sufficient manpower must be made available for the task.

c) Combat under cover of darkness:

1. The Russians often attack at night because the artillery is less effective then, and thus they can make up for their inferior artillery and bring the mass of their infantry into play. The Russians especially make use of moonlit nights, but can also attack without moonlight. At night the Russians often attack by means of infiltration. They are not very adaptable, however, and can be thrown back by even a weak counter-thrust in terms of numbers.

2. The Russians themselves are very susceptible to night attacks (bad leadership). Our night attacks were almost always successful. The one exception was mine barriers. It was almost impossible to remove these at night. It was necessary, for a night attack, to move along one or more roads. Cross-country travel was only possible under very favourable conditions (full moon, level terrain).

3. During a night attack, which must be practised as a drill, it is almost always the leading company alone which is directly involved in the action. Thus the remaining companies can be spread out along the whole length of the attack column to protect the other units.

4. If the night is dark, the enemy should be lit up by firing incendiaries into the houses and haystacks.

5. Very signal lights often betray the presence of an attacker. They should therefore only be used at night by experienced soldiers.

6. Sometimes we had great success when no shots were fired while approaching the enemy.

7. Only the commander at the head can see if it is possible to launch a night attack. It must be left to his discretion whether he wants to attack at night or the next morning.

8. Night marches, night assemblies and night attacks all require suitable roads. If these are not available there will be regular breakdowns. The unit will arrive too late and will be overtired. Night movements of motorised units on bad roads also leads to a loss of matériel. Therefore they should be the exception rather than the rule.

Question 25: Particular experiences:

I General

a) With all due respect for the achievements of the infantry, it can be seen, from a simple comparison of the number of combat days, that the regiments in the Panzer Division have to fight the most. They can only do this, in the long term, when their heavy losses are made up for by good replacements. Until now there have been conflicting regulations. It is vital for the success of the war that the Home Army sends the best replacements to the Pz. Divs.

b) It has often been said that successes were not exploited to the full. In most cases the unit was not to blame but rather the shortage of fuel, i.e. the failure of the supply services.

Command in the East is mainly a problem of supply support. To solve this, convoys must be made larger and a supply base must be set up at the start of each operation.

Supplies of oil, spare parts and vehicles failed time and again. Due to inadequate deliveries, for example, during the thrust to the rear of Kiev, 50% of the Division's tanks and motorcycles broke down.

c) Delivery of winter kit was far too late. The result was hundreds of case of frostbite in 4th Pz. Div. alone. The same goes for the delivery of winter equipment for the vehicles.

II Tanks (See also report by Pz. Rgt. 34 which was submitted to the General der Schnellen Truppen at Army High Command, together with 4th Pz. Div. Ia Nr. 32/42 geh. of 18 February 1942).

a) It is difficult to fight against Russian heavy tanks because they usually open fire at a distance of 800 metres or more, so that only field guns from the 8.8 cm anti-aircraft gun upwards are able to fight them. It is, however, hard to bring these field guns into position without their being fired on and destroyed by the enemy before they fire a shot. Here we found the following to be true:

When attacking, the 8.8 cm AA gun and the 10 cm cannon must follow close behind the panzer attack in a leap-frog operation. They must get into position in such a way that they are hidden from sight, behind the hill-crest or the edge of the village or the woods, otherwise they will be fired upon on the long climb, or while being put into position, before they can have any effect. Heavy artillery and dive-bombers must try to destroy the Russian tanks; alternatively, our tanks must attack and then, by moving backwards and to one side, try to draw the enemy along behind them so that they get within range of the 8.8 cm AA guns and 10 cm cannon. If these methods are not successful, then there is only one course of action left in order to get at the enemy – assault units carrying 3-kilogram charges.

Question 35: Motor vehicles:

b) Average fuel consumption (per 100 kilometres)
The actual fuel consumption levels are between 1 ½ and 3 times the theoretical levels depending on terrain and weather. The following figures give an idea:

Tank: 450 litres, on soft ground up to 800 litres;
Light armoured scout car: 40–45 litres;
Heavy arm. personnel carrier (8 wheeler): 80–90 litres;
Half-track vehicle: 60 litres;
Medium-sized truck: 60 litres.

When the Div. alternated between march and combat the average distance per unit of consumption fell from 100 kilometres to around 35 km.

On average an engine consumes 4–5% of its motor oil; when the engine is worn out this increases to 20% and more.

When the engines have to be left running because of the low temperatures, the fuel consumption of a stationary vehicle in 24 hours is equivalent to a distance of about 20 km, if the battery had to be charged at the same time.

Question 36: Extremely good Russian equipment and vehicles:

a) Russian T-34 tank, 27 tons, very wide track and thus highly mobile across country, good fording ability, superior speed, superior armour due to sloping surfaces, excellent engine, superior weaponry (7.62 cm cannon with high penetration and very good sighting mechanism). Disadvantage: high fuel consumption.

Certified correct:

Signed in draft:
Eberbach
Lt.-Col. (G.S.)

Source: 4. Pz. Div., Abt. Ia, Nr. 71/42 geh. of 12 March 1942 (RH 27-4/37).

Appendix IV

Orders of Battle

THE ARMOURED FORCE IN THE POLISH CAMPAIGN

Gen. Kdo. XIV. A. K. mot. (von Wietersheim)	1. le. Div. (von Loeper) 13. Inf. Div. mot. (Otto) 29. Inf. Div. mot. (Lemelsen)
Gen. Kdo. XV. A. K. mot. (Hoth)	2. le. Div. (Stumme) 3. le. Div. (Kuntzen)
Gen. Kdo. XVI. A. K. mot. (Hoepner)	1. Pz. Div. (Schmidt) 4. Pz. Div. (Reinhardt)
Gen. Kdo. XIX. A. K. mot. (Guderian)	3. Pz. Div. (von Schweppenburg) 10. Pz. Div. (Schaal) 2. Inf. Div. mot. (Bader) 20. Inf. Div. mot. (Wiktorin)
Gen. Kdo. XXII. A. K. mot (von Kleist)	2. Pz. Div. (Veiel) 5. Pz. Div. (von Vietinghoff) 4. le. Div. (von Hubicki)

Source: K. Nehring, *Die Geschichte der deutschen Panzerwaffe 1916–1945*, Frankfurt am Main and Berlin 1969, p. 20ff.

Appendix V

THE ARMOURED FORCE DURING THE FRENCH CAMPAIGN
(1st Phase: May 1940)

	XIX. Pz. K* (Guderian)	1. Pz. Div. (Kirchner) 2. Pz. Div. (Veiel) 10. Pz. Div. (Schaal)
Panzergruppe von Kleist	XXXXI. Pz. K.* (Reinhardt)	6. Pz. Div. (Kempf) 8. Pz. Div. (Kuntzen) 2. Inf. Div. mot. (Bader)
	XIV. A. K. mot. (von Wietersheim)	13. Inf. Div. mot. (von Rothkirch und Panthen 29. Inf. Div. mot. (Lemelsen)

* The 'A. K. mot.' (motorised army corps), which consisted mainly of tank units, were already being called Panzerkorps in the summer of 1940.

In the autumn of 1940 the following were renamed:
XXII. A. K. mot. was renamed Panzergruppe 1 (von Kleist);
XIX. A. K. mot. was renamed Panzergruppe 2 (Guderian);
XV. A. K. mot. was renamed Panzergruppe 3 (Hoth);
XVI. A. K. mot. was renamed Panzergruppe 4 (Hoepner).
During the first phase of the campaign there was a Panzergruppe Hoth under AOK 4 from 14 to 30 May 1940.

THE ARMOURED FORCE DURING THE FRENCH CAMPAIGN
(2nd Phase: from 8 June 1940)

	XIV. Pz. K. (von Wietersheim)	10. Pz. Div. 13. Inf. Div. mot. Inf. Rgt. mot. Großdeutschland
Panzergruppe von Kleist	XVI. Pz. K. (Hoepner)	3. Pz. Div. 4. Pz. Div. SS-Verfüg. Div. SS-Leibstandarte "Adolf Hitler"
	XV. Pz. K. (Hoth)	5. Pz. Div. 7. Pz. Div. 2. Inf. Div. mot.
Panzergruppe Guderian	XXXIX. Pz. K. (Schmidt)	1. Pz. Div. 2. Pz. Div. 29. Inf. Div. mot.
	XXXXI. Pz. K. (Reinhardt)	6. Pz. Div. 8. Pz. Div. 20. Inf. Div. mot.

Appendix VI

THE 2nd PANZER ARMY IN RUSSIA (1941)

	XXIV. Pz. K. (von Schweppenburg)	3. Pz. Div. (Model) 4. Pz. Div. (von Langermann) 1. Kav. Div. (Feldt) 10. Inf. Div. mot. (von Loeper)
2. Pz. A. (Guderian)	XXXXVII. Pz. K. (von Wietinghoff)	10. Pz. Div. (Schaal) SS Inf. Div. Das Reich (Hauser) Inf. Rgt. Groß-deutschland von Stock-hausen)
	XXXXVII. Pz. K. (Lemelsen)	17. Pz. Div. (von Arnim) 18. Pz. Div. (Nehring) 29. Inf. Div. mot. (von Boltenstern)

2nd Panzer Army, which was still called Panzergruppe 2 until 6 October 1941, was placed under H. Gr. Mitte, commanded by Field Marshal von Bock, for Operation Barbarossa.

THE 3rd PANZER ARMY IN RUSSIA (1941)

3. Pz. A. (Hoth)	XXXIX. Pz. K. (Schmidt)	7. Pz. Div. (von Funck)
		20. Pz. Div. (Stumpff)
		14. Inf. Div. mot. (Fürst)
		20. Inf. Div. mot. (Zorn)
	LVII. Pz. K. (Kuntzen)	12. Pz. Div. (Harpe)
		19. Pz. Div. (von Knobelsdorff)
		18. Inf. Div. mot. (Herrlein)

3rd Panzer Army, which was still called Panzergruppe 3 until the beginning of 1942, was planned under H. Gr. Mitte commanded by Field Marshal von Bock, for Operation Barbarossa.

Appendix VII

Types of Tanks in Use between 1939 and 1941

Renault M 1935 R (France)

Until 1940 about 2,000 of this type of tank were built. Over terrain the 10-ton tank, with its engine of only 82 hp (metric), was far too slow. Also, the crews complained that the visibility was inadequate.

Total weight:	9.9 metric tons
Length:	4 metres
Width:	1.85 metres
Height:	2.10 metres
Engine:	Renault, 4-cylinder, water-cooled, 82 hp/2,200 rpm
Speed:	19 kph
Fuel tank volume:	170.5 litres
Radius of action:	80–138 km
Weaponry:	1 37 mm gun, 1 machine gun
Ammunition:	58 37 mm shells, 2,500 rounds
Front armour:	45 mm
Crew:	2
Number built:	about 2,000
Year:	1935/40

Somua S 35 (France)

This 20-ton tank reached speeds of 40 kph on the road and gave the crew good visibility (in contrast to the Renault M 1935 R) due to an excellent telescope system. The turret with its 40 mm thick armour was cast from a single mould.

Total weight:	20 metric tons
Length:	5.30 metres
Width:	2.12 metres
Height:	2.62 metres

Engine:	Somua, 8 cylinder, water-cooled, 190 hp/2,000 rpm
Speed:	40 kph
Fuel tank volume:	413 litres
Radius of action:	129–260 km
Weaponry:	1 47 mm gun, 1 machine gun
Ammunition:	118 47 mm shells, 1,250 rounds
Front armour:	55 mm
Crew:	3
Number built:	about 500
Year:	1935/40

Renault B 1 bis (France)

This heavy tank possessed very thick armour, with the result that German anti-tank crews were told to aim at the hatches. Even when the turret hatch was closed the 4-man crew had excellent visibility. Also new was the emergency exit in the base-plate.

The bogie wheels were well protected against light fire by armour plates on each side.

Total weight:	31.5 tons
Length:	6.98 metres
Width:	2.49 metres
Height:	2.79 metres
Engine:	Renault, 6 cylinder, water-cooled, 307 hp
Speed:	29 kph
Radius of action:	209 km
Weaponry:	1 75 mm gun, 1 47 mm gun, 2 machine guns
Front armour:	20–60 mm
Crew:	4
Number built:	about 500
Year:	1940

Mark II A 'Matilda' III (Great Britain)

This British tank was quite impregnable for the German anti-tank guns with its almost 80 mm thick armour. Its only real enemy was the 8.8 cm AA gun. 'Matilda' tanks were employed above all in North Africa, while some were sent to the Red Army for training purposes.

Total weight:	27 tons
Length:	5.61 metres

Width:	2.59 metres
Height:	2.52 metres
Engines:	2 Leyland E 148 and E 149 or E 164 and 165, 6 cylinder, water-cooled,
	95 hp/2,000 rpm (per engine)
Speed:	24 kph
Fuel tank volume:	211.4 litres
Radius of action:	128–257 km
Weaponry:	1 40 mm gun, 1 machine gun, 1 light machine gun
Ammunition:	93 40 mm shells, 2,925 rounds machine gun, 600 rounds light machine gun
Front armour:	78 mm
Crew:	4
Number built:	2,987
Year:	1939/42

Panzer II, Model F (Germany)

The German Army Command decided upon the Panzer II as an interim measure because the planned Panzer III and IV were taking longer than expected to come into production. The Panzer II began to be produced in the mid-thirties, and during the French campaign in 1940 the German armoured force had 955 tanks of this type. Although these tanks were only ordered for training purposes, they were surprisingly successful on the battlefield.

Total weight:	9.5 tons
Length:	4.81 metres
Width:	2.28 metres
Height:	2.02 metres
Engine:	Maybach HL 62 TR, 6 cylinder, water-cooled, 140 hp/2,600 rpm
Speed:	40 kph
Fuel tank:	170 litres
Radius of action:	125–175 km
Weaponry:	1 20 mm gun, 1 machine gun
Ammunition:	180 20 mm shells, 2,550 rounds
Front armour:	35 mm
Crew:	3
Number built:	650 (Model F)
Year:	1940/44

Panzer III, Model F (Germany)

This tank was originally seen by the German Army Command as the main combat vehicle. In May 1940 there were 349 Panzer III ready for action, and the initial German successes in the Russian campaign would scarcely have been possible without the great numbers of Panzer III which were committed.

Total weight:	22.3 tons
Length:	5.41 metres
Width:	2.92 metres
Height:	2.51 metres
Engine:	Maybach HL 120 TRM, 12 cylinder, water-cooled, 300 hp/3,000 rpm
Speed:	40 kph
Fuel tank:	327 litres
Radius of action:	175–257 km
Weaponry:	at first 1 37 mm gun then 1 50 mm gun, 1 machine gun
Ammunition:	99 cannon shells, 2,000 rounds
Front armour:	30 mm
Crew:	5
Number built:	5,650 of all types
Year:	1939/43

Panzer IV, Model J (Germany)

The Panzer IV was at first only meant to be a support vehicle for the light Panzer I and II. With the short-barrelled L/24, however, there could be no real success against enemy tanks, and thus it is no wonder that this tank failed in the first year of the Russian campaign. After the 75 mm L/48 gun was fitted in 1942 the Panzer IV became standard equipment in the German panzer regiments. It remained in service until the end of the war because the new cannon enabled it to fight against all types of tanks known at the time up to a distance of 1,000 metres.

Total weight:	25 tons
Length:	7.02 metres
Width:	3.18 metres
Height:	2.68 metres
Engine:	Maybach HL 120 TRM, 12 cylinder, water-cooled, 300 hp/3,000 rpm

Speed:	38 kph
Fuel tank:	680 litres
Radius of action:	210–320 km
Weaponry:	1 75 mm gun 40 L/48, 2 machine guns
Ammunition:	87 75 mm shells, 3,150 rounds
Front armour:	80 mm
Crew:	5
Number built:	about 6,000 of types H and J
Year:	1937/45

T-34 (Soviet Union)

Designed by Morosov, the T-34 was not produced on a grand scale until 1940. Its direct forerunners were the A-20, the A-30 and the T-32. While the T-34's shells went through the German tanks like a hot knife through butter at a great distance, the Russian tank was immune to the 37 mm and 50 mm shells fired by the Panzer III because of its almost perfect shape. The tracks, about 60 cm wide, gave the T-34 a big advantage in snow and mud over the German tanks with their 20 cm narrower tracks. It is no exaggeration to call the T-34 the best tank of its time.

Total weight:	27 tons
Length:	6.58 metres
Width:	3.00 metres
Height:	2.44 metres
Engine:	V 2, 12 cylinder diesel, water-cooled, 500 hp/1,800 rpm
Speed:	51.5 kph
Fuel tank:	614 litres, extra fuel in tanks which could be jettisoned!
Weaponry:	1 76.2 mm gun, 2 machine guns
Ammunition:	77 76.2 mm shells, 2–3,000 rounds
Front armour:	60 mm
Crew:	4
Number built:	about 40,000
Year:	June 1940 onwards

KW I and KW II (Soviet Union)

This series of KW tanks fulfilled the demands in Russia for heavy tanks which were able to withstand anti-tank bombardment. In 1939 the KW (Kliment Woroshilov), developed by J.S. Kotin, went into mass production. Together with the legendary T-34, the KW tanks formed the backbone of the Red Army's tank force until 1942.

	KW	KW II
Total weight:	48 tons	52 tons
Length:	6.75 metres	6.80 metres
Width:	3.32 metres	3.35 metres
metres		
Height:	2.74 metres	3.25 metres
metres		
Engine:	Diesel, 12 cyl., water-cooled, 600hp/2,000 rpm	Diesel, 12 cyl., water-cooled, 600 hp/2,000 rpm
Speed:	35 kph	26 kph
Radius of action:	335 km	250 km
Weaponry:	1 76 mm gun, 3 machine guns	1 152 mm howitzer 3 machine guns
Ammunition:	111 76 mm shells, 3,024 rounds	unknown
Front armour:	130 mm	110 mm
Crew:	5	6
Number built:	large numbers	large numbers
Year:	1940/42	1940/42

Source: A. Halle and C. Demand, *Panzer, Illustrierte Geschichte der Kampf-wagen*, Berne, Munich, Vienna 1971; B. Perrett: *Fighting Vehicles of the Red Army*, London 1969; J.G. Andronikov and W. Mostovenko, *Die roten Panzer*, Munich 1963; F.M. von Senger und Etterlin, *Die Kampfpan-zer von 1916–1966*, Munich 1966; C.F. Foss, *Armoured Fighting Vehicles of the World*, London 1971; P. Chamberlain and Ch. Ellis, *Britische und amerikanische Panzer des Zweiten Weltkriegs*, Munich 1972; J. Milsom, *Russian tanks 1900–1970*, Harrisburg 1971.

Sources and Literature

BOOKS

GERMAN

Anderle, A., and Basler, W., *Juni 1941. Beiträge zur Geschichte des hitlerfaschistischen Überfalls auf die Sowjetunion*, Berlin, 1961.

Andronikov, J.G., and Mostovenko, W., *Die roten Panzer. Geschichte der sowjetischen Panzertruppen 1920–1960*, ed. by F.M. von Senger und Etterlin, Munich, 1963.

Antonov, A.S., and Artamonov, B.A., *Der Panzer*, Berlin, 1959.

Bauer, E., *Der Panzerkrieg*, Bonn, 1964.

Berben, P., and Iselin, B., *Die Deutschen kommen*, Hamburg, 1969.

Bernhard, K., *Panzer packen Polen*, Berlin, 1940.

Besymenski, L., *Sonderakte 'Barbarossa'*, Stuttgart, 1968.

Boerner, H., *Mit Stukas und Panzern nach Frankreich hinein!*, Berlin, Leipzig, 1943.

Bor, P., *Gespräche mit Halder*, Wiesbaden, 1950.

Borchert, H.W., *Panzerkampf im Westen*, Berlin, 1940.

Brehm, W., *Mein Kriegstagebuch 1939–1945. Mit der 7. Panzerdivision fünf Jahre in West und Ost*, Kassel, 1953.

Carell, P., *Unternehmen Barbarossa. Der Marsch nach Rußland*, Frankfurt am Main, Berlin, Vienna, 1963.

Chales de Beaulieu, W., *Der Vorstoß der Panzergruppe 4 auf Leningrad, 1941*, Neckargemünd, 1961.

——, *Generaloberst Erich Hoepner. Militärisches Porträt eines Panzer-Führers*, Neckargemünd, 1969.

Chamberlain, P. and Ellis, Ch., *Britische und amerikanische Panzer des Zweiten Weltkriegs*, Munich, 1972.

Clausewitz, C. von, *On War*, Princeton N.J., 1976.

Deutsches Militärlexikon, ed. by a team within the Militärakademie der Nationalen Volksarmee 'Friedrich Engels', 3rd edn, East Berlin, 1971.

Dwinger, E., *Panzerführer. Tagebuchblätter vom Frankreichfeldzug*, Jena, 1941.

Ettighofer, P.C., *44 Tage und Nächte. Der Westfeldzug 1940*, Stuttgart, 1953.

Fey, E., and Rehkämpfer, J., *Stählerne Gemeinschaft*, Essen, 1941.

Franke, H., *Handbuch der neuzeitlichen Wehrwissenschaften*, vol. 2, Berlin and Leipzig, 1937.

Fretter-Pico, M., *Mißbrauchte Infanterie. Deutsche Infanteriedivisionen im osteuropäischen Großraum 1941–1944. Erlebnisskizzen. Erfahrungen und Erkenntnisse*, Frankfurt am Main, 1957. Extended edn entitled: . . . *Verlassen von des Sieges Göttern*, Wiesbaden, 1969.

Fuchs, K.H., and Kölper, F.W., *Militärisches Taschenlexikon*, 2nd revised edn, Frankfurt am Main, 1961.

Fuller, J.F.C., *Die entartete Kunst Krieg zu führen, 1789–1961*, Cologne, 1964.

Geschichte der 3. Panzerdivision Berlin-Brandenburg, 1935–1945, ed. by Traditionsverband der Division, Berlin, 1967.

Gliederungen der Panzertruppen im 2. Weltkrieg, 1939–1945, ed. by Bundesministerium für Landesverteidigung, Militärwissenschaftliche Abteilung, Vienna, 1962.

Grams, R., *Die 14. Panzer-Division, 1940–1945*, Bad Nauheim, 1957.

Greiner, H., *Die Oberste Wehrmachtführung 1939–1943*, Wiesbaden, 1951.

Groener, W., *Das Testament des Grafen Schlieffen*, Berlin, 1927.

Guderian, H., *Achtung – Panzer. Die Entwicklung der Panzerwaffe, ihre Kampftaktik und ihre operativen Möglichkeiten*, Stuttgart, 1937.

——, *Mit den Panzern in Ost und West. Erlebnisberichte von Mitkämpfern aus den Feldzügen in Polen und Frankreich 1939/40*, Berlin, Prague, Vienna, 1942.

——, *Die Panzertruppen und ihr Zusammenwirken mit den anderen Waffen*, 4th extended edn, Berlin, 1943.

——, *Erinnerungen eines Soldaten*, Heidelberg, 1951. English edition: *Panzer Leader*, with a foreword by B.H. Liddell Hart, New York, 1952.

——, *Panzer-Marsch. Aus dem Nachlaß des Schöpfers der deutschen Panzerwaffe*, ed. by O. Munzel, Munich, 1956.

Guillaume, A., *Warum siegte die Rote Armee?*, Baden-Baden, 1950.

Halder, F., *Kriegstagebuch vol. 1: Vom Polenfeldzug bis zum Ende der Westoffensive (14 August 1939–30 September 1940)*, ed. by H.A. Jacobsen, Stuttgart, 1962.

——, *Kriegstagebuch vol. 2: Der Rußlandfeldzug bis zum Marsch auf Stalingrad (22 Juni 1941–24 September 1942)*, ed. by H.A. Jacobsen, Stuttgart, 1964.

Halle, A., and Demand, C., *Panzer. Illustrierte Geschichte der Kampfwagen*, Berne, Munich, Vienna, 1971.

Hartog, L.J., *Und morgen die ganze Welt. Der deutsche Angriff im Westen, 10. Mai bis 17. September 1940*, Gütersloh, 1961.

Haupt, W., *Kiew, die größte Kesselschlacht der Geschichte*, Bad Nauheim, 1964.

——, *Sieg ohne Lorbeer. Der Westfeldzug 1940*, Preetz/Holstein, 1965.

——, *Heeresgruppe Mitte 1941–1945*, Dorheim, 1968.

Heidkämper, O., *Witebsk, Kampf und Untergang der 3. Panzerarmee*, Heidelberg, 1954.

Heigl's Taschenbuch der Tanks, Part III: Der Panzerkampf, ed. by G.P. Zezschwitz, Munich, 1971.

Hess, F., *Der Sieg im Osten*, Berlin, 1940.

Hesse, E., *Der sowjetische Partisanenkrieg 1941–1944 im Spiegel deutscher Kampfanweisungen und Befehle*, Göttingen, 1969.

Hillgruber, A., *Hitlers Strategie. Politik und Kriegführung 1940–1941*, Frankfurt am Main, 1965.

——, *Deutschlands Rolle in der Vorgeschichte der beiden Weltkriege*, Göttingen, 1967.

——, 'Unternehmen "Barbarossa"' in *Probleme des Zweiten Weltkrieges*, ed. by A. Hillgruber, Cologne and Berlin, 1967.

Hoth, H., *Panzer-Operationen. Die Panzergruppe 3 und der operative Gedanke der deutschen Führung, Sommer 1941*, Heidelberg, 1956.

Hubatsch, W., *Hitlers Weisungen für die Kriegführung, 1939–1945. Dokumente des OKW*, Frankfurt am Main, 1962.

Imhoff, C. von, *Sturm durch Frankreich*, Berlin, 1941.

Irving, D., *Die Tragödie der deutschen Luftwaffe. Aus den Akten und Erinnerungen von Feldmarschall Milch*, Frankfurt am Main, 1970.

Jacobsen, H.A., *Dokumente zur Vorgeschichte des Westfeldzuges 1939–40*, Göttingen, Berlin, Frankfurt, 1956.

——, *Fall Gelb. Der Kampf um den deutschen Operationsplan zur Westoffensive 1940*, Wiesbaden, 1957.

——, *Dünkirchen. Ein Beitrag zur Geschichte des Westfeldzuges 1940*, Neckargemünd, 1958.

——, *Kriegstagebuch des OKW, vol. 1, 1 August 1940–31 Dezember 1941*, Frankfurt am Main, 1965.

——, *1939–1945, Der Zweite Weltkrieg in Chronik und Dokumenten*, 5th enlarged and revised edn, Darmstadt, 1961.

Jeremenko, A.J., *Tage der Bewährung*, Berlin, 1961.

Jungenfeld, E. Frhr. von, *So kämpften Panzer!*, Berlin, 1941.

Kabisch, E., *Deutscher Siegeszug in Polen*, Berlin, 1940.

Kesselring, A., *Soldat bis zum letzten Tag*, Bonn, 1953.

Kielmannsegg, J.A. Graf von, *Panzer zwischen Warschau und Atlantik*, Berlin, 1941.

Knecht, R., *Kampfpanzer Leopard*, Munich, 1972.

Knobelsdorff, O. von, *Die Geschichte der niedersächsischen 19. Panzerdivision*, Bad Nauheim, 1958.

Kurtzinski, M.J., *Taktik schneller Verbände*, Potsdam, 1935.

Liddell Hart, B.H., *Strategie*, Wiesbaden, undated.

——, *Jetzt dürfen sie reden. Hitlers Generale berichten*, Stuttgart and Hamburg 1950. Engl. edn: *The German Generals Talk*, New York 1948.

——, *Geschichte des Zweiten Weltkrieges*, vol. 1, Düsseldorf and Vienna, 1972.

Liss, U., *Westfront 1939/40, Erinnerungen des Feindbearbeiters im OKH*, Neckargemünd, 1959.

Mackensen, E. von, *Vom Bug bis zum Kaukasus. Das III. Panzerkorps im Feldzug gegen Sowjetrußland 1941/42*, Neckargemünd, 1967.

Manstein, E. von, *Verlorene Siege*, Bonn, 1959.

Manteuffel, H. von, *Die 7. Panzerdivision im Zweiten Weltkrieg. Einsatz und Kampf der 'Gespenster-Division' 1939–1945*, Ürdingen am Rhein, 1965.

Mellenthin, F.M. von, *Panzer-Schlachten. Eine Studie über den Einsatz von Panzerverbänden im Zweiten Weltkrieg*, Neckargemünd, 1963, English edn: *Panzer Battles 1939–1945. A study of the Employment of Armour in the Second World War*, ed. by L.F.C. Turner, London, 1956.

Mendelssohn, P. de, *Die Nürnberger Dokumente*, Hamburg, 1947.

Middeldorf, E., *Taktik im Rußlandfeldzug. Erfahrungen und Folgerungen*, Darmstadt and Dortmund, 1956.

Minz, J.J., Rasgon, J.M., and Sidorov, A.L., *Der große Vaterländische Krieg der Sowjetunion*, Berlin, 1947.

Mostovenko, W.D., *Panzer gestern und heute*, Berlin, 1961.

Mueller-Hillebrand, B., *Das Heer 1933–1945*, vol. 2, Frankfurt am Main, 1956.

Munzel, O., *Panzer-Taktik. Raids gepanzerter Verbände im Ostfeldzug 1941/42*, Neckargemünd, 1959.

——, *Die deutschen gepanzerten Truppen bis 1945*, Herford and Bonn, 1965.

Nehring, W.K., *Panzervernichtung*, 3rd fully revised and enlarged edn, Berlin, 1941.

——, *Die Geschichte der deutschen Panzerwaffe 1916–1945*, Frankfurt am Main and Berlin, 1969.

Nekrich, A., and Grigorenko, P., *Genickschuß. Die Rote Armee am 22. Juni 1941*, published and introduced by G. Haupt, Vienna, Frankfurt am Main and Zurich, 1969.

OKH, *Begegnungsstätte. Studien zur Kriegsgeschichte und Taktik*, published by Generalstab des Heeres, Berlin, 1939.

OKH, *Kampferlebnisse aus dem Feldzug in Polen 1939. Nach Schilderungen von Frontkämpfern*, published by Generalstab des Heeres, Berlin, 1941.

OKH, *Kampferlebnisse aus dem Kriege an der Westfront. Nach Schilderungen von Frontkämpfern*, published by Generalstab des Heeres, Berlin, 1941.

OKH, *Kampferlebnisse aus dem Feldzug gegen Sowjetrußland 1941/42. Nach Schilderungen von Frontkämpfern*, published by Generalstab des Heeres, Berlin, 1943.

OKW, *Der Sieg in Polen*, Berlin, 1940.

OKW, *Sieg über Frankreich – Berichte und Bilder*, Berlin, 1940.

OKW, *Kampf gegen die Sowjets. Berichte und Bilder vom Beginn des Ostfeldzuges bis zum Frühjahr 1942*, Berlin, 1943.

Philippi, A., and Heim, F., *Der Feldzug gegen Sowjetrußland 1941–1945*, Stuttgart, 1962.

Popjel, N.K., *Panzer greifen an*, Berlin, 1960.

Rebentisch, E., *Zum Kaukasus und zu den Tauren. Die Geschichte der 23. Panzer-Division 1941–1945*, Esslingen am Neckar, 1963.

Reibig, W., *Schwarze Husaren. Panzer in Polen*, Berlin, 1961.

Reinecker, H., *Panzer nach vorn! Panzermänner erzählen vom Feldzug in Polen*, Berlin, 1939.

Reinhardt, K., *Die Wende vor Moskau. Das Scheitern der Strategie Hitlers im Winter 1941/42*, Stuttgart, 1972. English edn: *Moscow: The Turning Point?* (Studies in Military History series), New York, Oxford, 1991 (planned).

Rohde, H., *Das deutsche Wehrmachttransportwesen im Zweiten Weltkrieg*, Stuttgart, 1971.

Röhricht, E., *Probleme der Kesselschlacht*, Karlsruhe, 1958.

Rokossovski, K.K., *Soldatenpflicht. Erinnerungen eines Frontoberbefehlshabers*, Berlin, 1970.

Rommel, E., *Krieg ohne Haß*, Heidenheim and Brenz, 1950.

Rondière, P., *Der Angriff auf Sowjetrußland am 22. Juni 1941 . . . und die Welt hielt den Atem an*, Rastatt, 1968.

Samsonov, A.M., *Die große Schlacht vor Moskau 1941–1942*, Berlin, 1959.

Saslavski, W.J., *Kurzer Lehrkursus über die Berechnung von Kampfwagen und ihrer Mechanismen*, Moscow, 1932.

Schäufler, H., *So lebten und so starben sie. Das Buch vom Panzerregiment 35*, Bamberg, (undated).

Scheibert, H., *Bildband der 6. Panzer-Division 1939–1945*, Bad Nauheim, 1958.

Scheibert, H., and Wagener, C., *Die deutsche Panzertruppe 1939–1945*, Bad Nauheim, 1966.

Scheibert, H., and Elfrath, U., *Panzer in Rußland. Die deutschen gepanzerten Verbände im Rußlandfeldzug 1941–1944*, Dorheim, 1971.

Schramm, P.E., *Kriegstagebuch des OKW*, vol. IV, 2nd half-vol., Frankfurt am Main, 1961.

Senff, H., *Die Entwicklung der Panzerwaffe im deutschen Heer zwischen den beiden Weltkriegen*, Frankfurt am Main, 1969.

Senger und Etterlin, F.M. von, *Die Panzergrenadiere*, Munich, 1961.

——, *Die 24. Panzer-Division, vormals 1. Kavallerie-Division 1939–1945*, Neckargemünd, 1962.

——, *Die Kampfpanzer 1916–1966*, Munich, 1966.

——, *Der sowjetische mittlere Kampfpanzer der Baureihe T-34 bis T-62*, Munich, 1970.

Shilin, P.A., *Die wichtigsten Operationen des Großen Vaterländischen*

Krieges 1941–1945, Berlin, 1958.

Spannenkrebs, W., *Angriff mit Panzerkampfwagen*, Berlin, 1939.

Stoves, R.O.G., *1. Panzer-Division 1935–1945. Chronik einer der drei Stamm-Divisionen der deutschen Panzerwaffe*, Bad Nauheim, 1961.

Telpuchovski, B.S., *Die sowjetische Geschichte des Großen Vaterländischen Krieges 1941–1945*. Published and with annotations by A. Hillgruber and H.A. Jacobsen, Frankfurt am Main, 1961.

Teske, H., *General Ernst Köstring*, Frankfurt am Main, 1965.

Tippelskirch, K. von, *Geschichte des Zweiten Weltkrieges*, 2nd rev. edn, Bonn, 1956.

Tschimpke, A., *Die Gespenster-Division. Mit der Panzerwaffe durch Belgien und Frankreich*, Munich, 1940.

Vormann, N. von, *Der Feldzug 1939 in Polen*, Weißenburg, 1958.

Wallach, J.L., *Das Dogma der Vernichtungsschlacht. Die Lehren von Clausewitz und Schlieffen und ihre Wirkung in zwei Weltkriegen*, Munich, 1970.

Warlimont, W., *Im Hauptquartier der deutschen Wehrmacht 1939–1945*, Frankfurt am Main, 1962.

Wegener, C., *Moskau 1941. Der Angriff auf die russische Hauptstadt*, Bad Nauheim, 1965.

Weidinger, O., *Division Das Reich. Der Weg der 2. Panzer-Division 'Das Reich'* . . ., vol. 2, 1940–1, Osnabrück, 1969.

Werthen, W., *Geschichte der 16. Panzer-Division, 1939–1945*, Bad Nauheim, 1957.

Zhukov, G.K., *Erinnerungen und Gedanken*, Stuttgart, 1969.

Zimmermann, H., *Der Angriff ins Ungewisse. Die ersten Kriegstage 1940 beim XVI Panzerkorps im Kampf um die Dylestellung, 10.–17. Mai*, Neckargemünd, 1964.

English

Disney, P., *Tactical Problems for Armor Units*, Harrisburg, 1952.

Foss, C.F., *Armoured Fighting Vehicles of the World*, London, 1971.

Lewin, R., *Rommel as Military Commander*, London, 1968.

Macksey, K., and Batchelor, J.H., *Tank. A History of the Armoured Fighting Vehicle*, London, 1970.

Milsom, J., *Russian Tanks 1900–1970. The Complete Illustrated History of Soviet Armored Theory and Design*, Harrisburg, 1971.

Orgill, D., *The Tank. Studies in the Development and Use of a Weapon*, London, 1970.

Perrett, B., *Fighting Vehicles of the Red Army*, London, 1969.

——, *NATO Armour*, London, 1971.

Seaton, A., *The Russo-German War 1941–1945*, London, 1971.

——, *The Battle for Moscow 1941–1942*, London, 1971.

Shirer, L., *The Collapse of the Third Republic*, London, 1970.

Strawson, J., *Hitler as Military Commander*, London, 1971.
Turney, A., *Disaster at Moscow. Von Bock's Campaigns 1941–1942*, London, 1971.
Werth, A., *Russia at War, 1941–1945*, London, 1964.

French

Beaufre, A., *Le drame de 1940*, Paris, 1965.
Boucher, J., *L'arme blindée dans la guerre. Origine, évolution de la stratégie, opérations dans la deuxième guerre mondiale, rôle futur*, Paris, 1953.
Chtémenko, S., *L'Etat-Major Général Soviétique en Guerre, 1941–1945*, Moscow, 1971.
Degrelle, L., *Front de l'Est 1941–1945*, Paris, 1969.
Gaulle, C. de, *Mémoires de guerre, Vol. 1, L'appel 1940–1942*, Paris, 1954.
Goutard, A., *1940. La guerre des occasions perdues*, Paris, 1956.
Grigorenko, P., *Staline et la deuxième guerre mondiale*, Paris, 1969.
Horne, A., *Comment perdre une bataille*, Paris, 1969.
Kurowski, F., *La bataille des Ardennes et l'agonie à l'Ouest*, Paris, 1968.
Macjek, S., *Avec mes blindés. Pologne-France-Belgique-Hollande-Allemagne*, Paris, 1967.
Marot, J., *Abbéville 1940. Avec la division cuirassée De Gaulle*, Paris, 1967.
Napoléon, B., *Maximes de guerre et pensées*, Paris, 1874.
Préletat, *Le destin tragique de la ligne Maginot*, Paris, 1950.
Saurel, L., *La tragédie de juin 1940*, Paris, 1966.
Thomas, L., *Documents sur la guerre de 1939–1940*, Paris, 1941.
Tonvieille-Alquier, F., *Les Français dans la drôle de guerre*, Paris, 1971.
Vaselle, P., *Les combats de 1940, 18 mai–9 juin*, Montdidier, 1970.

NEWSPAPER AND MAGAZINE ARTICLES

German

Allmendinger, 'Panzertaktik', in *Die Kraftfahrkampftruppe*, No. 6, 1938, pp. 217–9.
Ananjev, J., "Die Panzerarmeen in den Angriffsoperationen des Großen Vaterländischen Krieges", in *Wehrwissenschaftliche Rundschau*, No. 12, 1962, pp. 737–50.
Belonkony, A., 'Der Krieg und das Problem der Straßen', in *Pioniere*, No. 3, 1970, pp. 105–7.
B.E., 'Die Flüsse in der russischen Kriegführung', in *Der Schweizer Soldat*, No. 12, 1943, pp. 226–8.
'Bewegliche Verteidigung', in *Allgemeine Schweizerische Militärzeitschrift*, No. 5, 1951, pp. 327–9.

Bolckheim, 'Betrachtungen über Kampfwagen-Organisation und Kampfwagen-Verwendung' special supplement of *'Wissen und Wehr'*, No. 5, 1924.

Bolckheim, 'Zusammenwirken von Panzertruppen mit Fliegern', in *Die Kraftfahrkampftruppe*, No. 4, 1937, pp. 101–4.

Brandt, W., 'Wie soll das Fußvolk den Tankangriff begleiten?' in *Militär-Wochenblatt*, 11 June 1935, cols. 237–8.

Bühler, K., 'Auszüge aus den Erfahrungen über den Einsatz einer Panzerartillerieabteilung (SFL) im Verbande einer Panzerdivision', in *Allgemeine Schweizerische Militärzeitschrift*, No. 2, 1953, pp. 122–41.

Bülow, Frhr. von, 'Die Luftwaffe Sowjetrußlands', in *Militärwissenschaftliche Rundschau*, No. 6, 1936, pp. 797–824.

Doege, 'Infanterie und Panzer', in *Militär-Wochenblatt*, 29 April 1938, cols. 2810–15.

Donat, G., 'Der Munitionsverbrauch der deutschen Wehrmacht im Feldzug gegen Sowjetrußland 1941–1945', in *Allgemeine Schweizerische Militärzeitschrift*, No. 3, 1964, pp. 155–8.

'Einzelschilderungen aus dem Feldzug in Polen', in *Militärwissenschaftliche Rundschau*, No. 1, 1940, pp. 16–69.

'Einzelschilderungen aus dem Krieg an der Westfront', in *Militärwissenschaftliche Rundschau*, No. 3, 1940, pp. 234–96.

Feddern, G.D., 'Psychologische Aufgaben des Truppenführers', in *Truppenpraxis*, No. 11, 1972, pp. 830–8 and No. 12, 1972, pp. 905–13.

Fretter-Pico, M., 'Herbst- und Winterkrieg im Osten' (Brochure) from *Europäische Sicherheit, Rundschau der Wehrwissenschaften*, Nos 2/3, 1951.

Gaul, 'Das sowjetrussische Heer', in *Militär-Wochenblatt*, 22 August 1941, cols. 211–16.

Görlitz, W., 'Die Wende vor Moskau (General Schukow bricht sein Schweigen)', in *Die Welt*, 16/17 November 1966, p. 5.

Groehler, O., 'Zur Einschätzung der Roten Armee durch die faschistische Wehrmacht', in *Zeitschrift für Militärgeschichte*, No. 6, 1968, pp. 724–38.

Guderian, H., 'Kraftfahrkampftruppen', in *Militärwissenschaftliche Rundschau*, No. 1, 1936, pp. 52–77.

——, 'Schnelle Truppen einst und jetzt', in *Militärwissenschaftliche Rundschau*, No. 2, 1939, pp. 229–43.

——, 'Der Vorstoß auf Tula 1941', in *Allgemeine Schweizerische Militärzeitschrift*, No. 10, 1949, pp. 746–52, and No. 11, 1949, pp. 823–31.

Hansen, K.A., 'Zusammenwirken mit Pionieren beim Überwinden von Gewässern', in *Kampftruppen*, No. 4, 1972, pp. 113–17.

Hartung, H.J., 'Forcieren oder Überwinden von Gewässern', in *Kampftruppen*, No. 4, 1972, pp. 123–4.

Hofmann, 'Die Nacht, der Gehilfe des Panzermannes?', in *Die Panzertruppe*, No. 7, 1939, pp. 237–9.

Hoth, H., 'Das Schicksal der französischen Panzerwaffe im ersten Teil des Westfeldzuges 1940' in: *Wehrkunde*, No. 7, 1958, pp. 367–77.

Hoth, H., 'Der Kampf von Panzerdivisionen in Kampfgruppen in Beispielen der Kriegsgeschichte', in *Wehrkunde*, No. 11, 1959, pp. 576–84.

Kissel, H., 'Die ersten T-34', in *Wehrwissenschaftliche Rundschau*, No. 3, 1955, pp. 130–2.

Liddell Hart, B.H., 'Der Panzerkrieg und seine Zukunft', in *Wehrwissenschaftliche Rundschau*, No. 5, 1952, pp. 185–93.

Luckner, F., 'Die Versorgung der Wehrmacht mit Kraftfahrzeug-Ersatzteilen im 2. Weltkrieg', in *Logistik, Technik und Versorgung*, No. 2, 1972, pp. 58ff, and No. 3, 1972, pp. 88–92.

Magenheimer, H., 'Der deutsche Angriff auf Sowjetrußland 1941', in *Österreichische Militärische Zeitschrift*, No. 3, 1971, pp. 157–64.

Manteuffel, H. von, 'Marschtechnik motorisierter Verbände', in *Die Kraftfahrkampftruppe*, No. 6, 1938, pp. 219–21.

Martin, B., 'Tagebuch eines sowjetischen Offiziers vom 1. Januar 1942 bis 8. Februar 1942', in *Wehrwissenschaftliche Rundschau*, No. 6, 1967, pp. 352–7.

Moritz, E., 'Die Einschätzung der Roten Armee durch den faschistischen deutschen Generalstab von 1935–1941', in *Zeitschrift für Militärgeschichte*, No. 2, 1969, pp. 154–70.

'Panzerkampfwagen im Winter (Aus erbeuteten russischen Vorschriften)', in *Kampftruppen*, No. 6, 1963, pp. 12–13.

Philippi, A., 'Das Pripjetproblem', Supplement 2 to *Wehrwissenschaftliche Rundschau*, 1936.

'Pioniere in Panzerverband', in *Militär-Wochenblatt*, 4 June 1936, cols. 2061–4.

Raus, E., 'Die Panzerschlachten bei Rossienie, 23. bis 26. Juni 1941' in *Allgemeine Schweizerische Militärzeitschrift*, No. 1, 1952, pp. 57ff.

Reinhardt, H., 'Die Panzergruppe 3 in der Schlacht vor Moskau und ihre Erfahrungen im Rückzug', in *Wehrkunde*, No. 9, 1953, pp. 1–11.

——, 'Der Vorstoß des XXXXI Panzerkorps im Sommer 1941', in *Wehrkunde*, No. 3, 1956, pp. 122–36.

——, 'Die 4. Panzerdivision vor Warschau und an der Bzura vom 9.-20.9.1939', in *Wehrkunde*, No. 5, 1958, pp. 237–47.

Rjazanskij, A., 'Die Taktik der sowjetischen Panzertruppen im Zweiten Weltkrieg', in *Truppendienst*, No. 6, 1967, pp. 519–22.

Roos, H., 'Der Feldzug in Polen vom September 1939', in *Wehrwissenschaftliche Rundschau*, No. 9, 1959, pp. 491–512.

Rossiwall, Th., 'Die Winterschlacht 1941/42 in Rußland', in *Truppendienst*, No. 6, 1966, pp. 529–33.

Schmidtgen, 'Unser erstes Gefecht mit schweren russischen T-34-Panzern', in *Die Panzertruppe*, No. 6, 1942, pp. 92–5.

Schmilauer, O., 'Kampferfahrungen beim Panzereinsatz im 2. Weltkrieg' in: *Armee-Motor*, No. 5, 1969, pp. 145–53.

——, 'Gefechtsformationen der einstigen deutschen Panzerwaffe', in: *Armee-Motor*, No. 6, 1970, pp. 175–80.

Schweppenburg, Frhr. Geyr von, 'Elemente der operativen und taktischen Führung von Schnellen Verbänden des 2. Weltkrieges', in *Wehrwissenschaftliche Rundschau*, No. 2, 1962, pp. 93–110.

Senger und Etterlin, F.M. von, 'Die gepanzerte Kampfgruppe', in *Wehrwissenschaftliche Rundschau*, No. 5, 1953, pp. 220–7.

——, 'Der Marsch einer Panzer-Division in der Schlammperiode', in *Wehrkunde*, No. 3, 1955, pp. 85–91.

Siepert, H., 'Zusammenarbeit der Waffengattungen', in *Wehrausbildung*, No. 3, 1972, pp. 123–5.

Temmelsfeld, 'Der Nachschub (mot.)', in *Die Panzertruppe*, No. 11, 1941, pp. 172–5.

Tippelskirch, K. von, 'Hitlers Kriegführung nach dem Frankreichfeldzug im Hinblick auf Barbarossa', in *Wehrwissenschaftliche Rundschau*, No. 4, 1954, pp. 145–56.

'Verschiedene Kriegsberichterstatter' (Various War Reporters), in *Die Wehrmacht*, from No. 13, 18 June to No. 25, 3 December 1941.

Wiener, F., 'Höhepunkte des Panzerkrieges', in *Österreichische Militärische Zeitschrift*, No. 4, 1966, pp. 294–6.

Zeitzler, K., 'Krisenlagen', in: *Wehrkunde*, No. 1, 1961, pp. 2–8.

Zobel, H., 'Angriff einer gepanzerten Kampfgruppe im Osten', in *Wehrwissenschaftliche Rundschau*, No. 5, 1952, pp. 205–8.

English

Guderian, H., 'Armored Warfare', in *Armored Cavalry Journal*, No. 1, 1949, pp. 2–7.

Karslake, H., 'South of the Somme. May–June 1940', in *The Army Quarterly*, No. 1, 1972, pp. 231–2.

Lynn, J.A., 'French Armor: 1940', in *Military Review*, No. 12, 1967, pp. 78–84.

Ogorkiewicz, R.M., 'Armor in the Polish Campaign', in *Armor*, No. 5, 1959, pp. 4–7.

French

Cossé-Brissac, Ch. de, 'Combien de chars français contre combien de chars allemands le 10 mai 1940', in: *Revue de Défense Nationale*, July 1947, pp. 75–89.

Grouzdev, B., 'Le franchissement des bois et marais par les chars', in: *Revue Militaire Soviétique*, No. 1, 1972, pp. 20–2.

Merglen, A., and Regling, V., 'La percée allemande au sud d'Amiens (juin 1940)', in: *Revue Historique de l'Armée*, No. 1, 1970, pp. 75–102.

Mostovenko, V., 'L'histoire du T-34', in *Revue Militaire Soviétique*, No. 3, 1967, pp. 4–7.

Vaselle, P., 'Les divisions cuirassées françaises en mai 1940', in: *Revue Militaire Suisse*, No. 6, 1972, pp. 257–69.

FURTHER READING

German tanks in general

Doyle, H., and Chamberlain, P., *Encyclopedia of German Tanks of World War Two*, London, 1978.

German armour campaigns between 1939 and 1941

Battlefield-Tour 1983 (dealing with the campaigns of 1940), pres. by HQ Northern Army Group, Mönchengladbach, 1983.

Kennedy, R.M., *The German Campaign in Poland, 1939*, Washington, 1956.

Werrick, R., *Blitzkrieg*, Amsterdam, 1979.

German armour strategy

Macksey, K.J., *Guderian, Panzergeneral*, London, 1975.

——, *Panzer Division: The Mailed Fist*, New York, 1972.

Messenger, C., *The Art of Blitzkrieg*, London, 1976.

UNPUBLISHED SOURCE MATERIAL

All unpublished source material used in this book can be found in the Bundesarchiv-Militärarchiv in Freiburg im Breisgau.

Many of the files dating from the blitz campaigns against Poland and France were badly damaged in the fire in the Kriegswissenschaftliche Abteilung of the Heeresamt in Potsdam on 27 and 28 February 1942. Thus it is unfortunately no longer possible to speak of a complete documentation for this period.

File	Archive Code

OKW

KTB vom Wehrwirtschafts- und
Rüstungsamt, Wi.Rü.Amt/Stab. vom
1 November 1941–31 März 1942   (RW 19/166)

OKH

Kdo der Panzertruppen, Id, Nr. 3,770/37
  Besichtigungsbemerkungen des
  Kommandierenden Generals der
  Panzertruppen im Jahre 1937   (AD–RH/928)
Merkblatt für Gliederung und Kampfweise
  der Schützenkompanie zu 12 Gruppen,
  vom 13 Oktober 1939   (in RH 27–18/208)
Merkblatt für alle Waffen. Flußübergang,
  Feldbefestigung und Minenverwendung
  bei strengem Frost. Gen.St.d.H./
  Gen.d.Pi. u.Fest. beim OB d.H. 34/Pi 2,
  120/40   (in RH 27–18/208)
Merkblatt für den Einsatz der
  Sturmartillerie, Chef der Heeresrüstung
  und OB des Ersatzheeres, AHA/In 41E,
  Nr. 3,082/40 geheim vom 20 Mai 1940   (in RH 27–18/208)
Heeres-Druckvorschrift 470/1,
  Ausbildungsvorschrift für die
  Panzertruppe, vom 2 Oktober 1938
  (Berlin, 1938)   (in RH 27–18/208)
Heeres-Druckvorschrift 470/7,
  Ausbildungsvorschrift für die
  Panzertruppe, vom 1 Mai 1941   (in RH 27–18/208)
Heeres-Druckvorschrift 299/11d, OB d.H.,
  Gen.St.d.H./Gen. der Schnellen
  Truppen, Entw. vom 1 März 1941   (in RH 27–18/208)
Richtlinien für Führung und Einsatz der
  Pz. Division vom 3 Dezember 1940   (B II 2 D g 66)
H.Q. Vorläufige Richtlinien für Führung
  und Kampf des Schützen-Regimentes
  und des Schützenbataillons, undatierter
  Entw.   (RH 10/13)
Taktische Erfahrungen im Westfeldzug,

File	Archive Code

Gen.St.d.H./Ausb.Abt. (Ia) Nr. 2,400/40
geh. vom 20 November 1940   (RH 19 II/142)
Kampferfahrungen aus dem Ostfeldzug,
Gen.St.d.H./Ausb. Abt. (Ia) Nr. 1,550/42
geh. vom 10 Juni 1942   (RH 19 II/142)

H.Gr.Mitte

KTB Nr. 1, Band August 1941	(RH 19 II/119)
KTB Nr. 1, Band Sept. 1941	(nicht belegt)
KTB Nr. 1, Band Okt. 1941	(RH 19 II/120)
Anlageband A zum KTB Nr. 1, Band Dezember 1941	(RH 19 II/122)
Anlageband B zum KTB Nr. 1, Band Dezember vom 1 Dezember 1941 – 18 Dezember 1941	(RH 19 II/136)
Anlageband C zum KTB Nr. 1, Band Dezember vom 19 Dezember 1941 – 31 Dezember 1941	(RH 19 II/137)

Pz.AOK 2

Abt. Ia, Planspiel, Nr. 16/41 Geh.Kdos. vom 13 März 1941	(RH 21–2/v. 86)
Abt. Ic, Planspiel, Nr. 113/41 Geh.Kdos. vom 26 Februar – 28 Februar 1941	(RH 21–2/v. 87)
Abt. Ia, Nr. 25/41 Geh.Kdos. Chefs. vom 14 März 1941	(RH 21–2/v. 84)
Abt. Ia, Nr. 301/41 Geh.Kdos. Chefs. vom 8 Juni 1941	(RH 21–2/v. 88)
Abt. Ia, KTB Nr. 1, vom 1 November – 5 Dezember 1941	(RH 21–2/v. 244)
Abt. Ia, KTB Nr. 1 vom 6 Dezember – 26 Dezember 1941	(RH 21–2/v. 277)
Abt. Ic, KTB Nr. 1,	
vom 22 Juni – 30 Juni 1941	(RH 21–2/v. 646)
vom 1 Juli – 9 Juli 1941	(RH 21–2/v. 647)
vom 10 Juli – 18 Juli 1941	(RH 21–2/v. 648)
vom 19 Juli – 25 Juli 1941	(RH 21–2/v. 649)
vom 26 Juli – 2 August 1941	(RH 21–2/v. 650)
vom 3 August – 9 August 1941	(RH 21–2/v. 651)

File	Archive Code
vom 10 August – 17 August 1941	(RH 21–2/v. 652)
vom 25 August – 31 August 1941	(RH 21–2/v. 654)
Abt. Ia, Anlageband zum KTB Nr. 1, vom 22 Juni 1941 – 31 März 1942	(RH 21–2/v. 756)
Abt. Ia, Anlageband Nr. 2b zum KTB Nr. 1, vom 22 Juni 1941 – 31 März 1942	(RH 21–2/v. 757)
Abt. Ia, Zustandsberichte unterstellter Verbände	(RH 21–2/171)

Pz.AOK 3

Abt. Ia, Anlagen zum KTB, März 1940 – Mai 1941	(RH 21–3/v. 39)
Abt. Ia, Besprechungen des Generaloberst Hoth, Frühjahr 1941, vom 30 März – 21 Mai 1941	(RH 21–3/v. 40)
Abt. Ia, Anlage 65, Kriegsspiel 'Barbarossa', vom 20/21 Mai 1941	(RH 21–3/v. 41)
Abt. Ia, Anlagen zum KTB, Tagesmeldungen, Bd. I, vom 21 Juni – 31 August 1941	(RH 21–3/v. 43)
Abt. Ia, Anlagen zum KTB, Ausgegebene Befehle, Bd. III, vom 25 Mai – 31 August 1941	(RH 21–3/v. 44)
Abt. Ia, Anlagen zum KTB, Eingegangene Befehle, Bd. III, vom 25 Mai – 31 August 1941	(RH 21–3/v. 45)
Abt. Ia, Erfahrungsbericht für Marschanweisung vom 22 Juni – 28 Juli 1941	(RH 21–3/v. 67)
Abt. Ia, Anlagen zum KTB, Tagesmeldungen, vom 1 September – 31 Oktober 1941	(RH 21–3/v. 70)
Abt. Ia, Anlagen zum KTB, Tagesmeldungen, vom 1 November – 31 Dezember 1941	(RH 21–3/v. 71)
Abt. Ia, Nr. 520/42 geheim, Gefechtsberichte Rußland 1941/42, vom 10 Februar 1942	(RH 21–3/v. 113)
Abt. Ic, Anlageband zum Tätigkeitsbericht Nr. 2, vom 1 Januar – 11 August 1941	(RH 21–3/v. 423)
Abt. Ic, Anlageband D, zum	

File	Archive Code
Tätigkeitsbericht Nr. 2, vom 22 Juni – 11 August 1941	(RH 21–3/v. 430K)
Abt. Ic, Anlageband B, Teil I, zum Tätigkeitsbericht Nr. 2, vom 1 Januar – 21 Juni 1941	(RH 21–3/v. 425K)
Abt. Ic, Anlageband B, Teil II, zum Tätigkeitsbericht Nr. 2, vom 22 Juni – 20 Juli 1941	(RH 21–3/v. 426K)
Abt. Ic, Anlageband B, Teil III, zum Tätigkeitsbericht Nr. 2, vom 26 Juli – 6 August 1941	(RH 21–3/v. 427K)
Abt. Ic, Anlageband C, Teil I, zum Tätigkeitsbericht Nr. 2, vom 12 März – 4 Juli 1941	(RH 21–3/v. 428)
Abt. Ic, Anlageband C, Teil II, zum Tätigkeitsbericht Nr. 2, vom 4 Juli – 8 August 1941	(RH 21–3/v. 429)

XV.Pz.K.

File	Archive Code
Abt. Ia, KTB vom 19 August – 13 Oktober 1939	(RH 21–3/v. 2)
Abt. Ia, Anlagen zum KTB, vom 25 August – 5 Oktober 1939	(RH 21–3/v. 3)
Abt. Ia, Anlagen zum KTB, vom 13 September – 5 Oktober 1939	(RH 21–3/v. 4)
Abt. Ia, Karten und Skizzen	(RH 21–3/v. 5)
Abt. Ia, Eingegangene Meldungen und Funksprüche	
vom 17 September – 28 September 1939	(RH 21–3/v. 12)
vom 17 September – 8 Oktober 1939	(RH 21–3/v. 13)
vom 23 August – 31 August 1939	(RH 21–3/v. 14)
Ausgänge von Fernschreiben	
vom 31 August – 8 September 1939	(RH 21–3/v. 15)
vom 9 September – 22 September 1939	(RH 21–3/v. 16)
Abt. Ia, Die Bereitstellung an der Pilica und Einsatz zwischen Bzura und Warschau, vom 15 September – 18 September 1939	(RH 21–3/v. 24)
Abt. Ia, Anlagen zum KTB, vom 30 August – 5 Oktober 1939	(RH 21–3/v. 23)

File	Archive Code

XIX.Pz.K.*

Abt. Ia, Erfahrungsbericht über den
Einsatz in Polen, vom 17 Februar 1940   (RH 21–2/v. 583)

Abt. Ia, KTB Nr. 1, vom 1 September –
25 September 1940   (RH 21–2/v. 3)

Abt. Ia, Anlagen zum KTB Nr. 1, Einsatz
Ost, II. Teil, Erfahrungsberichte über
den Feldzug in Polen bis 9 Oktober 1939   (RH 21–2/v. 29)

Abt. Ia, Anlagen zum KTB Nr. 1, Einsatz
Ost, II. Teil, Tägliche Aufzeichnungen
vom 7 September – 24 September 1939   (RH 21–2/v. 9–24)

Abt. Ia, Anlagen zum KTB Nr. 1, vom
20 Juni – 31 August 1939   (RH 21–2/v. 2)

Abt. Ia, Anlagen zum KTB Nr. 1,
Gefundene Feindunterlagen, vom
1 September – 6 September 1939   (RH 21–2/v. 28K)

Abt. Ia, Befehle der H.Gr.Nord, vom
15 August – 15 September 1939   (RH 19 II/353)

Abt. Ia, Akte III, Morgen- und
Abendmeldungen des Ia, vom 10 Mai –
28 Mai 1940   (RH 21–2/v. 44)

Abt. Ia, Akte IV, Morgen- und
Abendmeldungen des Ic, vom 11 Mai –
31 Mai 1940   (RH 21–2/v. 625)

Abt. Ia, Akte V, Tätigkeit der Luftwaffe,
vom 10 Mai – 31 Mai 1940   (RH 21–2/v. 45)

Abt. Ia, Akte, VI, Verlauf des Tages beim
Kommandierenden General, vom
10 Mai – 29 Mai 1940   (RH 21–2/v. 46)

Abt. Ia, Akte VII, Funksprüche, vom
12 Mai – 17 Mai 1940   (RH 21–2/v. 47 + 8)

Abt. Ia, Akte VII, Funksprüche, vom
23 Mai – 29 Mai 1940   (RH 21–2/v. 50)

Abt. Ia, Akte X, (title burned), vom
7 April – 1 Juni 1940   (RH 21–2/v. 54)

Abt. Ia, Akte XII, Bericht über Einsatz der
Korps-Nachrichten-Abteilung 80, mit

---

* During the 2nd phase of the campaign in France XIX Pz.K. was reorganized
to form Panzergruppe Guderian. Cf. App. V, p. 143.

File	Archive Code
Anlagen, vom 10 Mai – 25 Mai 1940	(RH 21–2/v. 56)
Abt. Ia, Akte VII, Funksprüche, vom 2 Juni – 22 Juni 1940	(RH 21–2/v. 51)
Abt. Ia, Akte D, Tätigkeitsbericht des Ia, vom 22 November 1939 – 22 Juni 1940	(RH 21–2/v. 37)
Abt. Ia, Akte F, Gefechtsberichte, vom 19 Mai – 6 Juli 1940	(RH 21–2/v. 63a)
Abt. Ia, Tätigkeitsbericht des Kommandos, vom 25 Juni – 24 Dezember 1940	(RH 21–2/v. 64)
Abt. Ia, Anlagenhefte Juni 1940 bis Dezember 1940	(RH 21–2/v. 65–71)

XXII.Pz.K.*

Abt. Ia, KTB Nr. 2, vom 1 Oktober 1939 – 5 März 1940	(RH 21–1/15)
Abt. Ia, Anlagen zum KTB Nr. 2, vom 22 November 1939 – 4 März 1940	(RH 21–1/16)
Abt. Ia, KTB, vom 10 Mai – 11 Juli 1940	(RH 21–1/22)
Abt. Ia, KTB Nr. 3, vom 6 März – 9 Mai 1940	(RH 21–1/18)
Abt. Ia, Anlagenheft 1 zum KTB Nr. 3, vom 2 März – 7 Mai 1940	(RH 21–1/19)
Abt. Ia, Anlagenheft 2 zum KTB Nr. 3, vom 21 März – 8 Mai 1940	(RH 21–1/20)
Abt. Ia, Anlagenheft 1 zum KTB Nr. 4, vom 10 Mai – 17 Mai 1940	(RH 21–1/23)
Abt. Ia, Anlagenheft 2 zum KTB Nr. 4, vom 18 Mai – 23 Mai 1940	(RH 21–1/24)
Abt. Ia, Anlagenheft 3 zum KTB Nr. 4, vom 24 Mai – 31 Mai 1940	(RH 21–1/25)
Abt. Ia, Anlagenheft 4 zum KTB Nr. 4, vom 1 Juni – 10 Juni 1940	(RH 21–1/26)
Abt. Ia, Anlagenheft 5 zum KTB Nr. 4, vom 11 Juni – 17 Juni 1940	(RH 21–1/27)
Abt. Ia, Anlagenheft 6 zum KTB Nr. 4, vom 18 Juni – 24 Juni 1940	(RH 21–1/28)
Abt. Ia, Anlagenheft 7 zum KTB Nr. 4,	

* During the 2nd phase of the campaign in France XXII Pz.K. was reorganized to form Panzergruppe von Kleist. Cf. App. V, p. 143.

File	Archive Code

vom 25 Juni – 12 Juli 1940   (RH 21–1/29)
Abt. Ia, Chef des Generalstabes, Anlage B
zum KTB Nr. 3, 'Vorläufige Erfahrungen
mit großen motorisierten Verbänden',
vom 10 August 1940   (RH 21–1/36)
Abt. Ia, Tätigkeitsberichte vom 12 Juli –
31 Dezember 1940   (RH 21–1/34)
Abt. Ia, Anlagen zum Tätigkeitsbericht
vom 12 Juli – 31 Dezember 1940   (RH 21–1/35)
Abt. Ia, Chef des Generalstabes,
Richtlinien für die Führung Schneller
Gruppen, Entwurf vom 20 Oktober 1940   (RH 21–1/37)

XXIV.Pz.K.

Abt. Ia, Anlagen 229–308b zum KTB Nr. 8,
vom 5 Oktober – 21 November 1941   (RH 24–24/122)

XXXIX.Pz.K.

Abt. Ia, KTB, vom 27 August –
27 Dezember 1941   (23 584/2)
Abt. Ia, Nr. 291/40 geh. 'Richtlinien für die
Führung der Panzerdivision', vom
9 Oktober 1940 (in Anlagenheft Oktober
1940 der Panzergruppe Guderian)   (RH 21–2/v. 69)

XXXXVI.Pz.K.

Abt. Ia, KTB Nr. 2, I. Teil, vom 19 Mai –
7 Juli 1941   (30 241/1)
Abt. Ia, KTB Nr. 2, II. Teil, vom 8 Juli –
23 August 1941   (30 241/2)
Abt. Ia, Gefechts- und
Verpflegungsstärken der unterstellten
Truppen, vom 21 Mai – 21 August 1941   (30 241/2)
Abt. Ia, Anlagen zum KTB Nr. 2, Befehle
der Pz. Gr. 2 und vom AOK 4, vom
23 Mai – 23 August 1941   (30 241/4)
Abt. Ia, Anlagen zum KTB Nr. 2,
Meldungen an Pz.Gr. 2, vom 6 Juni –

File	Archive Code
23 August 1941	(30 241/5)
Abt. Ia, Anlagen zum KTB Nr. 2, Befehle des Korps, vom 31 Mai – 22 August 1941	(30 241/6)
Abt. Ia, Anlagen zum KTB Nr. 2, Meldungen der 10. Pz.Div., vom 10 Juni – 1 September 1941	(30 241/7)
Abt. Ia, Anlagen zum KTB Nr. 2, Meldungen und Gespräche der 5. Pz.Div., vom 27 September – 31 Dezember 1941	(30 241/29)
Abt. Ia, Anlagen zum KTB Nr. 2, Meldungen und Gespräche der 11. Pz.Div., vom 27 September – 31 Dezember 1941	(30 241/30)
Abt. Ia, Anlagen zum KTB Nr. 2, Meldungen zeitweise unterstellter Divisionen, vom 31 Juli – 8 August 1941	(30 241/31)
Abt. Ia, Anlagen zum KTB Nr. 2, Meldungen und Gespräche der 2. Pz.Div., vom 12 Oktober – 14 November 1941	(30 241/32)

XXXXVII.Pz.K.

File	Archive Code
Abt. Ia, Anlagen zum KTB Nr. 2, 401–500, vom 27 Juli – 17 August 1941	(RH 24–47/7)
501–600, vom 18 August – 30 August 1941	(RH 24–47/8)
601–700, vom 31 August – 8 September 1941	(RH 24–47/9)
701–800, vom 9 September – 22 September 1941	(RH 24–47/10)
Abt. Ia, Anlagen zum KTB Nr. 3, 1–150, vom 22 September – 6 Oktober 1941	(RH 24–47/20, 21)
151–300, vom 7 Oktober – 15 Oktober 1941	(RH 24–47/22, 23)
301–450, vom 16 Oktober – 5 November 1941	(RH 24–47/24, 25)
451–600, vom 6 November – 26 November 1941	(RH 24–47/26, 27)

File	Archive Code
601–750, vom 26 November – 15 Dezember 1941	(RH 24–47/28, 29)

LVII.Pz.K.

Abt. Ia, KTB Nr. 1, vom 15 Februar – 31 Oktober 1941	(15 683/1)
Abt. Ia, KTB Nr. 2, vom 1 November – 31 Dezember 1941	(15 683/1a)
Abt. Ia, Anlagenband zum KTB, Morgen-, Zwischen- und Tagesmeldungen, vom 21 Juni – 31 Dezember 1941	(15 683/2–6)
Abt. Ia, Anlagenbände Nr. 1-10 zum KTB, Anlagen 1–1041, vom 1 März 1941 – 2 Januar 1942	(15 633/2–11)

1. Pz.Div.

Abt. Ia, Anlage d zum KTB Nr. 4, Gefechtsberichte, Juni 1940	(RH 27–1/17)

2. le.Div.*

Abt. Ia, Erfahrungsbericht über Polen und Tschechei, vom 22 März – 1 November 1939	(RH 27–7/2)

3. Pz.Div.

Abt. Ia, KTB Nr. 3, vom 11 Juli – 18 September 1941	(RH 27–3/14)
Abt. Ia, KTB Nr. 3, vom 19 September 1941 – 6 Februar 1942	(RH 27–3/15)
Abt. Ia, Anlagen zum KTB Nr. 3, Allgemeines, vom 7 Mai – 28 Juli 1941	(RH 27–3/18)
Divisionsbefehle, vom 5 Juni – 3 Juli 1941	(RH 27–3/19)
Divisionsbefehle, vom 15 September – 29 Dezember 1941	(RH 27–3/21)

* During the Western Campaign: 7. Pz.Div.

File	Archive Code

Gefechts- und Erfahrungsberichte, vom
    6 Juli 1941 – 19 Februar 1942   (RH 27–3/30)

4. le.Div.**

Abt. Ia, KTB, Feldzug in Polen 1939   (RH 27–9/79)
Abt. Ia, Anlagen zum KTB, vom
    22 August – 22 Oktober 1941   (RH 27–9/80)

4. Pz. Div.

Abt. Ia, Anlagen zum KTB, Gefechts- und
Erfahrungsberichte, vom 22 Juni 1941 –
26 März 1942; especially Nr. 71/42 geh.
Beantwortung Fragebogen OKH betr.
Erfahrung Ostfeldzug in Führung,
Ausbildung und Organisation, vom
12 März 1942   (RH 27/4–37)

7. Pz.Div.

Abt. Ia, Kurzberichte, Der Kampf im
    Westen, vom 10 Mai – 19 Juni 1940   (RH 27–7/191)
Abt. Ia, Anlagen zum KTB, Gefechts- und
Erfahrungsberichte über den West-
feldzug, vom 10 Mai – 24 Juni 1940   (RH 27–7/29)
Abt. Ia, Tagesmeldungen, vom 20 Juni –
    10 Juli 1941   (RH 27–7/52)
Abt. Ia, Tagesmeldungen, vom 11 Juli –
    25 Juli 1941   (RH 27–7/53)
Abt. Ia, Tagesmeldungen, vom 26 Juli –
    12 August 1941   (RH 27–7/54)
Abt. Ia, Morgenmeldungen, vom
    19 August – 21 September 1941   (RH 27–7/55)
Abt. Ia, Tagesmeldungen von unterstellten
Truppenteilen, vom 28 September –
20 Oktober 1941   (RH 27–7/56)

** During the Western Campaign: 9. Pz.Div.

File	Archive Code

10. Pz.Div.

Abt. Ia, Anlagen I zum KTB, vom
25 August – 14 September 1939   (RH 27–10/1)

Abt. Ia, Anlagen II zum KTB, vom
15 September – 4 Oktober 1939   (RH 27–10/2)

Abt. Ia, Anlagen III zum KTB, vom
1 September – 23 September 1939   (RH 27–10/3)

Abt. Ia und Ic, Anlagen zum KTB Nr. 2,
vom 10 Oktober – 31 Dezember 1939   (RH 27–10/5)

Abt. Ia, KTB Nr. 3, vom 9 Mai –
29 Juni 1940   (RH 27–10/10)

Abt. Ia, Anlagenbände III–VI zum KTB
Nr. 6, undatiert   (RH 27–10/40–43)

Abt. Ia, Bericht über den Einsatz der
10.Pz.Div. im Ostfeldzug, vom 22 Juni –
5 Dezember 1941   (RH 27–10/109)

12. Pz.Div.

Abt. Ia, Anlagenmappe Nr. 6 zum KTB
Nr. 1, vom 1 August – 31 August 1941   (RH 27–12/9)

Abt. Ia, Anlagenmappe Nr. 10 zum KTB
Nr. 1, vom 1 November – 15 November
1941   (RH 27–12/13)

Abt. Ic, Tätigkeitsbericht vom 1 Juni –
15 Dezember 1941 und Aufstellung über
Gefangene und Beute   (RH 27–12/48)

Abt. Ic, Anlagenmappe Nr. 1 zum
Tätigkeitsbericht, vom 1 Juni –
15 Dezember 1941   (RH 27–12/49)

Abt. Ic, Anlagenmappe Nr. 3 zum
Tätigkeitsbericht, vom 1 Juni –
15 Dezember 1941   (RH 27–12/51)

17. Pz.Div.

Lebenserinnerungen des Generaloberst
Hans-Jürgen von Arnim, Teil VI,
Polenfeldzug, Westfeldzug   (N 61/1)
Teil VII, Der Krieg in Rußland, Vormarsch

File	Archive Code

der 17. Pz.Div. bei der H.Gr.Mitte bis
Orel   (N 61/2)
Abt. Ib, KTB, Teile 1–4, vom 25 Mai 1941 –
15 Januar 1942   (RH 27–17/18–2)

18. Pz.Div.

Abt. Ia, Anlagen zum KTB,
   Zustandsberichte der Division und
   unterstellter Einheiten, vom 22 Juni –
   26 Oktober 1941   (RH 27–18/32)
Abt. Ia, Gefechtskalender, Teil I, vom
   22 Juni – 19 August 1941   (RH 27–18/63)
Abt. Ia, Gefechtskalender, Teil II, vom
   20 August – 29 September 1941   (RH 27–18/64)
Abt. Ia, Gefechtskalender, Teil III, vom
   30 September – 19 Oktober 1941   (RH 27–18/65)
Abt. Ia, Anlagen zum KTB, Allgemeines,
   vom 1 September 1941 – 10 März 1942   (RH 27–18/72)

19. Pz.Div.

Abt. Ia, Anlagen zum KTB, Gefechts- und
   Verflegungsstärken, vom 1 Juni 1941 –
   31 Dezember 1942   (RH 27–19/8)

20. Pz.Div.

Abt. Ia, Anlagenband D 1 zum KTB Nr. 2,
   Einsatz-, Gefechts-, Bergungs- und
   Lageberichte, Lagekarten, vom 20 Juli –
   31 Dezember 1941   (RH 27–20/96)
Abt. Ia, Anlagenband D 3 zum KTB Nr. 2,
   Zustandsberichte, vom 15 August 1941
   – 30 April 1942   (RH 27–20/98)
Abt. Ia, Anlagenband D 4 zum KTB Nr. 2
   vom 16 August – 15 November 1941   (RH 27–20/99)
Abt. Ia, Anlagenband H zum KTB Nr. 2,
   vom 11 Juni 1941 – 30 April 1942   (RH 27–20/104)

Abbreviations

Abbreviation	German	English
Ia	Erster Generalstabsoffizier	G.S.O. 1 (G1)*
Ib	Zweiter Generalstabsoffizier	G.S.O. 2 (G2)
Ic	Dritter Generalstabsoffizier	G.S.O. 3 (G3)
Abt.	Abteilung	battalion, detachment, unit, section
AK or A.K.	Armeekorps	army corps
AOK	Armeeoberkommando	army headquarters (AHQ)
Art.	Artillerie	artillery
Bat.	Bataillon	battalion
Brig.	Brigade	
Chefs.	Chefsache	see Kdos. Chefs.
Div.	Division	
Div. Gef. Std.	Divisionsgefechtsstand	div. headquarters
Flab.	Fliegerabwehr	anti-aircraft
Flak	Fliegerabwehrkanone	anti-aircraft gun
Gef. Bericht	Gefechtsbericht	combat report
geh.	geheim	secret
Gen. Kdo.	Generalkommando	corps HQ
Gen. Ob.	Generaloberst	(Colonel-)General
Gen. Qu.	Generalquartiermeister	see Ib; at field HQ
Gen. St.	Generalstab	general staff
H.	Heer	the Army (as distinguished

* Ia = for command matters, at Div., Army Corps, Army and Army Group
Ib = for supply matters, Div. only
Ic = for intelligence and counter-intelligence, at Div., Army Corps, Army and Army Group.

Abbreviation	German	English
		from Armee, a tactical unit)
H. Dv.	Heeresdruckvorschrift	Army Manual
HG	Handgranate	hand grenade
H. Gr.	Heeresgruppe	army group
HQ	Hauptquartier	headquarters
I.D.	Infanteriedivision	infantry division
Kan.	Kanone	field gun, cannon
Kav.	Kavallerie	cavalry
Kdo.	Kommando	order, command; HQ (Div. and larger); detachment, party, detail
Kdos.	Kommandosache	confidential military document
Kdos. Chefs.		top secret military document (TSM)
Kol.	Kolonne	column, train (supply) convoy
Kfz.	Kraftfahrzeug	motor vehicle
Kpfw.	Kampfwagen	tank, armoured car, combat car
KTB	Kriegstagebuch	war diary (WD)
le.	leichte	light
mech.	mechanisiert	mechanised
MG	Maschinengewehr	machine gun
MTW	Mannschaftstransportwagen	personnel, troop carrier
mot.	motorisiert	motorised
OB	Oberbefehlshaber	C-in-C, Supreme Commander
Ob d. H.	Oberbefehlshaber des Heeres	Army C-in-C
OKH	Oberkommando des Heeres	Army High Command
OKW	Oberkommando der Wehrmacht	Armed Forces High Command
Op.	Operation	operation, mission
Pak.	Panzerabwehrkanone	anti-tank gun
Pz.	Panzer	tank
Pz. A.	Panzerarmee	Panzer Army

Abbreviation	German	English
Pz. Gr.	Panzergruppe	Panzer Group
Pz. Gren.	Panzergrenadier	Armoured Infantry
Pzj. Abt.	Panzerjägerabteilung	anti-tank battalion
Pz. K.	Panzerkorps	Panzer Corps
Pz. Sp. Wg.	Panzerspähwagen	armoured scout car
Rgt.	Regiment	
Sch.	Schützen	infantry
SPW	Schützenpanzerwagen	armoured personnel carrier
WFst.	Wehrmacht-Führungsstab	Armed Forces operations staff
Zugkw.	Zugkraftwagen	tractor, prime mover

The Author

Rudolf Steiger
Professor, Dr. phil I; Lecturer in Military Educational Theory and Rhetorics (Militärpädagogik und Rhetorik) in the Military Sciences Department and the Military Command College (Militärische Führungsschulen) at the Swiss Technical College in Zürich.

He holds lectures at foreign military academies and conducts seminars in Management and Leadership (Menschenführung) for civilian and military executives. Prof. Steiger holds the rank of Colonel and General Staff Officer in the Swiss Army. Between 1984–7 he commanded an armoured battalion, and since 1989 he has headed the Working Party on Military Sciences under the auspices of the Army's Chief of Education (Ausbildungschef der Armee).

He has published numerous papers as well as the following books:

Panzertaktik im Spiegel deutscher Kriegstagebücher 1939–1941, Vol. 12 of 'Einzelschriften zur militärischen Geschichte des Zweiten Weltkrieges', Rombach Verlag, 4th edition (out of print), Freiburg im Breisgau, 1977.

Werden junge Menschen im Militärdienst überfordert? Fragen und Antworten zur militärischen Ausbildung und Erziehung, Huber Verlag, 2nd revised edition, Frauenfeld, 1988.

Lehrbuch der Vortragstechnik, Huber Verlag, 5th enlarged edition, Frauenfeld, 1990.

Lehrbuch der Diskussionstechnik, Huber Verlag, 5th revised edition, Frauenfeld, 1990.

Menschenorientierte Führung. Anregungen für zivile und militärische Führungskräfte, Huber Verlag, Frauenfeld, 1990.

Index

1. Soweit fG-Sachen ihrer Natur nach nicht zur Rechtsprechung im materiellen Sinne zu zählen sind, können sie durch einfaches Gesetz vom Richter auf die Verwaltungsbehörde oder den Rechtspfleger übertragen werden. Die Übertragung der tendenziell einfacheren fG-Angelegenheiten vom Richter auf den Rechtspfleger durch das RPflG von 1969 ist mit Art. 92 GG vereinbar. Den Rechtspflegern dürfen aber keine Aufgaben der materiellen Rechtsprechung übertragen werden, die gem. Art. 92 GG den Richtern vorbehalten sind (BVerfGE 101, 397, 405).

2. Die für materielle Rechtsprechung wesentlichen rechtsstaatlichen Regeln müssen Richter in fG-Verfahren auch dann beachten, wenn die einzelne fG-Angelegenheit der Natur nach lediglich Rechtsprechung im formellen, nicht im materiellen Sinne ist. Wenn diese Angelegenheiten nämlich zunächst einer Verwaltungsbehörde zur Erledigung anvertraut wären, wäre anschließend der Rechtsweg mit vollem gerichtlichem Rechtsschutz garantiert (Art. 19 Abs. 4 GG). Da diese fG-Angelegenheiten aber wegen ihrer gehobenen Bedeutung von vornherein den Gerichten anvertraut sind und nach dem fG-Instanzenzug weiterer Gerichtsschutz nicht gewährt wird, gebieten Art. 19 Abs. 4, 92 GG, daß in den fG-Verfahren vor dem Richter auch alle rechtsstaatlichen Regeln beachtet werden müssen, die für materielle Rechtsprechung wesentlich sind. Dies gilt nicht nur für die Beschwerdeinstanz, sondern schon für die erste Instanz (dazu näher: Kollhosser, Verfahrensbeteiligte, § 3 III, S. 56 ff.; a. A. Smid

S. 481 ff.). Die Einschaltung des Richters soll gerade die Anwendung der Garantien des richterlichen Verfahrens gewährleisten (BVerfGE 9, 89, 97).

14. Amtshaftung des Rechtspflegers

In notarieller Form verkauft V dem K ein Grundstück in Hamburg und verpflichtet sich zugleich, darauf für K ein Haus zu bauen. Kurze Zeit später läßt V das Grundstück an K – ebenfalls in notarieller Form – auf. K beantragt daraufhin unter Vorlage beider Urkunden und der Unbedenklichkeitsbescheinigung des Finanzamtes (§ 22 GrEStG) seine Eintragung als Eigentümer ins Grundbuch. Der zuständige Rechtspfleger R weist den Eintragungsantrag unter Hinweis auf BGHZ 69, 266 ff. gem. § 18 Abs. 1 S. 1 GBO zurück, weil der der Auflassung zugrundeliegende Werkkaufvertrag formnichtig (§§ 125 S. 1, 311 b S. 1 BGB sei. Die Baubeschreibung für das Haus, das von V auf dem verkauften Grundstück errichtet werden soll, sei nämlich der Vertragsurkunde nicht beigefügt worden.

Kurz danach verkauft V das Grundstück an X und läßt

I. **Beamter** im **haftungsrechtlichen Sinn** ist jeder, dem ein öffentliches Amt im funktionellen Sinn anvertraut ist, daher auch Richter (arg. e § 839 Abs. 2 BGB) und Rechtspfleger, also auch R. (Notare haften nach der Sondernorm des § 19 BNotO.)

Voraussetzung der beantragten Eintragung war nach § 20 GBO nur der Nachweis einer wirksamen Auflassung, nicht auch eines wirksamen Kaufvertrages (zu den Prüfungspflichten im Grundbuchverfahren s. Nrn. 182, 184, 186). Die Formnichtigkeit des Kaufvertrages wäre nur von Bedeutung gewesen, wenn sie gem. § 139 BGB auch die Nichtigkeit der Auflassung nach sich gezogen hätte. Der Anwendung des § 139 BGB steht aber das Abstraktionsprinzip entgegen (OLG Frankfurt NJW 1981, 876 f.). Da die Auflassung wirksam war, enthielt die Zurückweisung des Eintragungsantrags durch R eine schuldhafte Amtspflichtverletzung gegenüber K i.S.d. § 839 Abs. 1 BGB.

II. Zugunsten des R greift § 839 Abs. 2 BGB ein, wenn es sich bei der Zurückweisung um ein „**Urteil in einer Rechtssache**" handelt.

1. Das setzt zunächst voraus, daß die Entscheidung durch ein **Gericht** ergangen ist (BGHZ 10, 55, 57). Gem. § 1 Abs. 1 S. 1 GBO werden die Grundbücher von